We know what we are, but know not what we may be.
(Shakespeare, Hamlet 4.5.43)

An Anthology
Of
Essays by Ashraf

A Window into the Robust Tradition of Rich and Vibrant Art of
Essays on Philosophical, Religious, Cultural, and Current Affairs

MIRZA IQBAL ASHRAF

iUniverse®

AN ANTHOLOGY OF ESSAYS BY ASHRAF

iUniverse books may be ordered through booksellers or by contacting:

iUniverse
1663 Liberty Drive
Bloomington, IN 47403
www.iuniverse.com
844-349-9409

Because of the dynamic nature of the Internet, any web addresses or links contained in this book may have changed since publication and may no longer be valid. The views expressed in this work are solely those of the author and do not necessarily reflect the views of the publisher, and the publisher hereby disclaims any responsibility for them.

Any people depicted in stock imagery provided by Getty Images are models, and such images are being used for illustrative purposes only.
Certain stock imagery © Getty Images.

ISBN: 978-1-6632-4706-3 (sc)
ISBN: 978-1-6632-4708-7 (hc)
ISBN: 978-1-6632-4707-0 (e)

Library of Congress Control Number: 2022919646

Print information available on the last page.

iUniverse rev. date: 10/25/2022

Warmly dedicated to my younger brother

Dr. Mirza Maqbool Ashraf

And his wife

Abida Maqbool Ashraf

A Book of
Essays is a rich and
Intelligent tapestry of thoughts,
Which are woven in the dimension of time.
Even if every thought is an afterthought, it's viewed
And judged in the present. It stays in the mind
And as a collection of treatises it shares
With others the knowledge
Argued in the book.
(Ashraf)

CONTENTS

FOREWORD

After the success of my landmark work, *Introduction to World Philosophies: A Chronological Progression*, followed by *Islamic Philosophy of War and Peace, Rumi's Holistic Humanism: The Timeless Appeal of the Great Mystic Poet, Diversity and Unity in Islamic Civilization*, and *Human Existence and Identity in the Modern Age: A Socio-Philosophical Reflection*. I kept writing essays from a philosophical perspective, covering a vast range of knowledge. I have now collected those essays in *An Anthology of Essays by Ashraf* comprising two parts. Part 1 contains fifteen essays on the subjects of philosophy, science, and humanities, while Part 2 has another fifteen essays revealing the underpinning of philosophical thought of the world of Islam.

Whereas this work celebrates the rich and vibrant tradition of writing essays on philosophical, scientific, humanitarian, and socio-religious matters, it is also a window into the robust and vibrant art of essay writing by one author. *An Anthology of Essays by Ashraf* is a rich and intelligent tapestry of thoughts, woven in the dimension of time, depicting the unity of human experience that every person has within oneself. Even if every thought appears as an afterthought, I have viewed and judged them in the present. It stays in the mind, and as a collection of treatises it shares with others the knowledge argued in this work of distinctive discerning and entertaining writing.

An Anthology of Essays by Ashraf is a work of dynamic literary genre representing the everlasting tradition of essay writing beginning, from Classical Greek period, Ancient Rome, and the Golden Age of the Arabs, up to the modern age of artificial intelligence and cybernetic technology. I have presented this anthology in an easy-to-read style, which offers a feast of knowledge for the readers of every age and profession.

Mirza Iqbal Ashraf August 11, 2022

What I Have Lived For

I have existed as I am and have lived as I look.
(Ashraf)

Having been taught at home from nursery to my B.A. (Bachelor of Arts) by my father and missing the sociable atmosphere of school and college or experiencing an outlook of the world beyond the boundaries of my house, a complex of shyness developed in me. In order get rid of shyness I started seeking awareness of life through fine art. Though the secret of fine art "to know how to see" revealed to me when I was grown up, painting had become my first medium to express myself. From the age of nine to fourteen years, I painted everything from flowers to fauna, portraits to landscapes, and sketched geometrical patterns.

By the age of ten, having set my heart upon learning, I started my education by reading most of the subjects such as, history, geography, mathematics, and books on general knowledge in English language, I also started learning Urdu, Arabic, and Persian languages. During the second decade of my life I benefited from my grandfather's coherent commentary on Rumi's six volumes of Masnavi comprising twenty-five thousand verses written in Persian. I read most of the Muslim philosophers of the golden era of knowledge in the Islamic World during my academic study of Honors in Persian Language and Literature. In my twenties, I immersed myself in English literature with special interest in the works of William Shakespeare. After getting my Master's degree in English language and literature, I got deeply engrossed in the study of philosophy with greater interest in the writings of Bertrand Russell.

Overall, in my pursuit of learning, three great intellectuals and icons of knowledge, Jalaluddin Rumi (1207-1272), William Shakespeare (1564-1616), and Bertrand Russell (1872-1970) have overwhelmingly impacted my life. Benefitting from the intellectualism of these three great geniuses, I found within myself impressions of a spiritual Rumi who could view, listen to, and communicate with the Absolute's invisible intelligence; impacts of humanistic reason from an intellectual Shakespeare, who was capable of comprehending and expressing the intelligence of Nature through the medium of dialogue; and the epistemological magnetism of Russell, a philosopher whose love of wisdom through logical and rational arguments became the best subject of education and instruction in my life. Thus my encounter with these remarkable geniuses helped my life's spiritual, literary, and moral upbringing in becoming an author.

But in my quest for knowledge, I, influenced by the teachings of Rumi, Shakespeare, and Russell, I no longer suffered from perplexity, knew the order of Heaven, and heard it receptively. I could muse on the dictates of my heart and no longer in fragment I prepared myself for the best of life 'to become what I have lived for!'

1. **Jalaluddin Rumi:** the spiritual connects with the invisible Intelligence, with love and reason, through his heart and mind.

Gamble everything for love
If you're a true human being
If not leave this gathering.
Half –heartedness
Never reaches into Majesty.[1]

From Rumi I learnt life is a charisma of poetry to be composed, a song to be sung, and a dance to be danced. It is the creative eye, in a fine frenzy rolling, glancing from heaven to earth and from earth to heaven that exposes the "meaning of life." Charisma is a word, like a thunderstorm that sits flat on the page compared with the actual experience it tries to name, which I thought I understood. But when I met Rumi, who exuded a spiritual charisma like a wave of the sea, I realized his charisma made me an odd fit for the mystical business, most of which is more mundane than heroic. Day after day reading unforgettable stories about real life, I glided through his Masnavi, whose every verse seemed like a field of flowers following the sun—Shams. How thrilling it was to read him, to know him—a great man who had exactly the right blend of intelligence and an infectious hunger to be in the know, which is impossible to define, rather its essence has to be felt to be comprehended.

Fusing the physical and metaphysical excellence of man, Rumi defining the [w]holistic humanism within the context of man's inner or unconscious mind appeared to me as a source of an invisible bond for the human beings seeking harmony, connection, and love for the whole humankind, beyond the limits and boundaries of religion, polity, race, and color.

2. **William Shakespeare,** a man of reason and love who keeps company with Nature as the will of man is swayed by his mind and heart.

Judgment and reason
Have been grand-jurymen
Since before
Noah was a sailor.[2]

From Shakespeare, I comprehended that as imagination bodies forth the forms of things unknown, a creator's pen turns them to shapes, giving to airy nothing a local habitation and a name. Life is creating one's character, developing and unfolding it by re-conceiving oneself at the call of time. Reading Shakespeare's poetry and plays detailing the luxuriance of his imagination and the prodigiousness of his intelligence made it a pleasure for me to understand his art of "the invention of the human." His genius holds a mirror up to nature, reflecting and capturing in words what it feels like to be human. His conveying of complex but natural human emotions developed in me a new understanding of Rumi's mystical reasoning as well as the timeless appeal of his holistic humanism. Having plunged deep into Rumi's spiritual and moral poetry, I found myself comparing Shakespeare's outpouring of rational creativity to Rumi's spiritual reasoning and humanistic wisdom. I saw both of them as legends of intimate knowledge, perennially relevant for readers of all ages.

3. **Bertrand Russell,** a man of wisdom, philosopher, social activist, pacifist, educationalist, humanist campaigner against the nuclear arms, who wanted philosophy—love of wisdom—to speak to ordinary people.

I did not write in my capacity as a philosopher;
Rather I wrote as a human being,

Who suffered from the state of the World!
Wished to find some way of improving it,
And was anxious to speak in plain terms
To others who had same feelings.[3]

With my understanding of Rumi's holistic humanism and Shakespeare's secular humanism, I started reading Russell's philosophical vision of social humanism. Reading Russell as a philosopher, educationalist, pacifist, social activist, and humanist, I understood that to live a meaningful life one must abandon private and petty interests and instead cultivate an interest in love and peace for the whole of mankind, without any discrimination based on race, color, or gender. I followed with full interest what Russell said about himself: "Three passions, simple but overwhelmingly strong, have governed my life: the longing for love, the search for knowledge, and unbearable pity for the suffering of mankind."[4] Though in my life, I have read and tried to understand hundreds of scholars of almost every religion, including philosophies and literature available in English, Persian, and Urdu; however, delving deep into the teachings of these three great masters of knowledge, I learned that life in and of itself has no meaning. *Life is an opportunity to create meaning.*

But following a common trend of longing for love, searching for knowledge, and feeling pity for the suffering of mankind, as transmitted by the three great intellectuals, l was blown hither and thither in a wayward course over a great sea of curiosity. The concepts of gambling everything for love, judgement and reason, and philosophy as "love of wisdom" would lead me upward toward the heavens, but pity for humankind always pulled me back to earth. Cries of pain and suffering still reverberate in my heart and mind. Hungry children, victims tortured by oppressors, helpless old people burdening their young offspring, and the whole world of loneliness, poverty, killings, and destructions by war, would make for me a mockery of what human life should be. In every moment of my life, I long to wipe out this evil. When I cannot, I too suffer, but believing that when there is no choice besides suffering, the only way out is to tolerate it—if possible enjoy it—and start the struggle of dreaming up new ideas! I, thus, cane to believe suffering is a key that opens locked doors to creativity.

I entreated love for several reasons. First, because it brings ecstasy— ecstasy so joyful that I would often have sacrificed all the rest of my life for few hours of this joy. Next because it relieves loneliness—that terrible loneliness in which one's shivering consciousness looks over the rim of the world into the unfathomable, cold, and lifeless abyss. And finally, because in the union of love I have seen, in a mystic miniature, the prefiguring vision of the heaven that saints and poets have imagined. This is what I sought, and though it might seem too good for human life, this is what—at last—I have found. After reading Russell's *Skeptical Essays* as a part of the curriculum which helped me understand the philosophy of skepticism, that I already understood when it was debated by the Muslim thinkers at the *Dar-ul-Hikmah* (House of Wisdom), I picked up Russell's universally acclaimed and Nobel Prize-winning work *History of Western Philosophy*, and read it many times in my life. After that, I started reading almost every work of Bertrand Russell.

I have sought knowledge with a passionate wish to understand the heart and mind of the human beings. With the start of the third millennium, humankind has stepped into the mesmerizing Fourth Age of Scientific Revolution—the age of smart phones, robots, and conscious computers—humans are experiencing a loss of intellectual and spiritual *élan vital* (the vital impulse or life force). Humanism, instead of emerging from the heart and mind of geniuses, is now digitally articulated by the technology in the hands of everyone. It is the beginning of a new era, the era of Artificial Intelligence which is creating a Digital Double of Human Intelligence. Today, the Artificial Intelligence is everywhere—on our screens, in our pockets, and one day may even be walking to our home with us. We are using "Artificial Intelligence" as an all-encompassing umbrella term that covers everything that serves as an integral piece of the greater future of our technologies. But Artificial Intelligence can only impart knowledge which keeps changing and increasing every second of every day without asking us any question. Therefore, I would prefer to trade all this technology and its Artificial Intelligence for an afternoon with someone like Rumi, Shakespeare, or Russell, who would ask question after question, challenging my mind to find answers.

This has been my life from the day I was born, and as I am now in the last of my life for which the first was made, I have found it has been worth living. I would feel blessed to live it again if the chance were offered me.

MIRZA IQBAL ASHRAF

Notes:

1. Trans. Coleman Barks: *The Essential Rumi,* page 193 (Arberry 16b) The Three Fish
2. Shakespeare: *Twelfth Night,* 3.2.16.
3. Philip Stokes: *Philosophy: 100 Essential Thinkers,* page 161.
4. Russell: *The Autobiography of Bertrand Russell,* page 3.

PART 1

Essays on the Subjects of Philosophy, Science, and Humanities

CHAPTER 1

What Is Philosophy?

The unexamined life is not worth living ~ Socrates

Introduction

The term *philosophy* is a composite word derived from two Greek words: *philos,* meaning "love," and *sophia* meaning "wisdom," and is understood as "love of wisdom." The wisdom that philosophy teaches relates to what it might mean to lead a good life. According to Plato, "The wisest have the most authority." Philosophy is also concerned with knowledge of things as they are. One of the instincts leading human beings to philosophy is evident in the quest to know more and more about this universe. The subject of philosophy is to investigate general and fundamental principles that can be used to understand humankind, its responsibilities in this life and universe, through rational and scientific reflection.

In everyday life, people are usually too busy to think and argue in a philosophical manner. Most of their time is spent in the struggle for a livelihood. However, there have been people through the ages who ask straightforward but complex questions that do not bear practical answers: What is the true nature of reality? What is true and what is false? Do we have enough knowledge to be certain about anything? What are humans really like, and what is special about the human mind and consciousness? What are God and religion all about? Are humans free to choose who they are and what they do? Is scientific knowledge superior to other kinds of knowledge? There are many such questions. They concern the overall meaning of life and do not seem to have much to do with everyday survival, but those people we recognize as philosophers continue to look for convincing answers to them.

The early philosophers were usually individual sages asking questions and providing answers about everything. But today, philosophy is a comprehensive subject classified into various branches. These include

1

epistemology (theory of knowledge), metaphysics (theories about time, space, God, cause, and reality), ethics (principles of good and bad, value, and conduct), logic (theory of proof), aesthetics (art and beauty), political philosophy (law, politics, and society), social philosophy (society and social science), philosophy of religion (reason and religion), philosophy of history (knowledge and doctrines of civilizations), and many more. Generally philosophy, covering all these subjects, is the critical and systematic study of an unlimited range of ideas and issues, regulated by logical and rational argumentation.

Throughout history, every philosophy bears the mark of its origin. Ancient Greek philosophy, which is described as inquisitive, grew out of a way of thinking that emphasized strong reasoning. Chinese philosophy is humanistic—not in the modern sense of humanism, but focused on the intrinsic values of human life and relationships among social, moral, and political issues. Indian philosophy, having evolved out of the Vedic texts and traditions, is meditative. Islamic philosophy is spiritual, based on religious faith supported by reason. French philosophical conception is rationalistic, which emphasizes the belief that knowledge can be achieved through the use of reason. German philosophy is speculative, reconciling intellect and the senses, or in other words, rationalism and empiricism. British philosophy is recognized as empirical, stating that knowledge can be attained through sense experience. The American philosophical quest is founded on realistic considerations, such as truth being what works or is useful, and that all knowledge is pragmatic.

Philosophy is thinking about "Thinking"

According to some thinkers, philosophy evolves out of debate, argumentation, and criticism. For others, only deductive reasoning produces and develops philosophy. Some believe its development and evolution lie in the pursuit of knowledge. Others believe philosophy is "thinking about *Thinking*" and that its major role is to define or clarify ideas and remove misunderstandings. For Plato, "philosophy begins in wonder." Aristotle believed that "all men by nature desire to know," and to know, philosophers and thinkers are obliged to produce some kind of argumentative doctrine, explanation, idea, or proof. Philosophy is thus an attempt to answer ultimate, often agitating questions with reasoning and attentive, thoughtful scrutiny.

Al-Kindi, famously known the "First Arab philosopher" of the ninth century, held the view that "philosophy is the knowledge of the reality of things within man's possibility, because the philosopher's end in his theoretical knowledge is to gain truth and in his practical knowledge to behave in accordance with truth."[1] Many Muslim philosophers following al-Kindi have emphasized the importance of the practical role of philosophy. Bertrand Russell in his *History of Western Philosophy*, says, "Philosophy is merely the attempt to answer such ultimate questions, not carelessly and dogmatically as we do in ordinary life and even in the sciences, but critically, after exploring all that makes such questions puzzling, and after realizing all the vagueness and confusion that underlie our ordinary ideas."[2] Most importantly, he argued, "Philosophy is continually attacked by religion and science and thus it becomes its job to draw rational evidence upon science and religion." Philosophy, therefore, attempts to resolve those theoretical and abstract issues that are left unsolved by religions, and by social and natural sciences. It deals with questions about the nature and justification of knowledge, existence, belief, and many crucial concepts such as free will, God and truth, science and religion, etc. In short, a study of philosophers and their thought would probably yield a clearer idea of what exactly philosophy is.

Interestingly, philosophy is a unique activity that is not art, religion, or science, but is still closely connected with these subjects. Bertrand Russell in his work *The Problems of Philosophy* argues:

> Philosophy, like all other studies, aims primarily at knowledge. The knowledge it aims at is the kind of knowledge which gives unity and system to the body of the sciences, and the kind which results from a critical examination of the grounds of our convictions, prejudices, and beliefs. . . . It is true that this is partly accounted for by the fact that, as soon as definite knowledge concerning any subject becomes possible, this subject ceases to be called philosophy, and becomes a separate science.[3]

In science, religion, and art, many questions are consensual in their answers. But there are some questions whose suggested answers fall short of reasonable answers; all such questions become subjects of philosophy. However, with their instinctive curiosity, philosophers often find it difficult to agree. This is understandable, since philosophical problems are complex and deal with questions over which people generally disagree. Confucius the Chinese sage said, "He who learns but does not think is lost. He who thinks but does not learn is in great danger."[4] The business of philosophers is to learn by thinking and to challenge concepts and assumptions so that new ideas can emerge to deal with the all-time hardest-to-solve problems. For these individuals, thinking and arguing is an ongoing adventure and its journey far beyond the limits of human thought and understanding is endless, but philosophers have made the subject of philosophy fascinating through their intriguing questions and issues, unsure where to begin and where to end. Here, I will take up two important subjects of philosophy which are generally the concern of our everyday life: religion and philosophy, and philosophy and science.

Religion and Philosophy

Although it is believed that religion by its very nature precludes philosophical investigation, and philosophy is continually attacked by religion and science since they address many of the questions tackled by philosophy, philosophy's job is to draw rational evidence upon religion and science. Bertrand Russell in his *History of Western Philosophy* speculates:

> Philosophy, as I shall understand the word, is something intermediate between theology and science. Like theology, it consists of speculations on matters as to which definite knowledge has, so far, been unascertainable; but like science, it appeals to human reason rather than to authority, whether that of tradition or that of revelation. All *definite* knowledge—so I should contend—belongs to science; all *dogma* as to what surpasses definite knowledge belongs to theology. But between theology and science there is a 'No Man's Land,' exposed to attack from both sides; this 'No Man's Land' is philosophy.[5]

Philosophy is the most critical and comprehensive thought process developed by human beings. It is quite different from religion in that

4

philosophy is both critical and comprehensive, while religion is viewed as comprehensive but is not necessarily critical. And yet, almost all great thinkers of the world's religions have been far more than dogmatic expounders of an uncriticized faith, because they have related their religious tenets to experience and have also subjected them to radical criticism. We find many thinkers in the history of philosophy who are also theologians, but who have advocated the need of religion for intellectual interpretation rather than criticism.

Religion is not an abstract idealism; rather, it is concrete and practical. It attempts to offer a view of all of life and the universe and to offer answers to most, if not all of the basic questions occurring to human beings. Though answers offered by religion, unlike philosophy, are not subject to careful scrutiny of reason and logic, religion asserts that ideals are not only abstractly valid in the "Platonic Kingdom of Ideas," but that they can be realized in the world of human beings' actual existence. Many religious beliefs that defy logic also seem to be unreasonable, but religion means something about the present visible life in the world, its judgment and exposure is directed toward the same way of human life that philosophy investigates. However, religion having its basis in belief often becomes a subject of criticism by philosophy which, by its nature, is a critic of belief and its systems. Philosophy, looking for rational explication and justifications for the tenets of belief, puts religious ideas through severe examination.

Theologians do think about religious beliefs in a rational manner and employ reason to make their religious beliefs appear more logical, but they presume beliefs as a matter of faith. Believing that reason has its limits, they do not examine their beliefs as philosophers examine theirs. For philosophers, ideas accepted on faith are subject to critical scrutiny and debate before proven as acceptable. Edgar S. Brightman writing in his essay, "Religion as a Philosophical Problem," in the book *Approaches to the Philosophy of Religion*, explains:

> It is obviously impossible that all religious beliefs can be true or all religious value-claims be true values. The question: Is religion true? Would therefore be undiscriminating. The rational problem of religion would take the form: Are any religious beliefs true? If so, which ones, and why? Are any religious value-claims truly

objective? If so, which ones, and why? The best possible answer to these questions is the best possible philosophy of religion. If no religious beliefs or value-claims are true, then religion is shown to be of no metaphysical importance, and thus, is of primary importance only to phenomenologists or psychiatrists.[6]

Philosophy of Religion deals with rational thought about religious issues and concerns without a presumption of the existence of a deity or reliance on acts of faith. Aldous Huxley (1894-1963) in his work *The Perennial Philosophy*, argued that all religions in the world were underpinned by universal beliefs and experiences. He professed that there is a lot of agreement between proponents of classical theism in Platonic, Jewish, Hindu, Christian, and Muslim philosophy over three main points: God is unconditioned eternal Being, our consciousness is a reflection or spark of that, and we find our flourishing or bliss in the realization of this.[7] But philosophers generally examine the nature of religion and religious beliefs by the same criterion that is applied in science and in daily life to detect the presence of error and to measure human beings' approximation to truth. Brightman, arguing on a separate criterion for religious truth, remarks in the same essay:

> In seeking religious truth, all that a priori logic can offer must be considered; all secular experience must be weighed; but the vital question of the truth and value of religion cannot be said to have been approached until actual evidence of religious experience is interpreted. Neither physics, nor psychology nor philosophy is competent to pass any judgment, favorable or unfavorable, on religion until religious values have been considered; one cannot know whether one is confirming or refuting religion until one knows what religion is.[8]

Religions are complex systems of theory and practice, but philosophers tend to examine claims of religious truth, seeking rational answers. Religion addresses most of same questions as philosophy, but unlike philosophy, religion sometimes emphasizes the importance of faith over the application of our power of reason. That is why many philosophers have also been theologians, and many of the greatest religious thinkers have been philosophers—both seek rational answers about belief in an unseen God and the system of divine revelation to the prophets. But like religious faith, reason has its limits. Philosophy applies the power of reason as well as, and as far, as it can.

Philosophy and Science

Close to two centuries before Socrates (c.469-399 BCE), the philosophy of science emerged from the Milesian School at Miletus—a Greek colony on the eastern coast of Modern Turkey—when Thales (c.620-546 BCE), the first Greek philosopher, sought a rational answer for one big question: "What is the world made of?" The answers given by the philosophers of that time laid the foundation of scientific thought in philosophy, forging an intimate relation between the two disciplines. Thales was followed by Pythagoras (c.571-496 BCE), who marked a key turning point in science and philosophy by projecting the world in terms of mathematics. He, and all those philosophers who followed him, described the structure of the cosmos in numbers and geometry.

Though pre-Socratic philosophers were both philosophers and scientists, in the history of philosophy Aristotle is viewed as a pioneer in integrating the two disciplines. Philosophy of science witnessed its golden period from the ninth- to thirteenth-century renaissance in the Islamic world when Baghdad, Cairo, and Córdoba became the intellectual centers for science, philosophy, medicine, and education. Introduction to philosophy and science was initiated by al-Kindi, al-Farabi, ibn Sina, and al-Khwarizmi, followed by a long line of philosophers of sciences in Baghdad. In Arab Spain, philosophical and scientific knowledge came to its peak, with massive translations and commentaries on Aristotle by Averroes and the Jewish philosopher Maimonides, and many more thinkers. This is known as the golden age of scholarship in the Islamic world, marked by both scientific and philosophical enquiries. Though this golden age was brought to an end by the Crusades, followed by the destruction brought by the savage Mongols, scientific discoveries and philosophical awareness had already paved the way for modern science.

According to Albert Einstein, "Philosophy is empty if it is not based on science. Science discovers, philosophy interprets." In our history of philosophy, the researchers we call "scientists" are also "natural philosophers" or simply philosophers. "The best doctor is also a philosopher" says Peter Adamson (born August 10, 1972, an American professor of philosophy in late antiquity and in the Islamic world) and that "the best philosopher is also a doctor." In his article published in *Philosophy Now* issue #114 Adamson says:

> Because Galen [129-216 BCE, philosopher, and physician of medicine and anatomy] became the indispensable authority for later medical writers, and because many of these writers were also philosophers, medicine and philosophy continued to be closely intertwined. The point applies to famous European thinkers such as Descartes. But it was never more crucial than in the Islamic world: a short roll call of thinkers who wrote on both medicine and philosophy would include al-Farabi, al-Razi, Avicenna, Averroes, and the Jewish thinker Maimonides. Galen's influence makes itself felt in their ideas about knowledge (that mix of experience and theory), anthropology, and even ethics, with moral instruction being understood as a kind of medicine that applies to the soul instead of the body.[9]

In the present age of greater scientific progression, philosophy plays a tremendous role in integrating the scientific knowledge and cognitive activity enshrined in philosophical fields. Indeed, we have philosophy that explores the thought behind scientific methods and practices. The relationship between philosophy and science has ever been a back-and-forth affair, with ideas from one informing the other.

Notes:

1. Sharif, 1961, p. 424.
2. Russell; 1912, pp. 9-10.
3. Ibid; pp. 239-240.
4. Waley, 1938, 2:15.
5. Russell, 1861. P.13.
6. Brightman, 1954, p. 5.
7. Huxley, 1945.
8. Brightman, 1954, p. 11.
9. Adamson, Philosophy Now #114, p. 33.

CHAPTER 2

The Present Nature and the Future of Philosophy

O philosophy, life's guide!
O searcher-out of virtue and expeller of vices!
What could we and every age of men have been without you?
Cicero (106-43 BCE)

Introduction

Philosophy is the most critical and comprehensive thought process created and developed by human beings. To me, the study of philosophy reveals that philosophy is a perennially running stream of awareness and wisdom, which, when falls into the sea of knowledge, creates ripples of wonder, curiosity, and creativity. Though philosophy is seemingly concerned with the knowledge of things as they are, it is at the same time more concerned about how they will be in the future. The term *philosophy* will perennially remain to be understood as "love of wisdom,"; it teaches and will keep teaching "what it might mean to lead a good life." Our societal, political, and technological changes have been bound up with the ideologies and philosophical outlook of thinkers and philosophers. Bertrand Russell remarked, "To understand an age or a nation, we must understand its philosophy, and to understand its philosophy we must ourselves be in some degree philosophers."[1]

Philosophy has helped great thinkers to introduce new ideologies which have played an important role in the formation of societies. Great nations like the United States and the Soviet Union were born of the philosophical conceptions of Thomas Paine (1737-1809) and Karl Marx (1818-1883). The present Saudi Arabian Kingdom stands on the theo-philosophical propositions of the eighteenth-century Muslim scholar Muhammad ibn Abd al-Wahhab (1703-1792). India's freedom from British rule was actuated by the philosophy of nonviolence of Mohandas Gandhi (1869-1948). The creation of the new state of Pakistan is the brainchild of philosopher-poet Muhammad Iqbal (1873-1961).

There are many intriguing questions to be answered concerning the meaning of life which do not seem to have much to do with everyday survival. However, in every period of our history, those we recognize as philosophers continue to look for convincing answers to these questions. By enlarging the human mind, their philosophies expand the intellectual horizon of humankind and expose the perspectives of good life. They help solve difficult and intricate questions by inspiring the realization that philosophy as love of wisdom is very important for human beings to live a meaningful life. Overall, philosophy is fundamentally vital in finding answers for many of the existential questions of mankind. Bertrand Russell in his work *The Problems of Philosophy*, remarks:

> What is the value of philosophy and why it ought to be studied? It is exclusively among the goods of the mind that the value of philosophy is to be found; and those that are not indifferent to these goods can be persuaded that the study of philosophy is not a waste of time. The Knowledge [which philosophy] aims at, is the kind of knowledge which gives unity and system to the body of the sciences, and the kind which results from a critical examination of the grounds of our convictions, prejudices, and beliefs. . . Philosophy liberates us from prejudices by suggesting many possibilities which enlarge our thoughts and free them from the tyranny of customs, by removing the somewhat arrogant dogmatism of those who have never traveled into the region of liberating doubt, by keeping alive our sense of wonder, showing us familiar things in an unfamiliar aspect.[1]

Philosophy in every age of our history has attempted to resolve those theoretical and abstract issues that are left unsolved by the natural and social sciences. It deals with questions about the nature and justification of knowledge, existence, belief, and crucial concepts such as free will, God, and truth. Philosophy in every age attempts to answer ultimate, often agitating questions with reasoning and thoughtful scrutiny. Only a study of philosophers and their thought can yield a clearer idea of what exactly philosophy is.

Progression of Philosophy

In the beginning, philosophy emerged from epistemological debates of individual intellectuals asking questions, seeking understanding, and providing answers. Today, philosophy of science is the branch of philosophy which applies critical examination of the sciences. Science is a systematic knowledge based on a procedure of principles sifting through observation and experiments concerning how an observed phenomenon behaves. Philosophy also uncovers principles but is not limited to what can be observed—rather, it holds that the unobservable aspects are far beyond reality. However, a couple of centuries ago, what we now call science or *natural philosophy* had split off from general philosophy. What remains as philosophy today is no longer science, and it does not ask the questions science usually asks. For philosophy, the most important question is, "Why is there anything at all?" Science, free from philosophical chains, explains the existence of the universe by positing a "big bang" that took place some thirteen and a half billion years ago creating all matter and energy—even time and space. But does this scientific explanation remove philosophy's question of "Why there is something rather than nothing?" Saying "No," the philosopher asks, "Why was there a bang rather than no bang?"

Philosophy is a progressive discipline of epistemology which does not prescribe rules or set principles the way religion, sciences, and many other branches do. It helps invent and prescribe rules according to the need of its contemporary society by analyzing the independent judgments of common reason. Therefore, in every age of human history, its importance cannot be underemphasized. Whether there is socio-political turmoil or a scientific discovery, it is not possible to know and establish what to do with such conditions without having a vision of what sort of society human beings want to live in.

This supports the role of philosophy as an intellectual discipline which is not only a key to the advancement of knowledge but a provider of meaning to life. At the same time, in its interpretation of the universe, philosophy appears as a study of everything within the broader perspective of knowledge which is an education of everything, as mused by the nineteenth-century British poet Matthew Arnold, "the best that has been thought and said," about the existential questions of human life.

Present Nature of Philosophy

Traditionally, philosophy has been divided into four basic categories: metaphysics, epistemology, logic, and ethics. These four categories have generally remained a cognitive ground for philosophical propositions in every age and society. The history of philosophy reveals thinkers in three major regions who have greatly contributed to the development of intellectual history: the ancient Greeks in Europe, the Chinese in East Asia, and the Indians in South Asia. But it was the Greeks who made a dynamic impact first in the Islamic world and then in Europe, laying the foundation of modern Western philosophy. On account of its dominant educational pattern, Western philosophy has overshadowed other regions' philosophical discourses. However, a study of the philosophies of every region shows that although thinkers and philosophers in different times have emphasized one discipline of philosophical approach and neglected or marginalized others, there is a common strand of universal wisdom, ethics, and morality running through all of them. The depth and range of thought and traditions of all ancient and modern thinkers alike reflect the saying of the Persian sage Sa'adi Sherazi: "Of one Essence is the human race."

Today, as we are connected by a network of instantaneous exchange of knowledge, we are impelled to think and act globally. Philosophy is understood through general science, neuroscience, linguistic analysis, and phenomenology. Linguistic analysis attempts to probe, through a systematic analysis of language, what it means to "make sense" and to explain what is semantically structured in language. It tries to get at and to give a coherent account of the categorical structure of experience and thought, and of the world as it is available to our epistemic power. Phenomenology—study or description of objects or appearances—strives to get at the essential structure of experience and thought and their objects by direct intuitive inspection; it is not characterized by argument, but intends to be descriptive and empirical without any presuppositions. However, the philosophy of linguistic analysis, viewed in broad perspective and with an understanding of its problems, seems a more systematic, ingenious, disciplined, responsible, and useful method than phenomenological intuition.

In the long history of philosophy, philosophers have been arguing and writing primarily for intellectuals and other philosophers. But now we have arrived at an epoch in world history where philosophy is studied and practiced by intellectuals and nonintellectuals alike. Many complex and conflicting arguments are being addressed to achieve a simple and clear intellectual vision for the common man and his civilization in today's world. In order to facilitate this approach, the grand role of philosophy as the supreme form of intellectual life, the queen of sciences, the chronicler of time and eternity, and the guide of religious or worldly life, has been demoted to that of handmaiden of science. This should not be seen as a change in philosophy's cognitive role as an intellectual discipline, nor as a gradual alienation of philosophy from man's life in favor of science. Rather, it is an act of progressive transformation of philosophy actualized by the scientific revolution in the West, where philosophy has attained a place in scientific circles.

The modern world is, day by day, projecting the increasing authority of science over other cultural, religious, and social fields that fall under the jurisdiction of philosophy. Science and technology have succeeded on account of their practical utility, changing from a complex system to a series of easy tasks. This is because science as a technique has presented in practice a different outlook from the one found in theoretical philosophy. Technology has conferred such a great sense of power that human beings tend to feel less at the mercy of the environment than they did in the past.

The last decade of the twentieth century's cutting-edge biotechnological research and the boundless frontiers of computer science have enabled the transfer of knowledge and power from the physically strong to the mentally smart, from the rich and elite to the common man. Research and successes in genetic engineering, neurobiology, and superfast communication systems are amazingly and progressively transforming philosophy from a theoretical to a practical approach, bringing it closer to science than ever. Consequently, many long-unanswered questions of philosophy have now been answered by science.

Philosophy as an exclusive subject of epistemology has only served to legitimize models of progress that are wholly ideological and mostly dealing in questions that people tend not to agree on. In science, however, many answers enjoy a general consensus because people accept the assumptions of questions and the application of concepts within that discipline. Science and logical reality are constructed by language, and many different constructions are possible. But it is impossible to know what to do with scientific discoveries in genetics or biology without a vision of what sort of society we want to live in and what duties we assign to each other or to our descendants. Such questions lie in philosophy's jurisdiction because the answers are based on our conception as human beings and what we think is the best way for us to live.

The Future of Philosophy

The study of philosophy has helped enhance a person's problem-solving capacities through its role in analyzing concepts, providing definitions, and inciting arguments. It has contributed to our capacity to organize ideas and issues, to deal with questions of value, and to extract what is essential from large quantities of information. In every part of our history, philosophy has remained a central intellectual discipline of humankind. As we go through the history of philosophy, we find great thinkers from ancient times to modern days as living voices of wisdom from the past and extending up to our present time and will continue well into the future.

Throughout its history, philosophy has remained dependent on the raw material of empirical world's social, political, moral, and cultural interpretations. But today, as we are plugged into devices projecting artificial intelligence and are instantaneously connected online by a network without any physical contact, we are impelled to think and act globally. The shrinking of the global spectrum is no longer confined to the provision of specific raw material; rather, modern internet technology is making it possible that none of the traditions and cultures will be left apart. This situation foretells that future of philosophy is the" philosophy of technology" which will be understood through the voice of science.

The mesmerizing achievements of scientific education and research, and its amazing computer technology dominated by the modern mind, has opened a new vista to philosophical studies. The growth of intellectual consortiums is providing a new role to philosophy as a "techno-intellectual" catalyst between science and the human mind. Since philosophy has never had its own resources and has always confined itself to rethinking, reconsidering, and reinterpreting the facts of other disciplines, philosophy in the future, still as an intellectual discipline, will find its raw material homogenized by cybernetic technology.

To speculate what philosophy might be in the future, it is very important to understand that concerning its basic role as an intellectual discipline, there can be no alternatives to philosophy. For example, in scientific research, the use of embryonic stem cells and matters regarding cloning are serious issues that can be clarified and justified by philosophy as morally acceptable. With the development of artificial intelligence and robots, it falls under the jurisdiction of philosophy to explain what challenges our digital doubles would pose to our social systems in the modern world. What are the rational ways of removing the threat of universal annihilation? The structure of social life is becoming more complex as new forms of human activity are appearing.

Philosophy in the past was the study of everything, but in the future, philosophy's concrete attitude will holistically determinate human lifestyle by engaging the whole of existence. It will be a holistic conversion which will turn our life upside down. By playing an important role in raising an individual from an inauthentic life which is darkened by unconsciousness and is harnessed by worries, philosophy, by itself or with the help of artificial intelligence, will help us develop an authentic state of mind in which one's life attains self-consciousness, instigating inner peace, socio-political freedom, and an exact vision of human life and the world. At the core of philosophy will be an art of living, rather than just a scientific invitation to transform one's own life. With the digitized transmutation of language and logic through computers and the evolution of artificial intelligence, philosophy will emerge as an integrated and holistic giver of a meaning and purpose of life by fully intelligent robots as digital doubles of the human mind.

Notes:

1. Russell, 1912, pp. xv and xvi.

CHAPTER 3

Introduction to the Philosophy of Holism

"The whole is more than the sum of its parts." — Aristotle

Introduction

The concept of "the whole as greater than the sum of its parts" has ancient roots. But the term "holism" (more reasonably but less often spelled "wholism") rarely appears in conversation except somewhat narrowly in that of the philosophers, sociologists, or health care providers. It is a scholarly word that originated from the Greek *holos,* meaning "whole." In its present context, as defined by military leader, statesman and philosopher General Jan Christian Smuts (1870-1950), holism is "The tendency in nature to form wholes that are greater than the sum of the parts through creative evolution." Smuts, in his work *Holism and Evolution,* (1926, v) is of the view that:

> This factor, called Holism in the sequel, underlies the synthetic tendency in the universe, and is the principle which makes for the origin and progress of "wholes" in the universe . . . this whole-making or holistic tendency is fundamental in nature, that it has a well-marked ascertainable character, and that Evolution is nothing but the gradual development of progressive series of wholes, stretching from inorganic beginnings to the highest levels of spiritual creation.[1]

In ancient philosophical as well as theological belief, per Heraclitus (c.535-475 BCE), the holistic concept was strongly reflected in the concepts of Logos and Pantheism. The Chinese philosopher Zhuangzi (c. 369-286 BCE) was an exponent of the holistic philosophy of life, projecting a way of understanding that is uncommitted to a fixed system—a way that is fluid and flexible and maintains a pragmatic attitude toward the applicability of the "multiplicity of diverse modes" of realization among different creatures, cultures and philosophical outlooks. Philosophers and thinkers even before Socrates (c.469-399 BCE) have speculated that wholes, both animate and inanimate, are real, while parts are abstract analytical distinctions, and that wholes are flexible patterns, not simply mechanical assemblages of self-sufficient elements. Implicit in this view is the idea that when individual components of a system are put together to produce a large functional unit, a holistic quality develops which is not predictable from the behavior of components in their individual capacity.

The Holistic Paths

Along genuine holistic paths, whether non-theistic or theistic, and whatever they are called, there is a potential evolutionary movement in human consciousness. It is a movement from the ordinary level of being, doing, and having that most of us know in our daily lives to something more fulfilling. In the ordinary level there exist many misunderstandings, frequent periods of frustration and stress, remittent moments of happiness and pleasure, a somewhat scattered attention, and for some an underlying sense that we are not living as fully as we might until it is too late. The holistic path—which is an evolutionary path for a non-theist and a mystical path for a theist—is intended to help us experience another level where life reveals a much deeper inner meaning. It is a level where our thoughts, feelings, and actions are integrated by a clear intelligence and knowledge, and a feeling of intimacy and participation with something greater than our normal selves. Plato called it higher knowledge, but a theist describes it as a level where a profound spiritual dimension appears.

Many great artists tell of mysterious creative moments. Speaking holistically, we might say that our ordinary daily level is fragmented and incomplete, one where experiences are driven by one part or another, such as a strong desire, a thought, or a physical urge. The higher level is experienced as more whole, more free, where fragments of formerly disparate and conflicting physical, emotional, intellectual, and spiritual energies are unified by a love-wisdom of the heart and a new sense of inner unity and oneness arises. The spirit is now filled with love and emerges as an active, creative, participating force in life.

The modern proposition of holism stems from an old idea that arose spontaneously in the ancient cultures of the Chinese, Babylonians, Egyptians, Indians, Homeric Greeks, and Native Americans. It viewed the human being as a compound of body and soul. Upon physical death, the soul was no longer considered a consciously living entity. In some cultures it would become a pathetic shade or ghost doomed to reside in a gloomy underworld. In others it would reincarnate in another body, and in still others, on account of being no longer whole without a body, the soul would dissolve into nothingness.

The theme of a soul unable to function without a physical body, still holding ground in the modern age, impregnated itself especially into most of the monotheistic faiths within the concept of an eschatological (religious belief of judgment and destiny) resurrection as basic theological concern with death, destiny, and day of judgment. Historically, these theological ruminations, originating systematically from Zoroastrianism, entered first into Judaism when the Jews, came into contact with Zoroastrian culture during their Babylonian exile. From Judaism this idea passed on to Christianity and Islam, where it formed into a belief that a human being is a compound whole of body, mind and soul or spirit, and that not one of these by itself is fully alive and whole without the other two.

Though the concept of holism was vividly and concisely reflected by Aristotle (384-322 BCE) in his *Metaphysics* (1045a10) as "The whole is more than the sum of its parts," holism in the mystical dimension of Western philosophy and sociology did not emerge strongly until Baruch de Spinoza (1632-1677) developed a holistic philosophy in a way reminiscent of Parmenides (c. 515-450 BCE). Spinoza conceived that all the visible divisions and differences in the world are in fact aspects of a single invisible substance. He speculated that there is only one substance, "God, or Nature," as nothing finite is self-subsistent. His holistic view proposed a pantheistic religious experience which was already reflected in the mystical thinking of many religious traditions as "spirituality." After Spinoza, George Wilhelm Friedrich Hegel (1770-1860), based his holistic philosophy on the idea that nature consists of one timeless, rational and spiritual reality and state—reflecting a mystical vision of the invisible unity underlying all visible objects. Hegel's underlying invisible, unitive state is a quasi-mystical collectivism of an "invisible and higher reality." He identifies the whole as the Absolute in a spiritual sense.

All modern exponents of collectivism in the political and social science spectrum, including Karl Marx (1818-1883), stress some higher collective reality—a unity, a whole, a group—though nearly always at the cost of minimizing the importance of the part and the individual. Against individualism, they emphasize the social whole, or social forces that somehow possess a character and a will over and above summation of the characters and wills of the individual members. Thus, in the past hundred years, holism has tended to represent a collectivism and is sometimes perceived as opposed to individualism.

Modern Holism

In the second half of the twentieth century, the concept of holism began to inspire a broader thinking that the wholes, whether in a biological organism, medicine, science, art, individual behavior, philosophy of language, culture, etc., are much more than the sum of their parts. In the philosophy of history and social science, holism asserts that the objects of social inquiry are collectives rather than individual actions. In Gestalt psychology, the focus is on "Gestalt"—an organized whole that is perceived as more than the sum of its parts—not on isolated or separate elements. In biology, holism opposes mechanism and vitalism, maintaining that life consists of the dynamic system of the organism. In physics, the holistic concept is reflected in the modern quantum field theory that describes all existence as an exhortation of the underlying quantum vacuum, as though all existing entities are like ripples on a universal pond—a very modern theory yet remarkably similar to an ancient Indian theory that compares all entities to waves forming and un-forming.

Viewing modern secularist humanism in holistic perspective, we find that humanism has historically been associated with two main groups. One is the fifteenth-century "Italian humanists" who were concerned with art and literature; the other is the present-day humanists with their secular outlook. Neither group, at least as of now, has defined humanism within the context of a human being's inner or unconscious mind, the source of an invisible bond between people seeking harmony, connection, and love. Rather, the key purpose of modern humanism is to project the power of an individual human being pursuing worldly status, material gains or social contribution.

Though secular elements have a role in the theist's realm, it is not typically secularist. A theist's holistic outlook is neither relative nor confined to one period's art and literature nor to the present time's secularist view. For the theist, the core of the human being is the mind, soul, or spirit that projects empowerment and self-actualization that in right relation produce harmony within an individual and within humanity. The ability of the human being to think and feel in all aspects of life, "material" and "spiritual"—to reason and intuit, to love, hate, and fear, to understand the physical world through one's senses and to perceive and believe beyond matter and form—is a vital element in the holistic essence of any human being or any philosophy related to modern humanism.

Renaissance of Holistic Humanism

After the two World Wars of the twentieth century, a new dimension of humanism among philosophers, theologians, and men of science began to emerge as a "Renaissance of Holistic Humanism." This view emphasizes that since human beings are holistically body, mind, and spirit, their appreciation must not be based only on matter and form. This type of humanism prioritizes our common human needs and seeks both rational and spiritual ways of solving our problems as physical, intellectual, emotional, and spiritual beings. Though many atheists and agnostics of twentieth-century humanism give primacy to humans in contrast to an ideology or a religion, they nevertheless profess faith in human beings' capacity to evolve further in the realm of reason and love, and in their ability to grow toward their potential. For religious people, reason and science have their systematic limitations. Meanwhile, human imagination, being a religious imagination—irrespective of the faith or ideology one follows—is intrinsically drawn to spirituality, meaning the mental aspect of life as opposed to the material and sensual aspects of life, or the religious sphere of light against the dark world of matter. For them, the spirit is the real substance, and the phenomenal world of intellectual and physical properties is a collection of its attributes.

Present-day humanists pose serious questions about the validity of religious traditions. Some reject religion outright, arguing that religions are intolerant of each other and thus create conflict, violence, and war. Yet history does not support the thesis that secularists have done less harm or damage to mankind. Religions have, throughout human history, often espoused moral behavior by and toward those within the group and have been a source of motivation for individuals to bind themselves into a society. Theists endorse the faith instinct, believing that it is hardwired into human nature. The prophets and sages who introduced religions are like different windows through which one light enters and is reflected differently to accommodate a diverse humankind. The consequences depend on the capacity of the receivers—how they accept this light and/ or manipulate it.

Hundreds of years before Spinoza developed a holistic philosophy, Hegel conceived a mystical vision of the unity of all things, or modern thinkers like Karl Marx (1818-1883) propounded a sociopolitical collectivism, a sophisticated and remarkable holistic development had already developed in Judaism, Hinduism, Buddhism, Christianity, Islam, and many other religions of the world. Holism emerges in the mystical branch of every religious tradition, identifying a mystic of a high level of consciousness, or a whole human being. It is important to add here that the famous philosopher of eighteenth century, Emmanuel Kant (1724-1804)—though not directly connected to the mystics—defined this concept of mystical unity as a transcendental unity of perception or self-consciousness. Albert Einstein (1879-1955) said this about mysticism: "The most beautiful and most profound experience is the sensation of the mystical. It is the sower of all true science. He to whom this emotion is a stranger, who can no longer wonder and stand rapt in awe, is as good as dead."[2] Mystical thinkers believed that the human spirit or soul has windows that can open to all directions in unlimited dimension and their contents.

Subsequently, more than a few renowned mystics, men and women both, have appeared in all religions, believing and preaching pantheism, or in the modern sense, holism. Pantheism maintains that everything is divine, that God and Nature are identical. The mystics expressed pantheism within their belief of the "unity of being," a concept tinged with metaphysics and a philosophical way of stating the same simple idea. Khalifa Abdul Hakim in *Metaphysics of Rumi,* is of the view:

> Even most of the evidently atheistic doctrines can be identified with it, to justify the witty remark of Schopenhauer that "Pantheism is the poetry of Atheism." Ethical Monism like that of Fichte or Penologism like that of Hegel, the One Substance doctrine of Spinoza with a number of others in so far as they are monistic are pantheistic.[3]

Muslim mystics—being the latest in the traditions of revealed and unrevealed religions—both experienced and unfolded a mysterious and invisible factor (called later "holism") that is enfolded but "hidden" within the fundamental synthetic tendency of the universe. Long sought by philosophers, mystics, and scientists, this factor brings an evolutionary leap in consciousness—a process with a phenomenal result we are describing as holistically human. Whereas a study of the ordinary outer mind highlights reason and projects the power of a human being as an individual, the study of the inner or unconscious mind reflects the importance of genuine passion and the power of a relationship between human beings—an invisible bond that yearns for and brings contact, connection, harmony, and wholeness. For the mystics, the "unconscious" is innate, emotional, and sensitive, capable of perceiving and creating brilliantly. It is the unconscious mind that wants to reach out, and aspires to love and commune with fellow human beings, emphasizing a feature of the inner or unconscious mind that the learned are as one soul; in particular, the oneness of all the monotheistic prophets that cannot be broken up into fragments. If one disbelieves in any one of the prophets, one's faith in any other prophet is fractured.

Muslim Thinker's View of Holism

Interpretation and development of a rational, Hellenistic-style philosophy by Muslim thinkers reached its highest point in the period between al-Kindi (801-873) and Averroes or Ibn Rushd (1126-1198). But in the twelfth century, the renowned Islamic theologians, most prominent amongst them al-Ghazali (1058-1111) stated in reaction to Neoplatonism that religion cannot be reconciled with philosophy. Jalaluddin Rumi (1207-1273), appearing at a relative high point in the development and perfection of philosophical thought and religious experience in Islam, was fortunate to inherit an exceptional wealth of intellectual and spiritual wisdom. He had the theoretical influences of Greek philosophical interpretation, Jewish and Christian religious understanding, and Islamic jurisprudence on the one hand and the influences of Persian and Indian traditions on the other. Rumi, an orthodox Muslim, was guided and inspired by his mentor Shams-i-Tabriz who in his *Maqalat* said: "The universe exists through the whole, not parts—and the whole universe is within one human being. When he knows himself, he knows all." Thus the concept of holistic humanism evolved to embrace all human beings as one "whole humankind."

Rumi, benefiting from his predecessors, viewed the human being as the sum of several distinct but interconnected energies within one body: namely, the physical, intellectual, emotional, and spiritual components. As these entities or systems of energy interact, the potential exists for both alignment and misalignment, for right or wrong relation. In ordinary daily activity, these energies are usually pulled in different directions. But, at moments, without notice, they can align—resulting in a new level of awareness and consciousness that is substantially greater than the sum of its previously separated or conflicting parts. For as long as it lasts, this wholeness brings a much greater sense of unity and oneness, an awareness of itself with a new integrity, and a new relation to its inner and outer environments. An ordinary person, living with conflicting thoughts, feelings, and impulses etc., cannot imagine how it will be when they are reconciled or resolved, what it will be like when "the conflicting desires and voices" (within) vanish, leaving a wholeness—one intention, a unity reflecting as a whole. In many but not in all cases, when this previously unimaginable wholeness occurs, the individual may be aware of a spiritual component or presence and recognize it as such. This paradigm of holism within an individual who experiences even a flash of holism is a clue to what may be possible for the larger whole of humankind. The universal "holistic humanism" for the species appears dependent on the same paradigm as a single human being seen as a whole, bearing a common strand of spiritual harmony, unity, and love.

Philosophically, an understanding of Al-Ghazali and Rumi's works allows the premise that the holistic human view of these great thinkers may have been the forerunner of modern trends toward spiritual pluralism, voluntarism, and activism. The impact on Latin philosophical thought of the translations and commentaries of Greek philosophers by the Muslim thinkers of the eighth to thirteenth centuries was so great that Western thought between the thirteenth and sixteenth centuries is inexplicable without considering the conceptual discourses of Muslim thinkers stating there are different routes to the same truth. This became the base for theoretical openness, political freedom, and religious tolerance in modern Western thought. Muslim thought helped shape philosophy in the post-Kantian period of Goethe and Spinoza, and is related with the cognitions of Nietzsche, Schopenhauer, Bergson, Iqbal, Tagore, and many other thinkers of East and West. One salient aspect in al-Ghazali and Rumi's work is their personal experiences in unraveling the religious problems that surround questions of free will, ego, and resurrection. Their theory of emergent evolution, creative development, and emphasis on intuition and love (as opposed to barren intellectualism) converge in a supreme philosophy that an individual's "self" is isolated, indeterminate, indistinct, and featureless, unless and until he can incorporate himself into the natural and social holism of humanity.

Notes:

1. Smuts, 1926, p. v
2. Einstein
3. Hakim, 2006, p. 14,

CHAPTER 4

On Human Consciousness

Introduction

Many great thinkers, philosophers, and scientists have agreed that consciousness is a unique human capability that arises when information is broadcast throughout the brain. But there is no central location in the brain to be defined as the seat of consciousness. This raises an important question: Is consciousness loaded into the brain through sensory experiences, perception, memory, and intelligence, or is it the brain's process of objectivity and subjectivity that our cognitive mind uses to process input? The question complicates itself further: Is consciousness an extra ingredient that we humans have in addition to our abilities of perceiving, thinking, and feeling, or is it an intrinsic and inseparable part of man who is a creature that can perceive, think, and feel? If it is an extra ingredient—as many of us think of our soul, an extra entity—then we are naturally inclined to ask, "Why do we have it as a telltale signature?" On the other hand, if it's an evolutionary trait, then we want to know how and why consciousness has only evolved in humans! For some thinkers, if human consciousness is intrinsic and has evolved, then any other creature that has also evolved to have intelligence, perception, memory, and emotions would also be equipped with consciousness.

Since the brain cannot be fossilized, the study of the origin of man as a thinking human being shows little evidence of the evolutionary journey of the human brain. Researchers in modern neurobiology believe that we all have three eyes, including one inside the head. Known as the pineal gland, it is located in the human brain and has the structure of an eye. It has cells that act as light receptors, just as the retina does, and a structure comparable to the vitreous—a gel-like substance between the retina and lens of the eye, in the shape of a lens. Scientists are still studying the pineal body as a possible seat of human consciousness, as well as a third eye.

Being Aware of Himself

Man, having himself torn away from nature and finding himself to be endowed with reason and imagination, needed to form a concept of himself. He yearned to feel, and to say: "I am 'I'." Thus, becoming self-conscious, man grew to be a "human." However, "self-consciousness" which gives an ineffable awareness of the self, is unique only to humans, that each one of us can think about the fact "I think, therefore I am." A human being's intellectual awareness inspired him to find out how the brain developed and how it displays a force known as "consciousness" that can directly influence the world. Today, researchers of neuroscience with the help of Brain Imaging Technology (BIT), are revealing functions and performances of different parts of the human brain, but the most intriguing function of brain is its ineffable and nonphysical performance, 'the charismatic human consciousness.'

Whereas scientists are busy discovering how the brain is intimately involved in consciousness, other thinkers, with the help of scientific and psychological evaluations, have emphasized a distinction between different levels of consciousness. Differentiating between human and animal consciousness, they have assumed that animals have simple-consciousness which, we can call the awareness that most animals have of their bodies and environment. Thus the animal, without trespassing the limits of its perceptive, sensory-brain capacities, is confined to its intrinsically managed consciousness. Generally the animal lives through biological laws of nature; it is part of nature and does not transcend it. It has no conscience of a moral nature, and no awareness of itself and its existence. It has no reason, if by reason we mean the ability to penetrate the surface and grasp the essence behind or within it. Though it may have an idea of what is useful and what is harmful, it has no concept of truth and falsehood, and no or little inwardness or imagination. Though some animals have the ability to learn whatever man teaches them, their simple-consciousness is whatever they perceive to be outward and explicit.

The level of human consciousness is an even greater wonder than mere inwardness. Everything we know about the universe tells us that reality consists of physical matter composed of atoms and their component particles, busily colliding and combining; while in human beings, consciousness is so distinct from and discontinuous with matter that it creates the illusion that it might have been created by a "Higher Consciousness." Rational theories regarding the nature of consciousness started emerging when man realized that the voices he hears in his head are his own, resulting from his own perceptions, and not from gods or spirits. He thus began to consider that the enigma of consciousness is a challenging puzzle of his own life, raising questions: Is man an evolved animal or a creation of intelligent design? Is consciousness the same as a soul or do both exist? If consciousness is a non-physical mental phenomenon, how could it cause physical things to happen, such as the feeling of pain or the impulse to jerk fingers away from the edge of a hot frying pan?

Emergence of Consciousness

Stepping out of nature, the first thing that emerged in human beings was cosmic consciousness—a capability that put humans far above the rest of creation. But the main reason for man's concern about the universe even today is an acute awareness of the true life and order of the universe, in which a person experiences oneness with the source of creation, which at an early stage was identified by him as a divinity and at a later stage as "universal energy." Cosmic consciousness needed an idealism to be interpreted intellectually, which appeared as religion. This defined both the present visible world and also the hereafter, where divinity is a conscious spirit without bodily form. Man viewed religion not as an abstract idealism but something concrete and practical. He believed that ideals are not only abstractly justifiable in the "Platonic world of Ideas," but are also, to some extent, realizable in the realm of actual existence.

Modern man's approach today is through reason and science or through his own consciousness. For him, divinity is a force, principle, or law with no "personal consciousness." Science in the present age has developed cosmology as a secular approach and a form of faith for the atheists whose preachers are scientists and cosmologists like Albert Einstein, Stephen Hawking, Carl Sagan, and many more. But cosmology basically undertakes the same issues as religions: How did the universe come into being? How did life begin? Not to mention the same old dilemma: What comes next? To answer such difficult questions, thinkers and scientists focused on the human brain and its consciousness.

Today, neurobiology or neuroscience is helping us to understand how our brain works. Here is an excerpt from a study of the human brain—in a short and simple paragraph—from *National Geographic's* special publication, *Your Brain: A User's Guide, 100 things You Never Knew*, which reveals:

> In this corrugated mass, a staggeringly complex symphony of electrochemical reactions plays out every second of every day. Much of it does so without a conscious conductor. The brain makes the lungs expand with the inrush of air and the heart pumps blood. It houses memories, processes sounds and sights, smells and tastes, and feelings ranging from the subtle to the sublime. But beyond the work the brain does automatically comes something far different. Out of the human brain arises consciousness and mind—the unique ability of *Homo-sapiens* the "thinking man," to be aware of being aware. ... An unconscious part of your brain "wills" an action before you are consciously aware of your will to direct it.[1]

Though we know an astonishing amount about the human brain, paradoxically, the 1.4kg lump of pinkish-beige tissue inside our skull, consisting of more than a billion neurons (nerve cells), with billions of connections that let us understand ourselves, our universe, and the cosmos far beyond our realm, *understands so little about itself.* Though we may understand many of the details of how the mind works, consciousness itself remains beyond our reach. Today, the hard problem that is challenging our brain is to define *what is consciousness?*

Daniel Dennett, a distinguished Arts and Science Professor, says in the beginning of his book *Consciousness Explained*, "Consciousness stands alone today as a topic that often leaves even the most sophisticated thinkers tongue-tied and confused." He argues: "Information comes into the senses and is distributed all over the place for different purposes. In all this activity there is no central place in which "I" sit and watch the show as things pass through my consciousness. ... Instead, the many different parts of the brain just get on with their own jobs, communicating with one another whenever necessary with no central control."[2] After speculating and reasoning through five hundred pages of his books he concludes, "My explanation of consciousness is far from complete. One might even say that it was just a beginning; but it is a beginning, because it breaks the spell of the enchanted circle of ideas that made explaining consciousness seem impossible."[3] Thus, there is so far no universally accepted definition of consciousness.

Even with a scientific understanding of the details of the human brain and how it works, consciousness itself is still unexplained. But we all know that consciousness makes the difference between our life and death or our overall existence and nonexistence. The concept of the evolution of consciousness from the brain is a relatively recent finding, yet we cannot ignore our inquisitive mind's quest to uncover the mechanisms of mind and its intelligent systems, through cognitive scientists and artificial intelligence researchers, that lead to our consciousness.

Some neurophysiologists have recently attempted to define consciousness in objective terms, arguing that it is a process in which information about multiple individual modalities of sensation and perception are combined into a unified multidimensional representation of the state of the system and its environment, integrated with memories and information about the organism's needs, generating emotional reactions and programs of behavior to adjust the organism to its environment. Ayn Rand (1905-1982) in her book *Philosophy who Needs It,* is of the view that:

> Existence exists—and the act of grasping that statement implies two corollary axioms: that something exists which one perceives and that one exists possessing consciousness, consciousness being the faculty of perceiving that which exists. ... If nothing exists, there can be no consciousness: a consciousness with nothing to be conscious of is a contradiction in terms. Before it could identify itself as consciousness, it had to be conscious of something. If that which you claim to perceive does not exist, what you possess is not consciousness.[4]

William James (1842-1910), the father of modern psychology, expounded that our conscious life feels like a continuously flowing stream of sights, sounds, smells, touches, thoughts, emotions, worries, and joys— all of which happen to us, one after another. James thus coined the phrase "the stream of consciousness." Carl Jung (1875-1961) said, "There are certain events of which we have not consciously taken note; they have remained, so to speak, below the threshold of consciousness. They have happened, but they have been absorbed subliminally." The Latin root of the word "subliminal" translates to "below the threshold." Psychologists employ the term to mean below the threshold of consciousness.

Cognitive scientists Stanislaus Dehaene and Bernard Baars, in *Scientific American Mind*, (May/June 2014, page 27) have suggested: "Memories, sensory perceptions, judgments and other inputs are stored in a type of short-term memory called the Global Workspace, and thus establish the buffer or a cushion of Global Workspace Model. This buffer gives rise to consciousness when the collected information is broadcast throughout the brain to stimulate cognitive process that engaging the motor system, spurs the body to action."[5] Christoph Koch, on page 26 of the same magazine, expresses:

> During the past several decades, two distinct frameworks for explaining what consciousness is and how the brain produces it have emerged, each compelling in its own way. ... One of these—the Integrated Information Theory—uses a mathematical expression to represent conscious experience and then derives predictions about which circuits in the brain are essential to produce these experiences. ... [Second] In contrast, the Global Workspace Model of consciousness moves in the opposite direction. Its starting point is behavioral experiments that manipulate conscious experience of people in a very controlled setting. It then seeks to identify the areas of the brain that underlie these experiences.[6]

Within the perspective of these theories it seems that consciousness is just brain-wide collecting and sharing of information in the memory of our "neural buffer blackboard."

The human brain, by the firing of more than a billion neurons and billions of interconnections, produces extraordinary potentialities of cognition, perception, learning, memory, reasoning, language, conscious, sub-conscious, and unconscious thought, and many other subjective and objective expositions. It is so intimately involved in consciousness that changes in the brain cause changes in consciousness. Information comes to the brain through the senses, but there is nothing centralized in it. By contrast, according to Susan Blackmore in her work *Consciousness*:

> Human consciousness seems to be unified. This 'unity of consciousness' is often described in three distinct ways—and the natural way of thinking about consciousness, in terms of a theater or a stream of experiences, implies all three. First, it implies that at any particular time, there is a unity to those things I am experiencing now; that is, some things are in my consciousness while many others are not. Those inside are called the 'contents of consciousness,' and form the current experiences in the stream or the show on the stage of the theater. Second, consciousness seems unified over time in that there seems to be a continuity from one moment to the next, or even across a whole lifetime of conscious experiences. Third, these conscious contents are experienced by the same 'me' that there is a single experiencer as well as stream of experiences.[7]

Consciousness: an Ineffable Qualia

Human consciousness is an "Ineffable Qualia: — "ineffable" meaning so great and powerful it's impossible to describe; "qualia" meaning a property distinct from any source it might have in a physical object. Qualia, which is the plural form of quale, are those aspects of a conscious experience considered subjective and based on sense perceptions, rather than objective material reality (for example, the smell of a rose or the way pain feels). They are commonly held to be directly accessible only from the first-person perspective of the conscious subject, and also often held to be intrinsic in that they cannot be analyzed into more basic elements or relations. It is true that animals can smell and experience pain, but their consciousness, being only external or objective, falls in the category of being simply aware of that experience.

Intellectualism, feelings, and experiences of human beings vary widely. For example, running fingers over rough surface, smelling a rose or a skunk, feeling a sharp pain in a part of the body, seeing a bright purple color, being happy or becoming extremely angry—in each of these cases, one is subjected to a mental state with a very distinctive subjective character. For such experiences philosophers use the term "qualia" to refer to the introspectively accessible phenomenal aspects of a human's mental experience. In this broad sense of the term, it is difficult to deny that qualia exist. The status of qualia is hotly debated in philosophy because it is central to a proper understanding of the nature of consciousness. Qualia are at the very heart of the mind-body problem, because human beings don't share consciousness, they share emotions.

Consciousness is a complete package of the working of human being's mental states involving qualia—that works [w]holistically as a sum of his conscious, sub-conscious, unconscious, memory, intention, imagination, and all the functions of the brain. Human consciousness is the mother of "I" where each individual is unique in his identity, intellectual representation, intention, and much more. Mental capacity for an animal species is all same—dogs are all dogs and cats are all cats—but each human being is different from the others where every individual is an "I"— and where his own specific consciousness is a seal of his distinctiveness, just as his fingerprint is a mark of his identity.

Though neuroscience as well as general sciences believe that nothing extra exists apart from the processes and abilities of the human beings, we still need to explain why we seem to be having ineffable-nonphysical conscious experiences. Since passage from the physics of the brain to the corresponding facts of consciousness is not only unthinkable but also unexplainable, it is here that the idea of consciousness as an illusion or a nonphysical substance named "soul" comes in. Mark Goldblatt, in his essay *On Soul* in *Philosophy Now* argues that the human soul, if it exists in an immaterial form, must be the "me-ness" of me, the sense of first personhood on which the rest of my conscious experiences hang. He further explains:

> The soul, in other words, is not your consciousness—unless you are a materialist. If you are not a materialist, however, then the soul is what's underneath your consciousness, the platform upon which your consciousness is constructed. Consciousness is the thing that emerges from sense data, memory and language have material components; they are rooted in the workings of the brain. The stuff of consciousness is definitely brain based. So if the soul is indeed immaterial, it must be more basic than consciousness.[8]

This means that soul and consciousness are two different entities. But in the brain there must be a place where everything comes together and consciousness happens. So far, neuroscientists have not discovered any center in the brain which is capable of corresponding to the emergence of a unified consciousness. All we know is that information coming in through the senses is distributed all over the brain. There is no central place in which "I" can sit, watch, and display things passing through "I's" consciousness.

The exponents of Darwin's evolutionary theory speculate that consciousness might have emerged during the part of our evolution when man became highly social, confronted by many complex relationships, and intrigued by intimate bonding with his fellow beings. One might also argue that since we are conscious, consciousness itself might have evolved independent of biological evolution. At the same time, since consciousness is inseparable from human beings' intelligence, thinking, perception, language, and many other evolved abilities, it cannot be an adaptation or infused into the mind by some power beyond man.

Notes:

1. National Geographic: *Your Brain: A User's Guide, 100 things You Never Knew,* 2011
2. Dennett, 1991, p. 22.
3. ibid., p. 455.
4. Rand, Any, 1984, p.32.
5. Dehaene and Baars: *Scientific American Mind*, May/June 2014, p. 27.
6. Koch, *Scientific American Mind,* May/June 2014, p. 26.
7. Blackmore, 2005, p.25.
8. Goldblatt, *Philosophy Now*, issue # 82.

—————————— CHAPTER 5 ——————————

Consciousness and Artificial Intelligence

Light of sun and moon cannot be outdistanced,
yet mind reaches beyond them.
Galaxies are as infinite as grains of sand, yet mind spreads outside them.
(Myoan Eisai - A Japanese Zen Buddhist)

Introduction

Since human consciousness is still a mystery, it is yet to be instituted or impregnated into the silicon brain of artificial intelligence. Until this point, humans have been following the way their consciousness directs, but the thinking machine is being designed to follow a way that is expected to digitally mirror billions of years of the brain and its consciousness. From ancient time to this day, the phenomenon of human consciousness has intrigued philosophers who have mostly discussed it in subjective terms. But Steven Arthur Pinker (born 1954) a Canadian-American cognitive psychologist, linguist, and popular scientist, author of *How the Mind Works* which advocates evolutionary psychology, and computational theory of mind says, "The brain, like it or not, is a machine. Scientists have come to this conclusion not because they are mechanistic killjoys, but because they have amassed evidence that every aspect of consciousness can be tied to the brain."[1]

Whereas the mystery of human consciousness from the time of Cartesian cognition—"I think; therefore, I am,"—became an open challenge for neuroscientists, the idea of the brain as a "thinking machine" opened a window into the human mind in order to create the human brain's digital double. Toby Walsh in *Machines that Think* writes, "Not without irony, Stephen Hawking (1942-2018), [an English theoretical physicist] welcomed a software update for his speech synthesizer with a warning that came in the electronic voice of that technology: 'The development of full artificial intelligence could spell the end of the human race."[1] But Ray Kurzweil, one of the world's leading inventors, thinkers, and futurists, in his works, *The Age of Spiritual Machines,* and *The Singularity is Near When Humans Transcend Biology,* followed by *How to Create A Mind,* is of the opinion that rather than heralding the end of the human race, artificial intelligence will bring an era in which the very nature of what it means to be human will be both enriched and challenged. Our species will break the shackles of its genetic legacy and achieve inconceivable heights of intelligence, mental progress, and longevity. It will be a union of human and machine, in which knowledge and skills embedded in our brains will be combined with the greater capacity, speed, and knowledge-sharing ability of our own creations (Kurzweil in *The Singularity is Near*).

Subjective to Objective Experiences

Although the "cognitive revolution" has introduced pragmatic methods of studying thought and other inner experiences of our mind, neuroscience, even assisted by modern technology, has not yet provided an easy way of answering the hard question of how the subjective experience of human consciousness arises from the objective activity of the human brain. How can our brain's physical network of neurons, with all its chemical action, electromagnetic system, and the interactions of billions of cells and circuits, create a mind that allows a unified awareness of thinking, recognizing, remembering, feeling, predicting, cognizing, innumerable experiences of our life and of the universe, repeating hundreds of millions of times in the neocortex, and finally, apparently giving birth to an instant output of all inner experiences in the form of "consciousness"? While we haven't been able to give a definitive or comprehensive delineation of human consciousness, we might get a scientifically created and defined answer from artificial intelligence. So far we know that at the root of artificial intelligence's technological appeal is the capability of the machine to perform many tasks characteristic of human intelligence.

According to Ray Kurzweil, a pioneering researcher in artificial intelligence, hybrids of biological and silicon-based intelligence will become possible, and one day the contents of a human brain can be transferred into a synthetic brain, as a CD-ROM uploads its software into a computer. Many thinkers, philosophers, and scientists agree that consciousness is a unique human capability, but have not identified the seat of consciousness in the brain where—like streaming data in the head—it can be mapped, copied, and downloaded.

Human Condition and Intelligent Machines

Before we argue about the role of intelligent machines and their capability of consciousness, we need a deeper understanding of the nature of human consciousness. The *Dictionary of Psychology* of the American Psychological Association gives a twofold definition of consciousness. The first part describes consciousness as the phenomena that humans report experiencing, including mental contents that range from sensory and somatic perception, to mental images, reportable ideas, inner speech, intentions to act, memories, semantics, dreams, hallucinations, emotional feelings, and "fringe" feelings (e.g., a sense of knowledge), and aspects of cognitive and motor control." The second part of the definition speaks of any subjective states of awareness in which conscious contents can be reported—for example, altered states such as sleeping—as well as the global access function of consciousness, presenting an endless variety of focal contents to executive control and decision making.

The history of human evolution reveals that at a certain point, when man transcended nature and ended his passive role as a mere creature, he emancipated himself from the bindings of nature, first by an erect posture and second by the growth of his brain. The evolution of man may have taken billions of years; but what matters is that a patently new species arose, transcending nature, recognizing life, "aware of itself." Self-awareness, reason, and imagination disrupted man's harmony with nature charactering his prehuman existence. Upon becoming aware of himself, man also realized the limitations of his existence, and his powerlessness and at being a finite being. Until today, man was never free from this dichotomy of his existence. He cannot rid himself of his mind, even if he wants to, and he cannot rid himself of his body as long as he is alive— rather, his mind and body create in him a strong urge to be alive, and live an infinite life. He cannot go back to the prehuman state of harmony with nature because he now views himself as a "special species." To assure himself that he is no longer an animal, man demonstrates his merits as a special species through his unique physical advantage and intellectual eminence.

The Human Mind and its Digital Double

The human mind, an evolutionary product of his biological brain, is now changing the course of evolution by creating a digital double in his own image, equipped with artificial intelligence and emotions. *Homo sapiens*, from the time of their appearance on this planet, have used their neural mechanism for building tools. This helped them initiate a new form of evolution that brought about a social culture of shared knowledge. As neurology gave birth to technology, the process of technology today has led us to the creation of an amazing tool we call the "computer." The computer has enabled us to expand our knowledge base, permitting extensive multiple layers of links from one area of knowledge to another. Perceiving our distinction from other animals and the uniqueness of our intelligence, our power of communication, and our capability of acquiring and sharing knowledge has given rise to a realization that humans are *special creatures*. But throughout our history, scientists have mostly remained reticent to evaluate and prove with scientific reasoning our claim of being a *special creature*, fearing that they might not be supporting the religious doctrine of exceptionalism of intelligent design.

Regardless of how humans got to be the way they are today, their intelligence and technology has enabled them to overcome biological hurdles in changing themselves in almost every aspect of their life. Hard scientific data cumulated across vast spheres, from ecology to epistemology, cognitive psychology to consciousness, affirms that human beings are truly remarkable and are the only species we know that are capable of achieving whatever in the first instance would seem unachievable. By developing artificial intelligence, humans are changing the course of evolution by creating digital doubles in their own image.

Being Aware of Himself

Today there are three proven players in our lives: human beings, nature, and machines. Emerging as *Homo sapiens*, from his first appearance on this planet, he has used his intelligence in building tools which helped him to invent newer tools for every phase of his life. But torn away from nature, endowed with reason and imagination, he needed to form a concept of himself. He yearned to feel and say: "I am I." Thus, becoming self-conscious, man grew to be human. Undoubtedly, the animation of "self-consciousness" is unique to humans and provides an ineffable awareness of the self. Each one of us can think about the fact of human being's consciousness and awareness which led the French mathematician and philosopher René Descartes in 1644 to proclaim *"Cogito, ergo sum"*—I think, therefore, I am—asserting that the ultimate reality lies in the mind.

Human intellectual awareness has inspired him to find out how the brain developed a force known as "consciousness" that can directly influence the world. Modern researchers of neuroscience, with the help of Brain Imaging Technology (BIT), are revealing functions and performances of different parts of the human brain, yet the most intriguing evolution and performance of the brain is its ineffable and nonphysical function, "the charismatic human consciousness." This is the sort of awareness in artificial intelligence we see in the movies, helping us believe that as compared to the billions of years' journey of the human brain's evolution, technology needs only decades to acquire and portray self-awareness and consciousness.

As we see sophisticated computerized devices arriving every day to supplant those of yesterday, we have begun to believe that a web of neurons similar to that in our own brain can be hosted in different material systems. We believe that human intelligence can make sufficiently powerful machines, self-aware and capable of holding consciousness in their circuits. However, in order to perform this great feat, we first need to understand much more comprehensively that elusive "something" we call human consciousness.

Though we have theological, philosophical, and psychological definitions of consciousness, we have no sufficiently convincing scientific definition, even with scientific knowledge of the functions of the human brain. But we all know that it makes the difference between our life and death, between overall existence and nonexistence. Since the concept of the evolution of consciousness from the brain is relatively recent, we cannot ignore our inquisitive mind's quest to seek the help of cognitive scientists as well as artificial intelligence researchers to uncover the mechanisms of the mind that leads to our consciousness. This means that artificial intelligence may be able to serve as a mirror of our own intelligence in which we would be able to see functions of our own consciousness in the brain of our digital double.

Mathematics and Consciousness

An important point that needs to be mentioned here: Is mathematics independent of human consciousness? Stephen Maitzen, a philosopher panelist of "Ask Philosophers" remarks in response to question:

> I am strongly inclined to say yes. If there's even one technological civilization elsewhere in our unimaginably vast universe, then that civilization must have discovered enough math to produce technology. But we have no reason at all to think that it's a *human* civilization, given the very different conditions in which it evolved: if it exists, it belongs to a different species from ours. So: If math depends on human consciousness, then we're the only technological civilization in the universe, which seems very unlikely to me.[3]

There is another argument that before human beings came on the scene, the earth orbited the sun in an ellipse, with the sun at one focus. This is a precise mathematical description of the earth's behavior, a description that was held true long before the element of consciousness emerged in the human mind. This means that mathematics predates human consciousness. It also supports the fact that as humans appeared their consciousness also appeared with them.

Research by neuroscientists has already proved how our state of mind is defined by electrochemical processing of information along neural pathways. We are in the age of super-computers and many people believe that artificial intelligence is going to solve our many hard problems.

According to Stuart Hameroff, a professor at the University of Arizona, "The human brain is the perfect quantum computer and the soul or consciousness is simply information stored at the quantum level." Today scientists and thinkers are working on quantum theory to explain the phenomenon of consciousness. But our *brain* is an indispensable guru in guiding us to understand the complexities of our mind and body and to solve the many problems of our lives.

Artificial intelligence is a machine's ability to perform tasks characteristic of human intelligence with more speed and greater memory capacity, which can be viewed as part of human endeavor to evolve digitally according to its own choices. So far, computers have excelled in doing simple tasks with greater speed than the human brain, which lags, getting tired and distracted, and sometimes fails to recall information with perfection and clarity. The brain might not work well when it fails to retain everything it encounters, whereas a computer's hard drive with its backup system functions as an ever-ready store of data available on deman. But the human brain's consciousness excels in its power to learn, adapt, think, compare, analyze and synthesize, cognize with wisdom, and make new connections and discoveries in ways that artificial intelligence is only beginning to do. One can imagine a step forward is required to create consciousness.

Notes:

1. Walsh, 2018, p. 8.
2. Pinker, *How the Mind Works* 2009, p 132.
3. Maitzen, Ask Philosophy (on-line).

CHAPTER 6

Wisdom and Artificial Intelligence

Science helps make a living; Wisdom helps make a life!
Can science create wisdom?

Introduction

We are living in an era of "scientific enlightenment" in which technological progress is changing everything in our life. At this point, past decades of the scientific and digital era have produced great comforts of life and easy access to knowledge. Today, we hear the alarming call, "The robots are coming! Artificial intelligence is coming!" No doubt, science rapidly introduces knowledge, enhancing our understanding of the natural world and the universe, but the important point is, *is it helping to enhance our wisdom?* Without wisdom human beings cannot decide how to ethically use scientifically developed instruments for the benefit of mankind. Scientists working on artificial intelligence are discovering how to equip digital computers with a brain performing as efficiently as the human brain. It seems possible that scientists may discover a way to upload an individual's brain with all the memory, perception, emotion, experience, wisdom, and consciousness, into an artificial neural network; in other words, a mind-transfer from a biological brain to a computational device. Some scientists believe that theoretically it's possible that a person's brain can be scanned, mapped, and its activities transferred to a computer hard drive. If this process becomes practicable, computers would be able at least theoretically to respond in the same way as the biologically evolved human brain.

Since the human brain is not a digital computer but a highly sophisticated neural network, the prospect of technological wisdom is still utopian. The brain's neural network is made up collections of hundred billion of neurons that constantly rewire and reinforce themselves after accomplishing a new task. It requires no programming but naturally performs with a hundred billion neurons firing instantly to learn and create something new. A digital computer, on the other hand has a fixed architecture, an operating system based on input, output, and processor. Therefore, the crucial questions before us are: Can artificial intelligence create or help us to receive or discover wisdom? Can a future super-computer be equipped with a wisdom chip to propound spontaneously and wisely as a incomputable and unpredictable situations demand?

Philosophy—Love of Wisdom

Throughout the history of mankind, two phenomena have shaped human life and virtually changed all of mankind. One is human wisdom, which proliferated philosophy—a composite of two Greek words, *philos* (love) and *sophia* (wisdom), meaning 'love of wisdom'—and the other is the development of natural sciences. Together, the social idealism of moral and ethical cognition and scientific rationalism form the foundation of human intellectualism. Man's evolution and his search, from his need to live a comfortable and well protected life to his exploration of the universe, has been the subject of science, but the belief about how life should be lived, what men and women should be, and how to treat one another, emerge from moral enquiry and wisdom. Though the great achievement of man is the development of science and technology, it is the ideological conceptions that have altered our way of life. Without science, humans would have lived in their natural habitat, a life like all other animals. But without wisdom they would have been uncivilized barbarians, not curious about where they came from, how they came to be where they are, or where they seem to be going.

The wisdom that philosophy teaches relates to what it might mean to lead an ideal life. In pursuit of this ideal life, human wisdom displays ethics and morality, setting out a systematic examination of the relations of human beings, how life could be lived, and how ethics and morality are applied to society. One of the instincts leading humans to philosophy is evident in their quest to learn about life and the universe. Its subject became the investigation of fundamental principles that can be used to understand mankind and its responsibilities through rational and scientific inquiries. Up till the end of twentieth century, philosophy led mankind to the pursuit of science which was understood through philosophical cognition. With the advent of twenty-first century, as humans have taken a big leap in the development of science and technology, philosophy is now understood through science. In the present era, the grand role of philosophy as the supreme form of intellectual life, the queen of sciences, the chronicler of time and eternity, the guide of religious or worldly life, seems to have been overtaken by science.

Stephen Hawking, the author of *A Brief History of Time,* while speaking to Google's Zeitgeist Conference in Hertfordshire said, "Most of us don't worry about these questions: Why are we here? Where do we come from? Traditionally, these are questions for philosophy, but philosophy is dead." He further said, "Philosophers have not kept up with modern developments in science, particularly physics. Scientists have become the bearers of the torch of discovery in our quest for knowledge, and new theories lead us to new and very different picture of the universe and our place in it."

"Philosophy is dead" is perhaps a bold statement, which is rather in itself a testimony of wisdom and philosophical judgment. When we use science we use reason; when we use reason we use philosophy. Therefore, philosophy is not dead. Without philosophy, Stephen Hawking could not have become a man of wisdom and the famous scientist he became.

However, to adapt a quote by Emmanuel Kant, "Philosophy without scientific input is empty, while science without philosophical guidance is blind." Today philosophers argue that the development of artificial intelligence should not be seen as a change in philosophy's cognitive role, nor is its wisdom to be subject to a gradual alienation from man's life in favor of science. But we need to know, when artificial intelligence surpasses human intelligence, will it be an act of progressive transformation of philosophy actualized by the immense scientific revolution in the world? Or is it going to be a crisis of human history that give us science without wisdom?

What Is Wisdom?

Before we deal with the subject of artificial intelligence, it is important to know what wisdom is, and what its relation with science is. According to Aristotle, "Wisdom must be intuitive reasoning combined with scientific knowledge." Wisdom, incited by human insight, is a golden-ticket tour of the human mind in all its dimensions. Knowing oneself is the beginning of all wisdom. It makes us know not to take second step before realizing at our first step that there are things we cannot and should not do, even if we have full knowledge of everything. Wisdom is higher than all knowledge, is ineffable to illustration, unintelligible to an intellect, unutterable in any word, unbound by any limit, and un-affirmable by any affirmation. It cannot be judged by any judge nor computed by any computer.

We must not mistake science or knowledge for wisdom. Science as a knowledge produces greater knowledge, facilitates the development of technology, and increases our power. Wisdom guides us how to act, apply, and make a best use of scientific knowledge and its achievements. In other words, wisdom helps us make a life, while science helps us make our living. Stephen Hall, in *Wisdom from Philosophy to Neuroscience,* presents a definition of wisdom:

> Many definitions of wisdom converge on recurrent and common elements: humility, patience, and a cleared-eyed, dispassionate view of human nature and the human predicament, as well as emotional resilience, an ability to cope with adversity, and an almost philosophical acknowledgment of ambiguity and the limitations of knowledge. Like many big ideas, it's also nettled with contradictions. Wisdom is based upon knowledge, but part of the physics of wisdom is shaped by uncertainty. Action is important, but so is judicious inaction. Emotion is central to wisdom, yet emotional detachment is indispensable. A wise act in one context may be sheer folly in another.[1]

Recent developments have sought to put the study of wisdom universally on a scientific basis—first the social sciences and now the natural sciences. It is a big challenge for neuroscientists to develop wisdom through artificial intelligence, particularly when its identity is the personal exposition of an individual's integration of his own self's microcosmic consciousness with the macrocosmic consciousness of the universe. Wisdom is a multi-dimensional human practice created through an individual's self-knowledge, self-transcendence, self-integration, non-attachment, compassion, and a deeper understanding of life, with diverse meanings from person to person. Just like human consciousness, wisdom has become a subject of study and research for neurobiologists. Trevor Curnow, a Professor of Philosophy at the University of Cambria and an internationally recognized authority on wisdom, argues on pages 196 and 203 of his book *Wisdom: A History*:

> Is wisdom a kind of knowledge? Or is it a kind of skill? Or is it a kind of perception? Or is it a kind of personality trait? Or is it a combination of some or all these things? ... If it becomes analyzable in terms of certain mental capacities, whether cognitive, reflective, affective or whatever, then it might be possible to identify neurobiological infrastructure associated with it. ... But wisdom is something esoteric that often passes from one wise person to another. It is universal. [its three forms are] First, wisdom is regarded as essentially divine. Second, humanity may receive it by revelation [or intuition] and preserve it by direct transmission from one person to another. Thirdly, the age of revelation is over, so wisdom is only accessible through tradition.[2]

Wisdom gives rise to compassion, and compassion gives rise to wisdom; truly, we can't have one without the other. For philosophy, wisdom and compassion are like two wings that work together to enable flight, or two eyes that work together to see deeply. Whatever we are learning and teaching in our schools, it is not wisdom; but as we are learning and teaching sciences and technologies we are giving and getting information. Wisdom is the ability to think and act by understanding and using knowledge along with experience, common sense, and above all personal insight. Wisdom is a capability or disposition to perform actions with the highest degree of adequacy under any given circumstance. It involves a deep understanding of people, objects, events, situations, and willingness, ability to apply perception, judgment and action. It is a disposition to find the truth coupled with the optimum judgment as to what actions should be taken in what sequence at an appropriate time in each situation.

What Is Science?

The word "science" comes from the Latin word *scientia,* meaning "knowledge, a knowing, an expertise." Science consists of knowledge based on a procedure of assessing theories impartially in the light of evidence. No thesis about the world is accepted permanently by science without solid, confirmable, and repeatable evidence. The scientific approach assumes that the universe has a kind of unified structure, which means it is pragmatically comprehensible. But a glance at the history of physics reveals that the comprehensible thesis of the universe keeps changing. In the seventeenth century, physics revealed that the universe consists of minute billiard ball-like corpuscles, which was later superseded by the discovery that the universe consists of point-particles surrounded by symmetrical fields of force. This gave way to yet another finding of a self-interacting field varying smoothly throughout space and time. Today, some scientists claim that everything is made up of quantum strings, embedded in ten or eleven dimensions of space-time. Tomorrow, physics could provide new assertions or proofs of the comprehension of our universe. The metaphysical assumption of the universe, though, remains the same, but being untestable it is problematic to the scientific mindset. However, based on human wisdom and knowledge, a common hierarchy regarding the comprehensibility of the universe between physics and metaphysics is that there is something—a cosmic purpose, a cosmic program, a physical entity, a final source of creation, or possibly even a God—present at all times in all phenomena.

According to science, human intelligence is a mechanistic process that happens in the brain, and there is no reason to assume that human intelligence is the only possible form of intelligence. Though scientists know that the brain is complex, it is an artifact of the blind progress of natural selection, which means it is still developing. Such assumptions leads scientists toward the possibility of developing artificial intelligence. But there is a risk, pointed out by Mathew Graves in his article "Why We should be concerned about Artificial Super-intelligence":

> The fact that artificial intelligence [AI] may be very different from human intelligence also suggests that we should be very careful about anthropomorphizing AI. Depending on the design choices AI scientists make, future AI systems may not share our goals or motivations; they may have different concepts and intuitions; or terms like "goal" and "intuition" may not even be particularly applicable to the way AI systems think and act. AI

systems may also have blind spots regarding questions that strike us as obvious. AI systems might also end up far more intelligent than any human.[3]

Today we are already encountering computer systems that act as if they are conscious. But we still consider them tools of integrated information and mere machines. We are not prepared for a machine that can be more intelligent than us.

Can Science Teach Wisdom?

For the past millennia, we have known that it is the job of a philosopher to wisely implement ideas of philosophical cognition and new scientific achievements, to be understood as scientific enlightenment. For social progression, scientific enlightenment involves social methodology as a primary inquiry. In other words, social inquiry is more fundamental than science. This would prioritize naturally evolved human intellectualism over artificial intelligence. Stephen Hall in *Wisdom from Philosophy to Neuroscience* argues:

> Could there be a "science" of wisdom? And if there is, can it provide us anything more at this point than a fuzzy geography of neural activity superimposed upon a vague definition of a human virtue? Can it shed light on the process by which each of us deals with the decisions and dilemmas of our own private 9/11s? Can it guide us to make the best decisions possible for our loved ones and ourselves, and help us find the right path when those interests collide? Might it even hint at ways we could train our hearts and minds to give us a better shot at achieving that lofty goal? [4]

Before the appearance of modern scientific enlightenment our emphasis on wisdom did not matter, because we were not overloaded with modern scientific advances that create many problems for ourselves and do greater damage to our planet. Today, the unprecedented powers bestowed upon us by science can create a new crisis if we have a science without wisdom. Our social progress depends upon our cognitive power, and our moral life on our wisdom. The irony is that our wisdom is being prevailed upon by artificial intelligence (AI), or artificial-general-intelligence (AGI), soon to be followed by artificial-super-intelligence (ASI), which poses a threat to our existence as humans.

In our quest to achieve social progress toward a wisely enlightened world, scientific knowledge must be combined with the insight of wisdom. It is a big challenge for computer scientists to re-produce human wisdom in the form of "artificial wisdom." While knowledge is a computable system, wisdom is spontaneously revealed by the imagination. Scientists working on artificial intelligence are trying to discover a way or a process of uploading the human brain with all its functions, such as memory, perception, emotion, experience, wisdom, and even consciousness from a physical brain to a computational device. Some scientists believe that theoretically it is possible that a person's brain can be scanned, mapped, and its activities uploaded to a computer's hard drive. This means that a mind-uploading program may make the human mind a figment of computer's imagination.

If we are able to capture a person's mental processes, then the reinstated mind will need a biological human body, because human thinking is directed toward physical needs and desires. According to James Barrat in his work *Our Final Invention,*

Throughout, it won't have feelings. It won't have our mammalian origins, our long brain building childhood, or our instinctive nurturing, even if it is raised as simulacrum of a human from infancy to adulthood. It probably won't care about you any more than your toaster does.[5]

Notes:

1. Hall, 2011, pp 18.
2. Curnow, 2015, pp 196 and 203.
3. Graves, Skeptic Magazine 2017.
4. Hall, 2013, pp 266.
5. Barrat Hall, 2011, pp 11.

CHAPTER 7

Science, Wisdom, and Consciousness

Science helps make a living; Wisdom helps make a life!
Consciousness holds science and wisdom.

Introduction

There are some big questions before philosophers and neuroscientists, such as how can we scientifically define or philosophically recognize wisdom and consciousness? For science, the most uphill task is determining how to measure or compute wisdom and consciousness. Another important question is, can a computer, equipped with a nonbiological intelligence, ever be able to match biologically evolved human wisdom and consciousness? We know that the human brain projects wisdom and causes consciousness by a series of specific neurobiological processes in the brain regarded as a crucial attribute of human beings which proliferates wisdom as an ineffable patchwork of different abilities developed by the human brain over millions of years of man's evolution. Neuroscientists, neurobiologists, and psychologists are still working to explore how the brain creates consciousness; uploading into an artificial intelligence chip is a big challenge. Michio Kaku in *The Future of Mind,* propounds:

> The brain is not a digital computer at all, but highly sophisticated neural network of some sort. Unlike a digital computer, which has a fixed architecture (input, output, and processor), neural networks are collections of neurons that constantly rewire and reinforce themselves after learning a new task. The brain has no programming, no operating system, no Windows, no central processor. Instead, its neural networks are massively parallel, with one hundred billion neurons firing at the same time in order to accomplish a single goal: to learn.[1]

The scientists considering the human brain as a kind of biological machine are trying to figure out how it works. They are trying to build an artificial brain that has a similar and an equal mechanism that can cause consciousness. But silicon-consciousness might need human emotions, their diversity of choice, their aims, and goals to achieve success.

We also have many human virtues like free will, aestheticism, creativity, and various natural as well as nurtured qualities which are not the same in every one of us. Intelligence, consciousness, and wisdom are multifaceted and their nature cannot be defined or computed as one standardized life form. We cannot distil down to few and final words the distinction of great masterpieces of art by Da Vinci, Picasso, or the music maestro Mozart, so that when uploaded into a computer other people will agree that it is the one and only definite description. What about the thoughtful expositions of great sages of past and present, for example: *"It is the part of a wise man to arrest the impulse of kindly feeling, as we check a carriage in its course"*— Cicero, 44 BC.

Shakespeare, (1596) in his play The Merchant of Venice opines:

> *The Quality of mercy is not strained.*
> *It drops as the gentle rain from heaven*
> *Upon the place beneath. It is twice blessed:*
> *It blesses him that gives, and him that takes.*

John Milton, (1667) in Paradise Lost propounds:

> *Only add.*
> *Deeds to your knowledge answerable, add faith,*
> *Add virtue, patience, temperance, add love,*
> *By name to come called charity, the soul*
> *Of all the rest: then will you not loath*
> *To leave this paradise, but shall possess*
> *A paradise within you, happier far.*

The novelist John Cheever remarks, "We do not receive wisdom. We must discover it ourselves after experiences which no one else can have for us and from which no one else can spare us."

The famous twentieth-century poet T.S. Eliot says:

Where is the wisdom we have lost in knowledge?
Where is the knowledge we have lost in information?

However, that will not stop scientists from continuing to do their homework of further insights into the nature and properties of wisdom, consciousness, and intelligence. If scientists are able to invent a silicon consciousness that would mean that consciousness can exist free from the constraints of the physical body. For those theologians and philosophers who assume consciousness is the human soul, it could help prove that after death the soul can exist for ever.

Moral Reasoning and Artificial Intelligence?

Before there was neuroscience, moral philosophies and theological invocations, the importance of the moral sense of goodness—doing right instead of wrong—had naturally assumed central importance in human societies. Morality is the effort to guide one's conduct by reason, to do what one has the best reason for doing, while giving equal weight to the interests of others who could be affected by what one does. But according to Stephen Hall,

> Neuroscientists have recently tunneled underneath all the lofty rhetoric by philosophers and theologians, and they have begun to discover that judging right and wrong, and making decisions that wisely discern between the two, can also be glimpsed in the activity of the brain.

On the same page, Hall quotes from Marc Hauser, a biologist at Harvard University and one of the leading researchers in this new field, who writes in his recent book *Moral Minds* that "moral judgments are mediated by an unconscious process, a hidden moral grammar that evaluates the causes and consequences of our own and others' actions." [2]

Moral reasoning depends upon how the human brain processes a moral dilemma and tells us what we should do. We know that moral reasoning, rationality, empiricism, and empathy are abstract virtues, not scientific distinctions. Wisdom tells moral reasoning what one "should" or "should not" do. Not surprisingly, the "should" or "ought" of moral behavior has been a subject of philosophic cognition over the past centuries. Morality deals with how one acts toward others, advising one to keep someone else's moral good in mind and refrain from acting in a way that leads to someone else's moral loss. Moral reasoning involves thoughts and actions that affect the instinct to live and the flourishing of sentient beings who are conscious, emotive, perceptive, sensitive, responsive, and able to feel and suffer. Instinctive acts are spontaneous, which for a digitized silicone-brain "is a big challenge" for scientists.

Moral reasoning is an evolutionary development of our behavior and characteristics from the time man first descended from the trees and started walking in groups. The human brain developed as man started walking upright, with hands free, along with his fellow beings. Cognitive power evolved as he perceived the mysteries of nature and realized the need for social life, which could not flourish without moral reasoning. The human brain is a "social brain" which produces moral reasoning—products of biological evolution and natural selection—and enjoins us to care for each other. A silicone brain producing artificial intelligence is not the same as the human mind, which depends on many factors: consciousness, intelligence, memory, goal, needs, plans, perceptions, preferences, feelings, psychological, and social capabilities.

The End of the Human Era

Human beings at the risk of computers and believing in scientific knowledge as their destiny are today on the road to a scientific civilization. Stephen Hawking remarks: "In contrast with our intellect, computers double their performance every eighteen months. So, the danger is real that they could develop intelligence and take over the world." Professor Vernor Vinge, a computer scientist, believes that "Within thirty years, we will have the technological means to create superhuman intelligence. Shortly after, the human era will be ended. Is such progress avoidable? If not to be avoided, can events be guided so that we may survive?" James Barrat mentions, "Ray Kurzweil defines Singularity as a 'singular' period in time (beginning around the year 2045), after which the pace of technological change will irreversibly transform human life. Most intelligence will be computer based, and trillions of times more powerful than today."[3]

Predicting the future of artificial intelligence and speculating on spiritual machines when computers exceed human intelligence, Ray Kurzweil, in his intriguing book, *The Singularity is Near*, imagines the unimaginable by making a compelling case that a human civilization with superhuman capabilities is closer at hand than we realize:

> A principal assumption underlying the expectation of the Singularity is that nonbiological mediums will be able to emulate the richness, subtlety, and depth of human thinking. But achieving the hardware computational capacity of a single human brain—or even of the collective intelligence of villages and nations—will not automatically produce human levels of capability. (By "human levels" I include all the diverse and subtle ways humans are intelligent, including musical and artistic aptitude, creativity, physical motion through the world, and understanding and responding appropriately to emotions) . . . Once a computer achieves a human level of intelligence, it will necessarily soar past it. A key advantage of nonbiological intelligence is that machines can easily share their knowledge.[4]

Given the incredible power of new technologies, and amazing development of artificial intelligence to super intelligence, we should be asking ourselves, how can we coexist with the machines? Ray Kurzweil answers, "Machines will follow a path that mirrors the evolution of humans. Ultimately, however, self-aware, self-improving machines will evolve beyond humans' ability to control or even understand them." But Ray does not reflect upon the fate of wisdom—whether these machines will be as wise as humans. While artificial intelligence is at or even above human level in the arena of knowledge and information, only a wise thinker can make wise decisions for the best of human beings. As James Barrat remarks, "Authorizing a machine [with artificial intelligence] to make lethal combat decisions is contingent upon political and military leaders resolving legal and ethical questions." [5]

Creativity is the most important theme of wisdom. It is thinking imaginatively and then coming up with the solution to a problem that is far from obvious. In other words, it is creative wisdom that helps inventors perform miraculous feats and provide solutions. Just as creativity is an individual's capability, the appearance of wisdom depends upon a person's own intellectualism. If scientists continue developing artificial intelligence without wisdom or prudence, the machines, designed to be human beings' servants may prove to be their executioner. In a provocative article, "The Future Does Not Need Us," Bill Joy argues,

> Our most powerful 21ˢᵗ century technologies—robotics, genetic engineering, and nanotech—are threatening to make humans an endangered species. ... This techno-utopia is all about I don't get diseases; I don't die; I get to have better eyesight and be smarter and all this. If you described this to Socrates [who said to know thyself is the beginning of wisdom] or Plato, they would laugh at you"[6]

Scientists can place chips in robots to shut them off if they become dangerous, or create fail-safe devices to immobilize them in an emergency. This means controlling the robot's artificial intelligence will still depend upon human wisdom. However, if robots are designed to possess the same consciousness and wisdom as we human beings have, it will be the end of the human era.

Today, science is busy developing artificial intelligence to be more like human intelligence. In February 2011, history was made when an IBM computer called Watson did what many thinkers believed impossible: it beat two human contestants on the TV game show *Jeopardy!* But the critics of artificial intelligence are of the view that that was merely a display of computational firepower. We know, science has, throughout history, broken new ground by following speculative lines of thought that involve a readiness to make do without the props and securities of the scientific method.

Whereas it is true; science has achieved some of its most notable advances precisely by venturing beyond the furthest limits of evidential proof, but we cannot overrule the fact that science also needs philosophy. In the near future, we will be able to develop the technological means to create 'Superhuman Intelligence' which can bring an end to the human era. Is such progress avoidable? If not to be avoided, can events be guided so that we may survive? We need to imagine philosophically that authorizing a machine to act with artificial intelligence and to make serious combat decisions is contingent upon circumstantial political and military judgements and wisdom of the leaders in charge of resolving many legal and ethical questions related to war and peace.

Notes:

1. Kaku, 2014, pp 220.
2. Hall, 2011, pp 100.
3. Barrat, 2013, pp 28.
4. Kurzweil, 2005, pp 145.
5. Barat, 2013, pp 135.
6. Joy, 2004, pp 67.

CHAPTER 8

The Quest for Techno-Power

**The Nature of Power and its Appearance
in the Hyperconnected World**
It has been asserted that man alone is capable
of progressive improvement;
that he alone makes use of tools or fire . . . mainly due to his power
of speaking and handing down his acquired knowledge.
(Charles Darwin, *The Descent of Man* pp 81-82)

Introduction

Whereas we find man developing fatherly power at the start of physical life, we also find a spontaneous appearance of power at the birth of social life. Arising from its root force, power started revealing its creative aspect when *Homo erectus*, using his freed hands and energetic imagination, began shaping his passion through "techno-power" to give meaning to life and his society. This power is constantly changing its many faces: emerging from the hands of a family head, passing to the control of a tribal chief, monopolized by nobility, exploited by religious and political leaders, dominated by the wealthy, dispensed by the sages, directed by ideologies, given principles by knowledge, systemized by science and technology, and managed by the elected authority, before today's hyperconnected world, power has been inaccessible to the common people it oppressed.

But whereas in the past, power has remained in the hands of centrally operating authority, just like a state-controlled currency, in our contemporary era of the network, in which everyone can be connected with everyone else in every corner of the globe, power is now like a current—accessible freely to everyone. Modern technology is a function of how smart we are, not how rich or physically powerful we could be. The power of hyperconnectedness has no central power-controlling authority. It works free from the shackles of hard power. It is developing new models, progressing by day and night, in which every individual is plugged into powerful gadgets. Heading rapidly toward a cyber-renaissance, technology is developing a borderless, nonracial, non-preferential, physically alienated, yet intellectually close-connected humanity, where the highest value would be the power of a smart brain. Thus, a culminating result of enlightenment in a cyber-renaissance would be that the spectrum of power, slipping out from the hold of rich and elite, will rapidly pass into the hands of those who were powerless in the past.

Power in the Hyperconnected World

Despite the ever-developing stages of power, from its root in force with many successive changes to the contemporary era with its miraculous bourgeoning in the hyperconnected world, power in its inmost core is still unchanged. Within its Hobbesian and Machiavellian perspective of raw power conquers all, and "military first," every nation has believed that a political outcome is determined by power and power along. For ages a power obsession has helped mankind achieve its intended effects by diverse acts of power practiced by human beings. Jeremy Heimans and Henry Timms in their work *New Power* are of the view that

> **Old power** works like a currency. It is held by few. Once gained, it is jealously guarded, and the powerful have a substantial store of it to spend. It is closed, inaccessible, and leader-driven. It downloads, and it captures. **New Power** operates differently, like a current. It is made by many. It is open, participatory, and peer-driven. It uploads, and it distributes. Like water or electricity, it's most forceful when it surges. The goal is not to hoard it but to channel it.[1]

The amazing developments of modern science—including the creation of robots and the introduction of artificial intelligence—have marked a radical break with the past not only in the growth of human power, but also in the sphere of power. In the past, there was a yawning gap between power in private hands and in the public sphere which is disappearing today. It is being replaced by the ethos of transparent and direct connectivity. Modern technology has made it possible for knowledge as an instrument and power as force to work horizontally from person to person. It is fast replacing the force vertically imposed by the sovereignty of God, gods, monarchs, governments, and wealthy magnates. The power of hyperconnectedness has devised an omnipresent link of connectivity, an ever-ready source in the hands of everyone to join together for a common cause with unprecedented speed in a stateless, borderless, and boundless system.

Furthermore, this new power may be merely an illusion. Heimans and Timms arguing against new power, have remarked:

> Those who are building and stewarding vast platforms that run on new power have become our new elites. These leaders often use the language of the crowd— "sharing," "open," "connected"—but their action can tell different story. Think of Facebook, the new power platform that most of us know best. For all those likes and smiley faces we create using what the company calls our "power to share," the two billon users of Facebook get no share of the vast economic value created by the platform.[2]

New power platforms set up by information technology, including youtube, skype, website, internet, Instagram, twitter, and the hashtag of #MeToo with almost one million tweets in forty-eight hours, are surging across the globe, an amazingly powerful cable-free-current. The power of hyperconnectedness, though a new technological innovation, is a reinforcement of the human instinctive passion for power in a superfast horizontal way. It's a way to share and cooperate rather than confront, compete, and impress; a way to enrich our brains instead of struggling for the survival of the fittest minds only; to refine, improve, and invigorate even the unfit or retarded minds rather than leave them behind to perish. It is ruminating-power that rewards everyone who shares freely his own assets or ideas, transmits them to others, and receives input to build on and improves his existing ideas.

Passion to Techno-Power in Today's World

Throughout history, in a world that is ruled by power, mankind has moved forward from one stage to another, never turning back. Our impulse to power instinctively drives us to fulfill our unlimited desires and do things just because we have the power to do them, regardless of whether they work for us or anyone else. Our intrinsic impulse to power driven by free will impels us to do anything we want. At every step of our life, our impulse to power has multiplied its force by inventing new technology. Byron Reese in his book *The Fourth Age*, propounds:

> Technology has fundamentally reshaped humanity just three times in history: 100,000 years ago, we harnessed fire, which led to language; 10,000 years ago, we developed agriculture, which led to cities and warfare; and 5,000 years ago, we invented the wheel and writing, which led to the nation-state. Now, we are on the doorstep of a fourth great change brought about by two technologies: artificial intelligence and robotics. We would soon be facing: machine consciousness, automation, drastic shifts in employment and the workforce, creative computers, radical life extension, artificial life, the ethics of artificial intelligence, autonomous warfare, superintelligence, and extreme prosperity, to name only a few.[3]

The free ideas of the Enlightenment and scientific inventions of past millennia are now being snapped up by the powerful new networked forces all around us. The new age of "network power" will confirm that "We are what we are connected to." But before the machines decide for us, we must start thinking about what the power of artificial intelligence means for us. As we look to our future, we find the prediction of "*Singularity*" by Ray Kurzweil is preparing us for wider participation in the technological powers that will drastically transform our lives. Singularity, according to Kurzweil is the union of human and machine, in which the knowledge and skills embedded in human brains will be combined with the greater capacity, speed, and knowledge-sharing ability of our own creation, the cyber-net power. Kurzweil, believing in human centrality, argues in the last lines *The Singularity is Near*:

> But it turns out that we are central, after all. Our ability to create models—virtual realities—in our brains, combined with our modest-looking thumbs has been sufficient to usher in another form of evolution: technology. That development enabled the persistence of the accelerating pace that started with biological evolution. It will continue until the entire universe is at our fingertips.[4]

Man's centrality in the cosmos was instilled in him an intense desire to perpetuate himself forever. His quest—his will to immortality—has been the foundation of his achievement. The wellspring of his passion to power in the beginning was reflected through his mythological stories, then religion, the muse of philosophy, and the impulse behind art and science. Man, as argued by Bertrand Russell, is framed in a dynamic pattern in the cosmos and, "While [all other] animals are content with existence and reproduction, men desire also to expand, and their desires in this respect are limited only by what imagination suggests as possible; some few find it difficult to admit the impossibility."

The Power of the Cyber-net

Modern technology has changed the natural way of our life. Our instinctive impulse to power has adopted the new passion to techno-power. Adults as well as children now contact with each other on Facebook, Twitter, and through text messages. Knowledge, information, teaching and learning, and life experiences, all come to everyone pre-managed, readymade, and above all filtered through digital devices. Even before the babies can walk they are exposed to screen media. Our children are plugged in seven to eight hours daily. They relate to each other without direct person-to-person contact, communicate mostly without speaking to each other. Teenagers woo each other by text; join up or break up on Twitter, tease and taunt, cheat and deceive—in some extreme cases commit criminal acts or get depressed to the point of suicide—all performed in cyberspace. The consequences of such a hyper-wired life-style are crippling us by creating a social isolation, intellectual introversion, and imaginational stagnation through emotional decadence and spiritual dissipation, yet it is keeping every one of us closely connected with everyone else across the globe.

Thanks to a powerful iPhone with an integrated camera in our hand, we have started thinking, communicating, and connecting with each other through pictures. Whereas the iPhone is creating a culture of non-physical connectivity, the camera heightens an existing culture of celebrity. The convergence of these technologies is helping us to be recognized and connected stripping off our natural identity. As the smartphone is creating a culture of physical separateness, the camera cultivates a culture of pictorial connectivity and celebrity exposure promoted by the "selfie" which has changed the way people contact, communicate, and present themselves to the world. It occupies a space of spontaneity, freedom in taking and sharing one's own image. Whereas this technology saves us from the fear of anonymity and validates our visibility, it is depriving our brain of its capabilities of direct intellectual investigation, interpersonal social skills, emotional bonds, spiritual peace, and the virtues of ethic and morality that older generations learned through everyday physical interaction.

Franklin Foer, in his book *World Without Mind* argues:

> The world has rushed to embrace the products and services of four titanic corporations. We shop with Amazon, socialize with Facebook, turn to Apple for entertainment, and rely on Google for information. These firms sell their efficiency and purport to make the world a little better place, but what they have done instead is to enable an intoxicating level of daily convenience.[5]

We have accepted an unstable culture of information which has put us on a path to a world without private contemplation, autonomous thought, or solitary introspection—a world without our own thinking mind.

Today, a big question lies before us all: Is modern science tyrannously changing our course of evolution? Is power of cyber-net technology taking over the intelligent-designed or the naturally evolved man and arbitrarily shaping him into an emotionless and spiritless figure subjected to Techno-Power sovereignty? We see our children, who were yesterday playing together, discovering themselves and exploring the world around them through their own perception, imagination, individually as well as by group contacts and interactions, being robbed of their childhood by internet technology. Those who once argued with friends, drew lots, chased each other, laughing, tumbling, bumping and bumbling around; those who talked and fought and resolved their conflicts face-to-face, are now plugged in computers. That which helped them to learn how to live with their parents, siblings, and friends, and not only staying physically active, but also lovingly connected, in which every interaction was direct, body to body and soul to soul, is taken away by the power of the network.

In today's complex web of hyperconnected world, the human passion to techno-power is facing new challenges from algorithmically creative computers, digitized machines, numerical ethics, the morality of artificial intelligence, and autonomous warfare, to name only a few. We have to learn how our next generation's natural passion to power, multiplied by the power of the silicone brain, would behave in their hyperconnected world, particularly of those who have experienced deprivation and oppression in the past. Let us hope that the complex of victimhood or deprivation, which is psychobiological and passes on generations to generations, does not trigger revengeful passions in that generation and that they will not resort to violent vengeance instead of upholding love and peace!

Notes:

1. Heimans and Timms, 2018, p. 2.
2. ibid., p. 11.
3. Reese, 1st inside flap of the cover, 2018.
4. Kurzweil, 2005, p. 487.
5. Foer, 2017, front-flap.

CHAPTER 9

The Rise of
Technocapitalism

Introduction

Technocapitalism is a new version of capitalism that generates new forms of corporate organization designed to exploit intangibles such as creativity and new ideas. Technology, being a subject of social intervention, affects and is affected by functional and cultural influences. It has also changed the way we conduct our daily social and business activities, such as shopping online for products, selecting them from pictorial display, paying online from our bank accounts, and communicating or chatting by texting. Having invented a techno-culture, we have laid the foundation of digitized technocorporatism by replacing the old economics of capitalism with the new scientific system of technocapitalism.

What is Technocapitalism?

For human beings, emancipation is not only freedom from socio-political oppression, but also from the economic conditions deployed over society through the power of business organizations or corporations. Corporatism as an agency of capitalism—an economic system based on the private ownership of the means of production and their operation for profit by few—colonizes human emancipation. Capital accumulation, competitive markets, price monopolies, private property, recognition of ownership rights, voluntary exchange, wage labor, and accumulation of wealth are central characteristics of capitalism. In a capitalist market economy, though prices and distribution of goods are determined by competition and services markets, the owner of wealth is the ultimate decision maker.

Capitalism, right from its origin, has been more comfortable with theocracies, autocracies, and monarchies, while its relationship with democracy has always been a tense one; in many cases it has remained a total contradiction. This is because capitalism is ruled by the owner of capital who individually or through a corporation controls the economy and people's needs, whereas democracy as a rule of the majority has neither capital nor reason to be identified with capitalism. Since capitalism's corruptive role of hoarding wealth gives free hand to the capitalist to control and deprive common people of access to money for their needs, it creates an economic slavery.

Though the creation of internet technology has multiple consequences—natural, social, political, and economic—it has given a new form to traditional capitalism as *technocapitalism.* Just as technology is the result of human creativity, technocapitalism, grounded in the power of corporatism and its exploitation of technological creativity, has now created *technocorporatism* as its agency. It has developed a new form of economics supported by technology—one which is not implemented by economists but is autonomously driven by the technology itself. It does not need to be defined by an expert in the field of economics; it is independent and does not seek the guidance of any hypothesis. Rather, the market is expressing itself through technology's operating system beneath our computer's interfaces and platforms, unrecognized even by the developers themselves is called technocapitalism and its operating system is called technocorporatism. This new version of capitalism is bringing about new forms of corporate power and organizations that will have major implications for human society during the twenty-first century. In new technocorporate regimes, technological creativity, which is primarily oriented toward research and intellectual appropriation, is turned into a commodity and is colonized by technocapitalism.

The Role of Technocorporatism

As, day by day, the new phenomenon of technocorporatism becomes ever more intrusive and rapacious through its control over technological creativity and innovation, it is likely to lead to major social, political, and economic consequences. However, the purpose of the technocapitalist operating system is same as capitalism has been from ancient times when agrarian societies were structured by religion-sponsored capitalist system: preventing common people from acquiring money for their betterment, keeping them away from access to wealth, and preventing widespread prosperity, which is fundamental to human emancipation.

Adam Smith's idea of commercial society, born in the eighteenth century in the midst of a period of organic economic growth which evolved into capitalism in the Western world, is today falling into an indistinguishable abyss. Adam Smith was well aware of the abstract nature of corporations and stressed that regulations would be necessary to keep them from destroying the marketplace. In the same way, today's "digital based business system" of technocapitalism is just software that converts real assets into abstract forms of shareholder value. The myth on which the techno-enthusiasts project their hopes is that new innovations will continue to create new markets and more growth—just as in our history. When agriculture reached its peak, we developed the steam engine; when electricity replaced the steam engine and radio and television emerged, they created new demand; when online retail slowed its growth, we developed data mining; and when data as a commodity seemed to plateau, we developed artificial intelligence, which needs massive supply of data in order to learn and progress.

Today's autonomous technologies, online markets, and free media have paralyzed our ability to think as humans, connect to each other meaningfully, and act constructively and purposefully. We are living in the age of digital culture which has given rise to technocapitalism controlled by a handful of IT organizations. As today's market is expressing itself through autonomous technologies, it is producing a bounty for a few technocapitalists. Four overpowering technocorporations, Google, Amazon, Facebook, and Apple—abbreviated as GAFA—have grown into wealthy giants. Whereas, during the traditional capitalist system, the CEO of a typical company in 1960 made about twenty times as much an average worker, today, the CEO of a technocorporation makes 271 times the salary of the average worker. This concentrates wealth in a few hands and is preventing the widespread growth of prosperity. Without thinking or questioning, we are relying on and trusting Google for information, shopping online with Amazon, socializing with friends on Facebook, and turning to Apple for entertainment.

The Birth of Digital Culture

Our cultural values and market transactions, which were once forces for human connections and expression, are now isolated, or rather, are becoming archaic. Digital culture and technological markets are repressing our natural human values. Our society is no longer together. We are individual players who find their souls in smartphones, introduce and recognize ourselves in selfies and on Facebook, seek information from digital media, shop online, and interact with friends and relatives through diverse mediums made available to us by IT. Among many transformations taking place in the global economy, none is more salient than the growth of gigantic "Internet Platforms" whose real danger is not that they distort markets, but that they threaten democracy. Google, Amazon, Facebook, Apple, Youtube, Twitter, and texting have been moving our daily activities online, and became even more popular during the COVID-19 pandemic, which helped today's "digital culture" gain firm ground in our social order.

At the same time, few technocorporations, despite having eighty-percent of the world's wealth in their control, are worried about the impoverished class staging an uprising—either now or after a disaster—and continue to hoard wealth, build real estate assets, control supplies, and mind their own security. The bounty produced by modern technocapitalists is more than offset by its dependence on nonrenewable resources and human slavery. The emergence of mega-dominant technocorporations is also ringing alarm bells—not just because they hold so much economic power but also because they wield so much control over the political and social order—they are posing threats to a well-functioning democracy.

We know that digital markets exhibit certain features that distinguish them from conventional ones; for example, its coin is data. Once a single technocorporation has amassed data on hundreds of millions of users, it can move into completely new markets and beat hundreds of established firms that lack similar knowledge. Moreover, technocorporations benefit greatly from so-called network efforts. The larger the network gets, the more useful it becomes to its users, creating a positive feedback loop that leads a single company to dominate the market. Unlike traditional firms, companies in the digital space do not compete for market share; they compete for the market itself, and can entrench themselves and make competition impossible. They can easily devour small companies and swallow up potential rivals, as Facebook did by purchasing Instagram and WhatsApp, and thus, can colonize human societies, turning our most precious human qualities into commodities.

The Power of Technocorporations

The concentrated economic and political power of the digital platform is like a loaded weapon sitting on a table. No liberal democracy, even based on the assumption of good intention, is prepared to entrust concentrated political power to an economically powerful technocorporation. The problem, however, is that neither the United States nor the European Union could likely break up Facebook or Google the way traditional corporations like Standard Oil and AT&T were broken up. Perhaps more important, it is not clear that a breaking up of Amazon, Google, or Facebook would solve the underlying problem. There is a very good chance that a baby created by such a breakup would quickly grow to replace the parent. Data probability faces a number of obstacles; chief among them is the difficulty of moving many kinds of data. Although it is easy enough to transfer some basic data—such as one's name, address, credit card information, and email address—it would be far harder to transfer all of a user's metadata.

The ideology of technocapitalism is part of a line of thought that relates science and technology to the evolution of traditional capitalism. At the core of this idea is that science and technology are not divorced from society nor do they exist in a vacuum, or even in a separate reality of its own. As technocapitalism is autonomously moving ahead supported by technological creativity, it is not out of reach of social action and human decision. This line of thought has encouraged philosophers to adopt and apply a theoretical and critical approach to internet technology and science in general, providing many important insights into how scientific and technological decisions and their outcomes are to be shaped by society—specifically, by capitalists and their institutions. Thus, the term *technocapitalism* has been used to denote aspects that diverge sharply from the corporate environment and relationships in a high tech-oriented local economy.

CHAPTER 10

The Human Situation

There is no other final cause beyond man;
And it is disclosed in his own self, that man is mankind.
(Sa'ad ud-Din Mahmud Shabistari)

Introduction

Today, we are living in a time when the human race is facing a serious threat of annihilation: through conventional and nuclear war, through population explosion, through moral dissipation, corruption, and many more cataclysmic acts of our own handiwork. But the major cause of the critical human situation today is an ever-increasing alienation of the human being from his own self, his fellow human beings, and from his lack of realization that *Man is the root cause and all other things are offshoots.* One major cause is that man, in his pursuit for superiority in this world is struggling to be "above man." Caught in the complex web of spiritual and material life, he is menacingly trespassing his limits of existing in this world as a "human being."

It is interesting to mention here that during World War II, Albert Einstein—a great thinker and scientist—brought to the attention of U.S. President Roosevelt that Germany might be working to develop an atomic weapon, and recommended that the United States begin similar research. Einstein's intention was to alert the Allied forces and prepare them to defend themselves, but he was not in favor of using an atomic weapon.[1] Once the U.S. had developed the nuclear weapon, Einstein, together with Bertrand Russell, signed the *Russell–Einstein Manifesto*, which highlighted the danger of nuclear weapons.[1] What an irony of the human situation that Einstein the scientist himself first suggested the production of nuclear technology and then as a humanist philosophized, "The unleashed power of the atom has changed everything, except our thinking. Thus, we are drifting toward a catastrophe beyond comparison. We shall require a substantially new manner of thinking if mankind is to survive." Just as Einstein the scientist and philosopher has speculated, we are tempted to indicate, "What a pathetic creature is man. Is he, even today, a brute trying to be god but traveling in the wrong direction?" Thus, we must probe the question: "What does the word 'man' mean and what is the concept of man?"

The Word "Man" and its Meaning

Before we reflect upon the concept of man and try to find an answer to this intriguing question, it is important to know, "What does the word 'man' mean?" According to one etymology the word "man" comes from the Proto-Germanic *mann*, or "person," originating from the Proto-Indo-European root, meaning "hand." The Old English *mann* also means man as "hand." Another view is that around 1.5 million years ago as *Homo erectus* appeared walking on two legs with a big brain, free hands, and opposable thumbs, the word "man" originated from the word "hand." Many words have "man" as suffix or prefix, but the word itself can designate an individual person, or all of the human race regardless of sex or age. In traditional usage, the word "man" also refers to the human species and mankind as a whole.

The increasing multiplicity of scientific views about man, valuable as they are, are severely impairing, which leads us to the thought that at no time in his history has man been so much a problem to himself as he is now. However, regarding the meaning of man, various irreconcilable ways of thinking are apt to come into conflict in our mind. Mark Scheler, in his book *Man's Place in Nature*, translated by Hans Meyerhoff writes:

> If we ask an educated person in the Western world what he means by the word "man" three irreconcilable ways of thinking are apt to come into conflict in his mind. The first is the Jewish-Christian tradition of Adam and Eve, including creation, paradise and fall. The second is the Greek tradition in which, for the first time, man's self-consciousness raised him to a unique place on the grounds that he is endowed with reason. Closely bound up with this view is the doctrine that there is a superhuman "reason" in the total universe in which man alone of all creatures participates.

> The third idea is that of modern science and genetic psychology, which also has a tradition of its own. According to this view man is a very recent product of evolution in our planet, a creature distinguished from its antecedents in the animal world only by the degree of complexity of energies and capacities already present on a subhuman level.[2]

These three ideas—one theologically revealed, one rationally theorized, and one scientifically advocated—are completely separate from each other. Due to the incompatibility of these ideas, we do not have a unified concept of man. Moreover, all these ideas tend to hide man's nature more than they reveal it. The only commonalities in these three meanings of man are his upright posture, his big brain, his grasping hand with opposable thumb, the recession of the jawbone and teeth, which help him in using the tool of language, and his brain which gives him the capability to think, behave, and act in his own unique way, so that in spite of his resemblance to the chimpanzee in morphological and physiological appearance, we define him as "human."

The Concept of Man as a Human

But the concept of man as a "human being" has an entirely different meaning, and a different origin which reduces man to a smaller section of the vertebrate world. The first concept of the creation of man is the "mythical man" whose appearance in this world is based on stories in pre-historical and early historical societies in different regions of the world. Mythology, which today is viewed as a kind of non-logical philosophy expressed in the form of a story or visual images, does not claim to be true. But it is expressive of human feelings about his creation and experiences in his life. Myths, on the whole being less dangerous—they are even read with great interest in the modern age — are viewed as more peaceful presentations of man and his life as compared to religious and scientific expressions.

Though different myths emerged in various parts of the world, one of the most popular story of man's creation is from Greek mythology which relates the supreme god Zeus giving the task of creating man and the animals to his sons Prometheus (meaning "forethought") and Epimetheus (meaning "afterthought"). Prometheus, who created man in the likeness of the gods, wanted to give man fire (the power of knowledge) but Zeus would not permit it. Prometheus defied Zeus and stole fire from the gods and brought it down to man. Epimetheus was to give special gifts for protection to all the animals, such as shells for turtles and claws for bears, and so on. He gave out all the special gifts to the animals and there was nothing left when it came to man.

Zeus believed man, created in the image of the gods and posessing the power of fire or knowledge, needed to be weakened. He thus ordered Hephaestus to create woman for this purpose. Hephaestus created the first woman, Pandora, in the likeness of the goddesses. Every deity contributed to the creation of woman and gave her not only beauty, grace, and charm, but also the art of lies, seduction, and guile. Zeus gifted Pandora a box and gave her to Epimetheus, who took her as his bride. Pandora was forbidden to open the box, but she could not resist her curiosity about what was in the box and opened it. Thus, out came all the plagues of mankind, such as disease, pain, envy, sorrow, and death. Pandora quickly shut the lid, trapping hope inside. Today the often-used term "Pandora's Box" refers to something that releases danger, unforeseen trouble, or confusion.

The second concept of the creation of man, known as "intelligent design" by a monotheistic God, is the Biblical story of Adam and Eve. The story, starting with the creation of the first couple, their life in paradise, and their fall from Divine Grace, is narrated in the scriptures revealed by God to his Prophets. These Scriptures assigned man the status of a human being as best of all the creatures created by God.

The third concept of man is the tradition of Classical Greek philosophers who, for the first time believing in man's self-consciousness, raised him to a unique place: a human being endowed with "reason" and "Logos"—which here means both speech and the capacity to grasp the nature of things. Closely bound up with this view is the doctrine that the man of "reason" in this universe is an intelligent "human being" amongst all the creatures.

The fourth concept is that of modern science, which tries to prove that man is a self-created creature and the human being is the product of a billions of years-long ongoing process of evolution. He is a creature distinguished from his antecedents in the animal world only by the degree of complexity of those energies and capacities present on a subhuman level. All these concepts—mythical, anthropological, theological, philosophical, and scientific—are separate and incompatible. Thus, we are still unable to define a unified concept of man as a "Human Being."

On Becoming a Human Being

The word "human" was first recorded in the mid-thirteenth century, and owes its existence to French word *humain,* "of or belonging to man," which, in turn, comes from the Latin *humanus,* thought to be a hybrid relative of *homo,* meaning "man," and *humus,* meaning "earth." When we raise the status of man to the level of "human being" we assign him unique characteristics which are not comparable to any other species. It is the task of anthropology, cognitive philosophy, and religion to identify how all man's achievements, such as language, conscience, philosophy, science, ethics and morality, ideas of right and wrong, art and literature, historical, religious, socio-political life, and the role of leadership, have arisen from the basic structure of man's nature to make him a "human being." The human status of man after progressing from the lower stage of his existence indicates that it was his inner impulse by which man became human. His consciousness of the world and his awareness of himself gave birth to a Cognitive Revolution.

With this Cognitive Revolution, in order to objectify his own psychophysical nature, the human being encountered the idea of his creation, first through mythical stories and then through his spiritual invocation of an Infinite Being beyond his world. During the Cognitive Revolutionary period, the human being started revising his behavior in accordance with the changing needs in his life. Yuval Noah Harari in his book *Sapiens* argues:

> The Cognitive Revolution is accordingly the point when history declared its independence from biology. Until the Cognitive Revolution, the doings of all human species belonged to the realm of biology, or, if you so prefer, prehistory. From the Cognitive Revolution onwards, historical narratives replace biological

theories as our primary means of explaining the development of *Homo sapiens*. To understand the rise of Christianity or the French Revolution, it is not enough to comprehend the interaction of genes, hormones and organisms. It is necessary to take into account the interaction of ideas, images, and fantasies as well.[3]

Humanity, starting from the Cognitive Revolution, arose entirely on its own through the driving force of its instinctive quest for creativity, the love of novelty, solving challenges, and disclosing new ones. At every step, during its evolution to explain human situation, humanity gave meaning to its existence. Thus, the human being in his attempt to picture the whole to himself first sought his place in mythical images, then in the image of divine activity, and then, emerging as an intellectual, figured out his place in the complex human situation facing subjective and objective challenges to his life.

The Complexity of the Human Situation

Human beings, governed by the laws of biology from the time they first appeared on the planet Earth, are constantly engaged with their biological needs. Influenced and constrained by their own genes and reproductive imperative, they are perennially concerned about the processes of their life and death. Their genetic imperative manifests itself in their emotional life describing love and hate, grief and mourning as natural behavior breaking down their emotional system into roughly two elements, "Love and Fear"—where love is of the heart and soul and fear is of the personality. Love unites man with his fellow human beings, and for the believer, with his God. Man is creative through his passion of love, while fear impels him to destroy. Long before Darwin's nineteenth-century work *The Origin of Species*, *Homo sapiens* sought relief from the fear of being alone in his world by connecting themselves with the supernatural realm. In order to seek an answer for whatever seemed mysterious to them, they first wove myths, then framed worldly religions, and after achieving spiritual awakening, humans found solace in revealed religions. Later on, guided by their cognitive power, human beings became rationalistic and scientific. Though today the man of science and intellectual insight is all over-powering, we find him still living in his religious and cultural domain of "man the mystic, the religious, and the intellectual."

Man the Mystic

Mysticism is an ancient doctrine or practice concerned with the mysteries of existence relating to man's spiritual and intellectual quest— about his own self, the origin of universe, its creator, and the Ultimate Truth or God. Mysticism universally covers both theistic and non-theistic dimensions. Mystical experience is not just a spiritual or an intellectual uncovering of information or facts; it is an experience of being and seeing the true nature of man's own self, mankind, the universe, and for a spiritual person, to establish communion with the Creator or God. Typically, the mystics (religious or non-religious) focus upon human transformation. It is a metaphysical branch of philosophy whose experience in a supersensory mode makes human experience mystical as well as spiritual. We can say that St. Augustine or Rumi and many others were spiritual mystics, while many great scientists and philosophers, like Isaac Newton, Albert Einstein, and others were natural mystics.

For a pure mystic, knowledge of the mysteries of existence is experienced mostly through the channels of direct intuition, including the possibility of direct communion with God or the first source of creation. Mystical experience can be monotheistic, polytheistic, agnostic, atheistic, or scientific. Most traditions agree that the aim of mystical practice is to actualize the highest stage of enlightenment—an actualization that brings freedom from destructive and self-defeating traits, such as vain ambition, greed, jealousy, anger, etc. It brings about a clear consciousness so that one can become—in mystical terms—a "perfect" or a "complete whole person." In different traditions, a person immersed in Divinity becomes a Qutab, Saint, Yogi, or Shaman, and in historical traditions, a "creative scientist" in the fields of science and art.

In the final analysis, a true mystic is a person whose inner life is driven by a passion for unity and oneness with Truth and Higher Knowledge and with humanity. It is an awakening which cannot be achieved by human reasoning alone but demands the brightening of hope, the leaping of faith, and the power of the unifying force of Love. A scientist advances with a firm faith in his knowledge of physical sciences and a desire to uncover what is hidden, helping to heal the body, while a spiritual heals the inner self of the man. This is one reason that a majority of psychologists are scientists as well as spirituals. In his lecture on "Man and Religion," included in the book *The Human Situation* edited by Piero Ferrucci, Aldous Huxley said:

> I take it that the mystical experience is essentially the being aware of and, while the experience lasts, being identified with a form of pure consciousness, of unstructured transpersonal consciousness which lies, so to speak, upstream from the ordinary discursive consciousness of everyday. It is a non-egoistic consciousness, a kind of formless and timeless consciousness, which seems to underlie the consciousness of the separate ego in time.[4]

Man the mystic is free from greed, intellectual pride, and blind obedience to custom or religious traits, or awe of persons higher in rank. This brings us to the famous saying about a mystic: *To be in the world but not of it.*

The earliest known theory of conscious evolution is of mystical origin based on metaphysics, which applies to the individual as well as to the whole human race. Though evolutionary theory is based on physics and natural science while mysticism is at the heart of human relationships, both seek the "self-existing essence" from the most fundamental meta-laws of physics to diverse kinds of consciousness, one of which could be a Divine revelation or a new scientific invention.

According to many religious traditions, our deepest values are expressed through our emotional and spiritual bonds. In the moral code of Confucianism, the health of a society derives from the maintenance of proper relationship with family, friends, and the community. Sacramental theory recognizes that physical relationships are reminders and reflections of man's spiritual relationship with other beings. The non-theistic or scientific approach of inter-being is based on the fundamental assertion that everything is connected to everything through a chain of attraction and gravity, which in philosophical terms is a passion of "love." Einstein in the book, *The Philosophy of Albert Einstein* edited by Walt Martin and Magoda Ott, says:

> The most beautiful and most profound emotion we can experience is the sensation of the mystical. It is the sower of all true science. He for whom this emotion is a stranger, who can no longer wonder and stand rapt in awe, is as good as dead. To know that what is impenetrable to us really exists, manifesting itself as the highest wisdom and the most radiant beauty which our dull faculties can comprehend only in their most primitive forms—this knowledge, this feeling is at the center of true religiousness.[5]

Whether it is within the perspective of natural science or the subject of humanities, for a mystic, the whole universe is woven together by a mystical relationship.

Man the Religious

Whereas according to the Abrahamic scriptures, Adam the first man created by the Intelligent Design was divinely aware of his religion, natural man was also actively involved in religious practices in his own way. The history of mankind reveals that for the human beings religious mechanism has perennially remained a source of bliss for them which even in the modern age seems to be part of their spiritual and social way of life. Billions of humans follow religion, giving legitimacy to a superhuman authority, and follow the laws ordained by an absolute, omnipotent, and supreme power. This human behavior reflects that religion is a system of mankind's norms and values embedded in the belief of a superhuman order.

Anthropologists believe that during the first millennium BCE, humans started following a natural system of religion emerging from their instinct to find an answer to the mysteries of natural events. They first believed in spirits, then in gods, but during the second half of the first millennium BCE, the belief in the One Supreme and Omnipotent God of Abraham appeared. A large percentage of mankind follows the three great revealed religions. However, man, impelled by his rational instinct to create new things, invented the knowledge of art and science. Discussing religion and science, Einstein argues that the two are not incompatible:

> [But] I maintain that cosmic religious feeling is the strongest and noblest motive for scientific research. It is cosmic religious feeling

that gives a man strength. A contemporary has said, not unjustly, that in this materialistic age of ours the serious scientific works are the only profoundly religious peoples. [Thus] science without religion is lame, religion without science is blind. The further the spiritual evolution of mankind advances, the more certain it seems to me that the path to genuine religiosity does not lie through the fear of life, and the fear of death [as it was with the primitive man] and blind faith, but through striving after rational knowledge.[6]

The religious image of man as a "creation of intelligent design" demonstrates that man is by nature a mystical-spiritual-intellectual human being with free will at his command—a capability that no other animal possesses. This free will permits man to bypass ordinary laws of cause and effect and thus, acting freely, he exercises a prerogative which some will attribute only to God or a Super-Power above man.

When we study the history of human culture, we find the first social discipline was established by religion. In the beginning, after the non-logical philosophy of mythical stories, religion appeared as a form of logical philosophy and was recognized as a perfect form of social discipline. Though in the history of mankind's biological and social evolution, the role of science and philosophy cannot be denied, billions of human beings believe that religion alone is capable of delivering mankind from its plight. When we begin the study of our cultural heritage by examining texts from the ancient Greek, Roman, Hebrew, Christian, and Islamic cultures, we find that the modern world is deeply rooted in these cultures. We are still inspired and shaped by Homer's epic poems, by Platonic philosophy, by the Old and New Testaments and the Qur'an. These key texts present compelling—though not always harmonious—insights into the human situation: *The excellences proper to humans, the character of the soul, relation to family, friends, lovers, strangers, and gods or God.*

The greatest thinkers of antiquity concerned themselves with the elaboration, criticism, and reconciliation of these powerful insights, and in doing so they took up the intriguing question of how to live one's life. The result of their efforts is a shared and open conversation concerning the most important matters for human beings. Aldous Huxley in his lecture on *Man and Religion* is of the opinion that:

> Religion as a system of beliefs is a profoundly different kind of religion, and it is the one which has been the most important in the West. The two types of religion—the religion of direct acquaintance with the divine and the religion of a system of beliefs—have co-existed in the West, but the mystics have always formed a minority in the midst of the official symbol-manipulating religions, and the relationship has been a rather uneasy symbiosis.[7]

Believers in religion generally concede that there are things and matters beyond human understanding. When human beings are unable to resolve the paradox of free will versus determination or solve the problem of good and evil, they end up in simple confession of faith. For the man of religion, the answer is a pious appreciation of God's redemptive power. Religion, according to Yuval Noah Harari, can be defined as *a system of human norms and values that is founded in a belief in a superhuman order.* In his book *Sapiens: A Brief History of Humankind,* he explains that religion involves two distinct criteria:

> That there is a superhuman order, which is not the product of human whims or agreements. . . Based on this superorder, religion establishes norms and values that it considers binding. . . In order to unite under its aegis a large expanse of territory inhabited by disparate groups of human beings, a religion must possess two further qualities. First, it must espouse a *universal* superhuman order that is true always and everywhere. Second, it must insist on spreading this belief to everyone. In other words, it must insist to be universal and missionary. . . The best-known religions in history, such as Islam and Buddhism, are universal and missionary. [8]

Those who believe in religion maintain that there is no natural evil; rather, it is a learned behavior. Evil is committed by humans, for and against themselves, and does not come from God. Though basic ethical and moral laws are fixed in religions, by the passage of time and the appearance of new cultures and traditions they can be re-interpreted by the rational consensus of religious scholars to become applicable in new situations.

Man the Intellectual and Scientific

The scientific image of man maintains that man is an animal that evolved according to the environmental and ecological rules of natural selection. Scientists present a strictly mechanistic and materialist interpretation of man who is free from any superstition and spiritual beliefs. Therefore, one image depicts man intrinsically possessing a spiritual part—an incorporeal soul and a mind—while the other image states that there is no such thing as a soul. The religious image reveals man's inner self or his spiritual nature, while science—focused on man's animal roots—unfolds the secrets of the external world. These images of man seem incompatible with each other, yet there is a common strand of mysticism between the two images, working as a "blazing lightning bolt." Such a view helps us to understand that it is because of man's mystical aspiration that both the images maintain an everlasting perception of what it means to be human.

A holistic view recognizes man as a conscious and unconscious being, aware of his free will, capable of self-knowledge to live rationally, morally, and meaningfully. Even today both characteristics of man are engaged in pursuing the source of his creation: science through physics, religion through metaphysics. Both images of man are involved in solving the mysteries of the universe—the scientific man researching through intellectual channels, the spiritual one trying to find the creator through the spiritual approach of his psyche. The scientific quest is materialistic and seeks only to see and present the abstract in physical form or shape, while the spiritual pursuit is collective of man's many intrinsic capabilities to feel, see, and experience the abstract in every possible form.

Humans are reminded in every period of their history that if they are to deal with new challenges of their era, they need to understand the intellectualism of their contemporary period. They are aware that no matter what happened in the past hour, it is history. They struggle to live every minute, every hour in the present, in the modern age and with the modern calendar. At this point, with an accepted modern technology reading time to an accuracy of nanoseconds, it becomes necessary to manipulate the analysis of all the variables of time and space, and find the reality of human existence and identity through the consensus of manageable ideas of knowledgeable intellectuals.

Despite our technological progress and the appearance of artificial intelligence, we, the human beings of the modern age, still display our religious traditions and philosophical cognitions in our political order, economic systems, social structure, and cultural traditions by the cognitive power of our minds. Since the culture of a time is a joint output of the leading minds of that time in the form of their discoveries, experiences, and scientific and philosophical ideas, today, as we live in a "scientific civilization" we mostly talk about scientific progress, and speak little of our spiritual and philosophical life. This situation is created by information technology which enables even our philosophical views, proliferated minute-to-minute, to be transmitted to every one. Though we consider science and philosophy as separate fields of knowledge, an insightful study of philosophical and scientific knowledge transporting ideas from mind to mind—ideas that are drivers of certainty, universality, unity and change, postmodernity, subjectivity, relativity, diversity and new narratives—reveal the dominant role of science in our life.

The digital revolution is shattering in every minute the narratives of the past minute and setting the stage for new ones. Technological advances have significantly transformed people's lives and ways they define themselves, so the digital age has given rise to existential fears, identity crises, and depression. This in turn has led people to question their identities along with the world surrounding them, and to seek out their true selves. The challenges posed by today's mega-tech to human existence and identity need to be faced through interdisciplinary sociological and philosophical reflections.

Humans instinctively seek meaning in their lives. Consciously or unconsciously, they want to know from where they came, why they are here, and where they are heading. Facing such intriguing questions, coming from an ordinary person to great literary and scientific scholars, we notice that mysticism keeps human beings sane and serene while science and reason fail to provide satisfactory answers. The secret is that a mystic—both in the religious and non-religious camps—can express faith in human beings, in their possibility to develop to ever higher stages, in their unity of a mankind, in their reason, love, tolerance, and peace, enabling them to realize that potentially "man is mankind." Though every living thing seeks to perpetuate itself, humans yearn and strive to perpetuate themselves forever.

Human beings' quest and will to immortality is the basis of their achievement; it is the source of religion and morality, the stimulus behind philosophy and literature, and the impulse behind science and art. Its combined expression is what we know as a "civilization of mankind." Human beings, guided by the sages to know themselves, have looked within themselves with global sweep—even in utterly disconnected cultures in a world of upheaval. Confucius taught morality in China, Buddha sought enlightenment in India, Plato and Aristotle examined the life of the mind and soul in Europe, and a chain of Abrahamic prophets penned a people of God into being in the Levant. The cultivation of inner life arose in an interplay with the startling proposition that the well-being of others beyond kin and tribe—the stranger, the orphan, the outcast—was linked as one's own being. Human beings have given voice to the questions that have animated religion and philosophy: What does it mean to be human? What matters in a life? What matters in a death? And how to be of service to each other and the world? These questions are being reborn, reframed, in our today's age of IT interconnectedness with far-flung strangers. Edward O. Wilson, in his book *The Meaning of Human Existence* writes:

> The advances of science and technology will bring us to the greatest moral dilemma since God stayed the hand of Abraham: how much to profit the human genotype? Shall it be a lot, a little bit, or none at all? The choice will be forced on us because our species has begun to cross what is the most important yet still least examined threshold in the techno-scientific era. We are about to abandon natural selection, the process that created us, in order to direct our evolution by volitional selection—the process of redesigning our biology and human nature as we wish them to be. No longer will the prevalence of some genes (more precisely alleles, variations in codes of the same genes) over others be the result of environmental forces, most of which are beyond human control or even understanding. Genes and their prescribed traits can be what we choose. So—how about longer lives, enlarged memory, better vision, less aggressive behavior, superior athletic ability? The shopping list is endless.[9]

When we conclude that man arose—on the only one planet which is our Earth—through an accumulated series of events during his evolution, he is not predestinated to reach any goal, not answerable to any power but only to himself, then only his wisdom based on his 'self-understanding' will save him from his annihilation on the planet Earth.

Notes:

1. Isaacson. 2007, pp 474 and 541.
2. Scheler, 1971, p. 5.
3. Harari, 2005, p.36
4. Ferrucci on Huxley, 1977, p. 212.
5. Einstein, 2013, p. 2.
6. Ibid. pp. 26-27.
7. Ferrucci on Huxley, 1977, p. 201.
8. Harari, 2005, p. 210
9. Wilson, 2014, p. 14.

CHAPTER 11

Human Passion for Power

Introduction

Power, by its nature is a neurophysiological property, an "instinctive impulse" that functions consciously or unconsciously in a mechanical way to fulfill the unlimited desires of human beings. It runs naturally as a force in every living being, creating both intended and unintended effects. But in human beings the impulse to power is an all-time active current ever ready to help them fulfill their desires by justified or unjustified acts. It began to expand when the descendants of an ancestral line of apelike creatures first picked up stones as tools and laid the foundation of the power of science and technology. Power's appearance as a brutish, cruel, and savage force determined its application as *unjustified* behavior. But due to its creative aspect, viewed as noble and altruistic, that helped man grow and develop into humanity, the passion to power is a *justified* and noble motive in mankind's evolution, growth, and progression.

In justified acts, power's appeal is noble and dignified, but its whetted appetite inspired the famous saying: "*Power tends to corrupt, and absolute power corrupts absolutely*,"—a quote from a letter by John Emerich Edward Dalberg Acton (1834-1902) to Bishop Mandell Creighton in 1887. Power can become unjustified, ignoble, graceless, and a devastating lust. It is the job of a sage or philosopher to determine when power is *justified* and when it is *unjustified*. Power, according to Bertrand Russell (1872-1970), "may be defined as the production of intended effects."[1] He further argued that "the fundamental concept in social science is Power, in the same sense in which energy is the fundamental concept in physics."[2] Russell, in his book *Power*, philosophizes:

> Between man and other animals there are various differences, some intellectual, some emotional. One of the chief emotional differences is that some human desires, unlike those of animals,

are essentially boundless and incapable of complete satisfaction. . . While animals are content with existence and reproduction, men desire also to expand, and their desires in this respect are limited only by what imagination suggests as possible. Every man would like to be [all powerful] God, if it were possible; some few find it difficult to admit the impossibility. These are the men framed after the model of Milton's Satan, combining, like him, nobility with impiety. By 'impiety' I mean something not dependent upon theological beliefs: I mean refusal to admit the limitations of individual human power. [3]

The intrinsic reverberation of power may change its appearance according to the situation and circumstances, but not its reality. Its natural appeal is always ready to face every challenge. According to Somali pirate Shamun Indhabur, "when evil is the only solution to achieve power, you do evil. That is why we are doing piracy. We know it is evil, but for us it is also a solution."

The Nature of Power

John Milton (1606-1674) in lines 242-264 of his epic *Paradise Lost* published in 1667, philosophically relates the nature of power by depicting the character of Satan and his desire for power and glory, after being stripped off his highest position of Archangel and declared by God forever an agent of evil in the world of human beings.

> *Is this the Region, this Soil, the Clime?*
> *Said then the lost Arch Angel, this the seat*
> *That we must change for Heaven, this mournful gloom*
> *For that celestial light? Be it so, since you*
> *Who now is Sovereign can dispose and bid*
> *What shall be right: farthest from Him is best*
> *Whom reason has equaled, force has made Supreme*
> *Above his equals [Iblees]. Farewell happy Fields*
> *Where Joy forever dwells; Hail horrors, hail*
> *Infernal world, and you profoundest Hell*
> *Receive your new Possessor [Satan]: One who brings*
> *A mind not to be changed by Place and Time.*
> ***The mind is its own place, and in itself***

Can make a Heaven of Hell, Hell of Heaven.
What matters where, if I be still the same,
And what I should be, all but less than He [God]
Whom Thunder [Power] has made greater?
Here at least we shall be free;
Here we may reign secure, and in my choice
To reign is worth ambition though in Hell:
Better to reign in Hell, than serve in Heaven.

Whereas Milton's lines are a paradox of *survival-will-of -power*, they are also the urge to the use of "force," a natural "struggle for existence," an instinctive "will to power," a passion to "grow and expand," and to be all powerful over land, sea and the sky.

Dr. Muhammad Iqbal (1873-1938)—the national poet of Pakistan and a famous philosopher-poet—in response to Milton's notion of "reason has equaled, force has made Supreme," set his view of human power in the "wedding of love and intellect." Iqbal, in his epic *Payam-i- Mashriq* (*Message of the East*) exhorts: "Man born of passive clay but a quintessence of creative and dynamic energy, gifted with the powers of love, action, and intelligence, and stirs the void of Universe to reconstruct it nearer to his heart's desire."[4] Iqbal argues for the natural power of man:

> *Nature worried that, out of passive clay has born a being,*
> *Self-creating, self-destroying, self-regarding!*
> *Word went around from heavens to the realm of Eternity,*
> *'Beware, O' veiled one, the tearer of veils is born!'*
> *Desire, unaware of its self, musing in the fold of life,*
> *Opened its eyes, and lo! a new world came into being.*[5]

Iqbal believes that man is the repository of unlimited powers waiting to be perfected. Whereas Milton in *Paradise Lost* portrays the spirit of confidence, courage, and passion to power in which man should set out on the undoubted perils of life, Iqbal in *Payam-i-Mashriq*—published in 1923—emphasizes the role of love in the spiritual and moral uplift of man's passion to power in the perfection of his self.

Thomas Hobbes (1588-1679), speculating on the restless desire of power of the human beings, argues in chapter 11 of his classic treatise *Leviathan* (published in 1651) on human nature and society:

I put for a general inclination of all mankind, a perpetual and restless desire of power after power that ceases only after death. And the cause of this is not always that a man hopes for more intensive delight than he has already attained to; or that he cannot be content with a moderate power: but because he cannot assure the power and means to live well, which he has present, without the acquisition of more.[6]

Hobbes, in the same work, conceives of human nature as mechanistic and deeply cynical, proclaiming man by his nature ruthless and selfish, with everyone struggling for his own sustenance and preservation, leading to "a state of nature in which it would be a war, as is of every man, against every man." They would inevitably kill one another, making life, "solitary, poor, nasty, brutish and short."[7] Paradoxically, Hobbes was speaking about the natural power impulse of man, where everyone seeks to overpower every other inspired by power's naked force.

Man's nature and his behavior as argued by Thomas Hobbes was profoundly probed and scientifically established, particularly in the light of biology, by Charles Darwin (1809-1892). His theory of evolution, based on biological changes of man and other living things over time, articulates the idea of Natural Selection, or the Survival of the Fittest. Within the biological and sociological perspective, it can be inferred that man's struggle through his long journey of the survival of the fittest was triggered by his intrinsic impulse of mental power. Darwin, throughout his works, has attributed every step of evolution to power, such as mental power, social power, emotional power, power of expressing desires, power of sexual selection, power of speaking, and man's numerous capabilities of overpowering other species, elements, traits, environments etc., leading him to the end result of Survival of the Fittest. Darwin argues:

It has been asserted that man alone is capable of progressive improvement; that he alone makes use of tools or fire, domesticates other animals, or possesses property; that no other animal has the power of abstraction, or of forming general concepts, is self-conscious and comprehends itself; that no animal employs language; that man alone has a sense of beauty, is liable to caprice, has the feeling of gratitude, mystery, etc.; believes in God, or is endowed with conscience. . . This is mainly due to his power of speaking and handling down his acquired knowledge.[8]

According to Darwin, the social instinct is the prime principle and chief factor of evolution of moral constitution. In Chapter III of *The Descent of Man*, Darwin propounds:

> In what manner the mental powers were first developed in the lowest organisms, is as hopeless an inquiry as how life itself first originated. These are problems for the distant future, if they are ever to be solved. . . [However] some intelligent actions, after being performed during several generations, become converted into instincts and are inherited. . . These actions may then be said to be degraded in character, for they are no longer performed through reason or from experience. But the greater number of the more complex instincts appear to have been gained in wholly different manner.[8]

The idea of evolution is basically biological change and development of human beings from a baser origin instead of his birth as a creation of intelligent design. Darwin in *The Origin of Species* proudly recounts his theory that "there is grandeur in this view of life, with its several powers."[8] The power impulse may well be an essential motivation that naturally runs through the inner being of every human being; but as a force in action, it is inherently relational. Force is at the root of power, and its appeal is evident in every phase of human life.

The Birth and Growth of Power

After understanding the nature of power, we need to learn how it was first born, what it first looked like as it developed itself into strength to overpower others and force them to obey. It is important to understand whether its appearance in human history is because of man's natural urge or nurtured process, or it evolved from his aggressive instinct. We now know love of power is an integral part of human nature and the source of his creative passion. Archaeologists have done amazing work in helping us to find the stemming of our social order in most of the human cultures evolving from a mother, who submitted herself to the authority of a male husband and conferred on him the role of a father with power over his wife and their offspring. Bertrand de Jouvenel, in his work *On Power*, propounds:

> The first authority to enter our lives is the parental. . . all authorities have agreed in seeing the family as the first society—as the primary cell from which the social structure afterwards grew, and paternal authority as the first form of command and stay of all the others.[9]

The father, beginning as the head of his family later on promoted himself as the head of expanded family and then extended families grouped together. The family became a tribe, then a political society, then a nation. Just as we find a father vested with power at the birth of physical life in a family, we can also draw a conclusion that power, which was naturally there before the appearance of society, emerged as a permanent tendency at the birth of our social life.

Throughout mankind's evolution, humans have tended to live and work in social groups. Whether, as argued by Hobbes, they were selfish individuals of innate wicked nature having no choice but to make reciprocal social contracts, or according to Jean-Jacques Rousseau (1712-1718), they were greedless noble savages that grouped together as good husbands and affectionate fathers following a faith of natural kindliness, human society would not have existed without a power superior to the power of individuals. Continuing the series of contrasts, conflicts, and power struggles, religion, headed by the sacred authority of an invisible "sovereign power" appeared to maintain discipline and social solidarity. Karen Armstrong in her work, *A History of God*, says, "My study of the history of religion has revealed that human beings are spiritual animals. Indeed, there is a case for arguing that Homo sapiens is also Homo religious."[10] For many millennia, the power of Divine sovereignty has been practiced by priests, Prophets, Caliphs, and monarchs as God's representatives on earth.

History is a chronicle of the conflicts, wars, and power struggles of mankind. In every culture, writers, particularly poets, have glorified power, depicting it as a graceful passion and eulogizing the virtue of being loved. But the love of power is also hypothesized by the ideologies of socio-political philosophers, giving free rein to hard force. Niccolo Machiavelli

(1469-1527) in his shocking political philosophy depicted in *The Prince*, propounded that force is basically an integral part of all political activities:

> All armed prophets have been victorious and the unarmed have come to ruin. Therefore, to survive, a ruler must be as cunning as a fox and as fierce as a lion, and every kind of power is necessary to attain political ends even if a ruler has to commit murder. He believed that power is for the one who possesses the art of capturing it in free competition.[11]

Friedrich Nietzsche (1844-1900), rejecting religious morality as belonging to slaves, pronounced that God must be dethroned to make room for earthly tyrants.[11] Changing its many faces, exploited by religious and political leaders, controlled by nobility, held by the elites, dominated by wealthy men, instructed by knowledge and ideologies, and in modern democracy controlled by the majority, power has remained inaccessible to those whom it has suppressed and subjected to obey.

Will to Power and Free Will

Friedrich Nietzsche in *Thus Spoke Zarathustra*, describes the will to power as "the unexhausted procreating will of life," indicating that it is creative, not merely controlling, and that it represents self-mastery, not just power over others. Further arguing on human beings' will to power he remarks, "Wherever I found a living thing, there I found 'Will to Power;' and even in the will of the servant, I found the 'Will to be Master.'"[12] By this he means that the will to power is man's intrinsic passion that motivates him in every phase of his life. It is the ability to direct or prevent actions of individuals and groups. Dan Barker states in his *Free Will Explained*:

> We don't locate love or free will by staring through a microscope. We don't find them analyzing antecedent material causes. They are qualities we human animals experience. . . Experiencing free will—socially true free will—is a huge part of what it means to be a moral species.[13]

For humans, one's personal will to power, free will, and freedom of expression are essential if one is to live a creative life.

In the make-up of power, the egoistical urge combined with the free will is its inner strength. Egoism in the human being encourages him to attain limitless power. His impulse to power is thus nourished by a vast variety of qualities such as useful or harmful, noble or sordid, great or small, etc. According to the argument of Bertrand de Jouvenel in his work *On Power*,

> As a self-proclaimed egoist, Power encounters the resistance of all the particular social interests with which it must have dealings. But let it call itself altruistic and give itself out for the executant of an ideal, and it will acquire such an ascendency over every concrete interest as will enable it to sacrifice them to the fulfilment of its mission and crush every obstruction to its triumphal march.[14]

Unfortunately, in human nature there is no such element that can naturally pacify or satisfy his passion of desire for power. However, an altruistic belief of "live and let live" would help man to nurture tamed passion and rid himself of his desire for unlimited power. In order to survive man needs to nurture a new manner. There is still time for mankind to seriously consider and act upon what Einstein has said: "We shall require a substantially new manner of thinking if mankind is to survive."[15] Instead of hard power, winning hearts and minds is necessary to change the role of power.

The Changing Nature of Power

The impulse to power is an ever-expanding, ever-changing urge, a desire so intense that every person wants to be all-powerful in every field of activity. In his quest to achieve this, man has been practicing power from hard to soft power on unlimited platforms in many spheres by the help of his multifunctional technological innovation. More than a century before Niccolo Machiavelli, a Muslim philosopher of history, ibn Khaldun (1332-1406) in his Prolegomena (*Muqaddimah*) to his *Universal History (Kitab al-Ibar)* depicted a comprehensive synthesis of social sciences. The core of ibn Khaldun's political and general sociology is his concept of *asabiyah*, or "social solidarity." Human beings, insofar as they display asabiyah, form into more or less stable social groups. His definition of society is a strong group feeling based on unity, loyalty, social cohesion, and powerful solidarity. For him, political process is cyclical, inexorable, transitory, and with no fixed direction. He equated cruelty, ferocity, oppression, tyranny, and use of hard power with primitive culture.

The havoc of "savage power"—probably the last of its kind—was unleashed by the Mongols between 1206 and 1368 and shattered the world of Islam. In sixteenth century, this old way of "savage power" was empirically interpreted by Niccolo Machiavelli in his notorious work of political theory *The Prince*. In chapter 17, "Cruelty and Mercy, and Whether It is Better to Be Loved or Feared, or the Contrary," he says; "The reply is that one should like to be both the one and the other, but as it is difficult to bring them together, it is much safer to be feared than to be loved if one of the two has to be lacking."[16] In his work *Discourses on Livy*, Machiavelli remarked on hard power, "He who creates a tyranny and does not kill Brutus [one of the murders of Roman Emperor Julius Caesar], and he who establishes a free state and does not kill the sons of Brutus, will not last long."[17]

After the French Revolution and the emergence of modern democracies, it was considered best to be both "feared and loved." But human beings' natural impulse of aggression, which had corrupted them in every period of their existence, had established such a tradition of hard power that mankind is still to see a change of power winning hearts and minds. The industrial revolution created new and horrible arsenals of war with the invention of steamships, airplanes, heavy guns, and atom bombs. During the twentieth century, the world was visited by two horrible World Wars, causing massive loss of property and life that came to an end by dropping atom bombs on Japan's cities of Hiroshima and Nagasaki. The second half of twentieth century saw wars in Korea, Vietnam, Afghanistan, Iraq, Libya, and Syria. It is unfortunate that even today mankind's savagery of "hard power" is a tool to keep the boundary between "us" and "them."

Military force is the most prominent and important form of power; it often takes the form of internal tyranny and foreign conquests. But international relations require both the *"carrot and stick"*—both punishment and reward. The carrot in the socioeconomic field might be a promise of economic aid from one nation to another, while the stick might be a threat of military action. But the function of power is not just to enforce domination or to create a winner and loser. Within its approach to peace, it has many forms of application. It organizes communities, societies, marketplaces, and world affairs.

Joseph Nye Jr., coining the term "soft power" in his book *Soft Power* is of the view that:

> Whereas hard power—the ability to coerce—grows out of a country's military or economic might, soft power arises from the attractiveness of a country's culture, political ideals, and polices. . . To win the peace, therefore the US will have to show as much skill in exercising soft power as it has in using hard power to win the war.[18]

He further argues: "The soft power of a country rests primarily on three resources: its culture (in places where it is attractive to others), its political values (when it lives up to them at home and abroad), and its foreign policies (when they are seen as legitimate and having moral authority)."[19] Soft power is an indirect way to exercise power by attracting other nations to follow the powerful due to admiring its values of democracy, emulating its example of freedom of thought, aspiring to its level of prosperity.

Soft power in a society embraces the power of humanism. It adopts democracy, based on the intelligence of a well-educated public. The core of democracy and humanism is tolerance, resolving differences by peaceful negotiation, not force or violence. Though inclinations to spirituality and religiosity are still dominating humanity, the virtues of secular humanism, free thought, agnosticism, and atheism—still in the minority—are a source of rapid change in humanity's outlook on power. Arguing on the changing nature of power, Nye Jr. is of the view:

> Power is like the weather. Everyone depends on it and talks about it but few understand it. Just as farmers and meteorologists try to forecast the weather, political leaders and analysts try to describe and predict changes in power relationships. Power is also like love, easier to experience than to define or measure, but no less real for that. At this most general level, power means the ability to get the outcomes one wants. . . [But] there are several ways to affect

the behavior of others. You can coerce them with threats; you can induce them with payments; or you can attract and co-opt them to want what you want.[20]

Today, technology is changing not only the role of power but also our behaviors and expectations; overall, we are changing fast. The revolution of modern technology is diffusing power from the hands of a centralized authority and is empowering individuals, even those who in the past have been victims of the rich and powerful.

Notes:

1.   Russell, 1967, p. 25.
2.   ibid., 1967, p. 9.
3.   ibid., 1967, p. 8.
4.   Saiyidain, 1938 p.72
5.   ibid., Payam-i-Mashriq p. 97 and 48.
6.   Hobbes, 2004, p. 69-70.
7.   Ashraf, 2007, p.164.
8.   Darwin, 1998, p. 67, 69, 81 and 82.
9.   Jouvenel, 1962, p. 65.
10.   Armstrong, 1994. p. xix.
11.   Ashraf, p. 157, 231, and 243.
12.   Nietzsche, 2005, p. xxiii and 100.
13.   Barker, 2018, p. 120.
14.   Jouvenel, 1962, p. 135.
15.   Einstein, 2013, p. 67.
16.   Machiavelli, 2003, p. 71-72.
17.   ibid., p. 196.
18.   Nye Jr., 2004, p. x-xi.
19.   ibid., p. 11.
20.   ibid., p.1.

CHAPTER 12

Peace: A Natural State of Human Mind

Only Peace itself can explain peace.
(Ashraf)

Introduction

Peace is an intrinsic state of mind, a virtue, a disposition for benevolence, love, confidence, and justice, which is by default natural and does not cost a single penny. War is a learned behavior and an institution which costs unlimited resources and wealth. Buried inside every human mind, peace is holistically alive unless a cause with a right or a wrong signal raises its head within the mind of an individual or a group, at which point it becomes normal to harm each other. There is no dearth of evidence that humans are inherently compassionate, intrinsically altruistic, innately generous, and naturally kind, even if they are in certain circumstances driven to act aggressively and violently. At the same time there is no lack of evidence for those who believe that humans are inherently aggressive, violent, and competitive, but still cooperate for personal gain or societal welfare.

Human beings are primarily peaceful, though sometimes to survive or to get what they need they are driven to violence. Peace quintessentially appears when an individual inertly and outwardly is in harmony with himself and the rest of creation. Its latent power is found in relaxation which gives rise to love; its mindfulness gives rise to vigilance; and its consciousness gives rise to reason—all these together give rise to a feeling of "Peace." Shakespeare in his play *Henry VIII* says:

> *I feel within me*
> *A peace above all earthly dignities,*
> *A still and quiet confidence.*[1]

But the enigma of peace challenges our mind when we find human beings to be imperfectly kind, unintentionally inconsiderate, and spontaneously helpful in near-equal measure; and at the same time acting ferocious, cruel, homicidal, and war-mongering. However, as kindness often transforms human beings in ways that lead to greater compassion and generosity, it is far more reasonable to perceive humans as capable of astonishing altruism, and most of the time, getting along fine together. According to Leslie E. Sponsel in his article "The Natural History of Peace: The Positive View of Human Nature and its Potential":

> From available evidence and interpretations, it appears that many prehistoric and prostate societies, probably the majority, were *relatively* nonviolent and peaceful in the sense that only sporadically and temporarily did intragroup or intergroup aggression occur, ranging from diverse kinds of fighting, feuding, and raiding to, in some cases warfare. Such cases lead to the potential for the development of a more nonviolent and peaceful world is latent in human nature as revealed by the natural history of peace. Here the phrase "the natural history of peace" refers to the possibility of a holistic and diachronic description of peace as the norm in most societies, which in this and other respects means that peace is natural.[2]

Since human beings are endowed with intellectual and spiritual powers of ethics and morality, it is a diehard fact that they do have biological underpinning emotional capacities of love and peace. Since a vast majority of human being are peaceful most of the time, peace seems to be ingrained in their nature. Mankind must end the institution of war.

Peace is hard to Define

Since peace is not a seamless web, it is not an orderly and simple subject matter which can be easily explained. Peace is a concept entangled in the development of activities conducive to making peace, or at least to preventing conflict and war. We know that war begins in the minds of human beings when peace, which is already there, foresees or faces the danger of being disrupted. Today, we find a peaceful society or a nation faced with a warlike neighbor—a society either hungry for power or more resources—alarmingly faces a bitter choice: either to be nonaggressive and submit or to stand up and resist. Submission leads to becoming a part of a larger warrior nation, while resistance means adopting the violent methods of a warlike culture. This leads societies to develop a war institution either for self-defense or offence, which today is a huge industrial complex, producing weapons more than capable of annihilating all of humanity from the face of the earth. By spending countless amounts of people's hard-earned money and depriving billions of food and shelter, power-monger nations are piling up arsenals of nuclear and biological weapons.

Peace is naturally viewed as an assumed condition of human relationships and therefore it does not invite our special attention. On the other hand, the matter of conflict and war is taken seriously because it disrupts peace. It is, therefore, unfortunate that we have not until today developed a peace-making machinery equivalent to the world-wide war machines. Moreover, peace, closely linked to almost a false assumption as the basal condition of human beings, appears less interesting as compared to the rattling chivalric virtues depicted in our literature, art, and history.

History delineates violent events as exceptional, which makes the institutions of peace undramatic; they do not clamor for our attention. Much of the sociological work concerning peace follows traditional directions based upon history and political science, analyzing empirical data about when and how actions contributing to peace have occurred. Most of our research and studies tend to be focused on conflicts and wars as units of analysis rather than the periods of peace in our history. This leaves us with the enigma of peace unfolding through conflict and war as a subject of history which is mind-blowingly expounded by the Roman historian Publius Cornelius Tacitus (56-120 CE): *"They make a wilderness and call it peace"*³—a rare flash of insight about the deadly role of war for peace.

Peace, like many other human ideals, such as happiness, justice, empathy, rule of law, love for all, etc., is basically a linchpin of social harmony. It is an ideal that every person, society, and culture naturally desire and venerate. We need to take up the subject of peace as a natural history within the holistic framework of *Homo sapiens* biology, ethology, ethnography, prehistoric archaeology, anthropology, and most importantly the philosophy of social sciences, rather than a general theory of war and peace. In the absence of what one might call solid empirical research and a coherent peace theory, the concept of peace can best be explained through an examination of peace thinking. The paradigm of peace as "no war" or "war for peace" has neither theoretical nor practical appeal. Since "negative peace" is an indispensable condition, it is exclusively the concept of "positive peace" that is worth exploring.

Levels of Peace

Sociologists have distinguished the concept of peace in two forms, "negative peace" and "positive peace." Negative peace is defined as the absence of any organized and direct physical violence between nations or major human groups of ethnic and racial standings. Positive peace is defined as a relation of cooperation and integration between major human groups or nations reflecting the absence of great inequalities in the lives of the people which might otherwise lead to unrest, violence, and conflict. Sociological researchers have further noted that the distinction between these two types of peace gives rise to a fourfold classification of relations between two nations: war, which is organized group violence; negative peace, where there is no direct physical violence; positive peace, where there is some cooperation interspersed with occasional outbreaks of violence; and unqualified peace, where absence of violence is combined with a pattern of cooperation.

People in the previous millennia thought of peace as the absence of war. War for them was *a temporary state of affairs—a violent but brief interlude between times of peace.* But the beginning of third millennium has given the word "peace" a new meaning, peace as the implausibility of war, which can be defined as "The New Peace." Yuval Noah Harari, in his book *Homo Deus: A Brief History of Tomorrow,* is of the view that:

> This New Peace is not just a hippie fantasy. Power-hungry governments and greedy corporations also count on it. When Mercedes plans its sales strategy in Eastern Europe, it discounts the possibility that Germany might conquer Poland. A corporation importing cheap laborers from Philippines is not worried that

> Indonesia might invade the Philippines next year. . . There is no
> guarantee, of course, that the New Peace will hold indefinitely.
> Just as nuclear weapons made the New Peace possible in the first
> place, so future technological developments might set the stage
> for new kinds of war. In particular, cyber warfare may destabilize
> the world by giving even small countries and non-state actors the
> ability to fight superpowers effectively. [4]

Political scientists mark the disruption of peace as a systemic breakdown or institutional failure. Once this systemic breakdown occurs, one group or nation attacks and causes losses to another, creating a psychological relationship of aggressor and victim, which most of the time endures for ages. The psychology of victimhood is in fact a very deep rooted and sensitive "psycho-physiological permanent state of alertness" on the part of victimized nations, groups, or individuals. They are always revengeful of the wounds of the past. It becomes difficult for them to be susceptible to rational acts of peace processes. At this stage it is more of a social scientist's job to look for a remedy. Just as violent individuals can be cured by psychiatric treatments, our remarkable achievements in the fields of neuroscience and instantaneous communication systems make it possible that societies and nations thousands of miles apart can be easily educated in psychologically based strategies of peace processes. Since human nature is capable of alteration by education, it is definitely within their power to create a peaceful society.

In our endeavor to present an analysis of the social dynamics relating to the achievement of a lasting peace we find that attempts to maintain peace have been made through religion, politics, but unfortunately mostly through warfare. Our experience through the ages shows that war and conflict are mostly the result of abuse of power, while peace is a practical matter of how human beings can live together harmoniously, dealing creatively and effectively with the differences, hurts, and fears that arise in their relationships. Peace is and has been as natural as life on this planet and its being there does not demand any justification. But any act which disrupts peace needs a reasonable justification. Though there are many reasons which have made the subject of peace very complex, most of all the aggressive and restless tendency of human beings has complicated this situation. Peace, once violated, has often been re-established by the use of force. Whereas the "just war" tradition considers war as morally justified for the sake of peace, hardened realists are of the view that we have not been able to present any moral justification for the use of force for the restoration of peace.

The French philosopher, Jean-Jacques Rousseau, in chapter three of his work *The Social Contract* has propounded, "The strongest is never strong enough to be always the master, unless he transfers strength into right, and obedience into duty. Force is a physical power, and I fail to see what moral effect it can have. To yield to force is an act of necessity, not of will—at most, an act of prudence. In what sense can it be a duty?" [5] Modern democracies believe that the use of force ensures a moral justification when an elaborate popular support of people's majority is present, which also reveals that with popular support it is hard to foresee what moral effect the use of force can have. But to prove that there is a moral justification for going to war against a certain nation, popular majority support for the use of force is often created through well-planned political, ideological, or religious propaganda. Since there is no ethical or moral standard that can justify the use of force and power, this leaves us with the alternative that war and conflict is a human activity which falls within the scrutiny of reason.

Peace versus Human Desire for Power

Whereas humans are naturally born as peaceful beings, they are embedded with boundless desires. One of the most interesting of these is the desire for power, which is so intense that man would like to be as powerful as God, creating an impulse to overpower his fellow beings. Those who profess to the theory of evolution believe this desire for power is one of the major causes of our wars and conflicts; paradoxically, it is also the cause of our evolutionary progress. Without the desire for power there would have been no progress in human society, and there would have been no history or any form of social order. The problem arises when this impulse for power corrupts and leads to an unjustified aggression. Aggression is a natural product of biology, but with the wrong combination of environments it predisposes a person to violence, which becomes a learned behavior.

From the emergence of society until today, the edifice of a family, clan, tribe, or nation, stands on the values of ethics and morality. Charles Issawi, in his book *An Arab Philosophy of History: Selections from the Prolegomena of Ibn Khaldun of Tunis*, an English rendition of the Arab scholar's Philosophy of History and Sociology writes:

> Societies are not static and social forms and laws change and evolve. These laws are sociological and not a mere reflection of biological impulses, or physical factors. ... It is, therefore, very important to keep shaping politics and social environment according to historically created norms of justice without interfering excessively with natural patterns of behavior. ... Conflict may stop if every person is clearly aware by the light of his reason, that he has no right to oppress his neighbor or a fellow citizen. Oppression and strife might therefore cease, if men undertake to restrain themselves.[6]

Human behavior is naturally flexible and variable, making it necessary for sociopolitical scientists to keep modifying social and political systems conducive to contemporary needs and environments. It is important to nurture love and brotherly relations to establish a tranquil, orderly, and peaceful society.

Our history is mostly a record of conflicts, wars, conquests, and empires, embedded with stories of chivalries and braveries of warriors. It is a veneration of war heroes and the greatness of generals, romanticized forever. Little effort has been made to analyze the causes and motives of the conflicts behind humanity's horrible acts of mass bloodshed. The glamorized myth of war and violence is based on the belief that we are aggressive and violent by nature, and in order to maintain peace we have to use force or struggle against this natural tendency toward aggressiveness. Peace represents order, harmony, and serenity, which is a very important characteristic of human nature. Human beings are creatures of habit and are capable of generating many patterns of thoughts and actions. Our habits and behaviors are learnt traits which are so plastic that we are amazingly capable of self-modification. We can shape our own behavior according to the prevailing environment, thus, we need to develop a culture where we can resolve our differences peacefully.

Cyber-Renaissance for Peace

In the present millennium, global society is at a very important juncture of our history. Religions and the ideologies of philosophy and social sciences are losing their central importance in the affairs of mankind. We are standing at the gateway of a cyber-renaissance. Just as the Renaissance in Europe changed the course of our social and political history, this cyber-renaissance would drastically change the course of our future history. The evolution of our progress is taking a new shape with an amazing speed that is happening before our eyes. Computer technology is rapidly shaping a society where the highest value would be the smart brain, not wealth or physical power. Thus, the culmination of the cyber-renaissance would be the spectrum of power passing from the grip of the rich and elite into the hands of the common and oppressed; from the physically strong to the intellectually smart generation.

One of the most salient features of the cyber-renaissance is that it would be free of ideological and religious strings which in the past have done massive damage to the cause of peace. Science has always been able to nurture a rational and humanistic outlook, even if its systematic and regimented stance has conflicted with the irregularity and diversity of human emotions. Science has done wonders in mastering the laws of the physical world, but our own nature is still less understood. It is important for the understanding of human nature to be the basis of our research in order to establish a peaceful and happy society. We have been neglecting the basic inclination of our desire for peace, which has always been an essential characteristic of all human beings.

This is the right time to develop the concept of peace as a part of the social sciences and introduce the subject of peace as a scientific philosophy based upon the moral and ethical principles of humanity. It is time to develop a *Scientific Philosophy of Peace* on the basis of humanity as one race, one culture, and one social order living in the only world we have. We are well aware that mankind started as one community, which we unfortunately lost sight of during the course of our evolution and cultural diversification. This might have happened due to many geographical and environmental variances. Because of our scientific and technological achievements, the geographical and environmental elements no longer dominate our evolutionary process. The whole world is like a global village where everyone is connected with everyone.

We humans are at the peak of our biological evolution and our physical perfection. The theory of biological evolution is now a chapter of our past history. Today we are less concerned about the questions of our own creation; rather we ourselves are now the creators. We are ready and excited to welcome our creations, the robots and artificial intelligence, which will mark the beginning of a new era in the history of mankind. We have arrived at the end of the evolutionary era of *homo sapiens* and are e ready to step into an era in which we will be proud to be known as *homo creators*. It is now within our own control to identify the progress-achieving methods of science and apply them wisely by equipping artificial intelligence with peace-projecting features and ideologies preaching love for all. It is predicted that within the next few decades, we will have the technological means to create artificial super intelligence, marking the beginning of an era in which machines will prevail upon biological humans. Given the incredible power of new technologies and development of artificial super intelligence, we have a golden opportunity to build self-aware, self-improving machines, which are not loaded with the tendencies toward oppression, conflict, and war.

Notes:

1. Shakespeare, Henry VIII, 3.2.378.
2. Gregor, 1996, Article by Sponsel, p. 95-96
3. The Roman historian, Publius Cornelius Tacitus (56-120 CE).
4. Harari, 2017, pp. 16-17
5. Rousseau, 1762, p. The Social Contract.
6. Issawi, 1987, pp, 8, 9, and 103.

---CHAPTER 13---

Why Only Man Is Addicted to War?

Only the dead have seen the end of war. ~ Plato

Introduction

When we raise the question: "Do human beings have a killer instinct that makes them homicidal and war mongers?" or "Why is only man addicted to war?" we are prompted by another question: "Why is war not woman's concern?" In other words, when we discuss human beings as killers and warmongers, we mean only males, leaving females out of the killer game. One assumption is that males have bigger bodies and greater physical strength than females, which has helped men evolve to be more aggressive than women. Thus, from the outset, their more aggressive pattern led them to a male-dominated war game. But our study of evolutionary science also suggests that male competition over mates and resources—an aspect the biologists call "sexual selection"—might have helped human males evolve to be more aggressive than females, which appears to be another reason why from the earliest phase of our evolution fighting and killing has been a male activity.

Though food in the earliest stages of evolution was acquired through foraging and gathering vegetables, hunting by men was taken to be an early development in hominid evolution. Once the tremendous leap to big-game hunting was made, meat-eating became a potential food source. Females, restrained by bearing and nurturing offspring, were relatively dependent on males for their meat supply. Whenever a male-the-hunter would bring meat for a female, he had to fight and compete with his fellow male to mate with the female. Emerging out of biological evolution and stepping into "societal evolution," man's aggressive behavior took a dangerous form of hostility—fighting, killing, and group battles which gradually became an everlasting learned behavior.

The Myth of War and Conflict

War, as the ancient Greeks and Romans viewed it, is a god and its worship demands human sacrifice. They would urge young men to go to war, making the slaughter they are asked to carry out into a ritual. Later religions and modern-day "patriotism" sanctified and immortalized this ritual as "martyrdom." Young men in nearly every corner of the world are schooled in the notion that war is an ultimate definition of manhood. They are taught to believe that their chivalry and bravery will be tested and proven in the heat of war.

In every page of our history, nothing reveals man the way war does, and in the same way nothing reveals peace the way war does by justifying war as being waged for the sake of permanent peace. Bertrand Russell mentions in his autobiography, "War should be treated as murder is treated. It should be regarded with equal horror and with equal aversion." But through the use of naked force, the prospect of war is portrayed as a sacred and exciting venture, creating a heroic myth out of murder. We speak of those we fight against only in the abstract and thus strip them of their human qualities. In war, we demonize the enemy to the point that they are no longer human, while those fighting against their enemy are portrayed as embodiments of noble souls.

War is a predatory phenomenon, and our history reveals that since ancient times, men have been continuously waging war somewhere on this planet. According to the American historian William James Durant (1885-1981), there have been only twenty-nine years in all of mankind's history during which war was not underway somewhere in the world. Another survey revealed that since 1776 when the United States became free, has been at war 223 years out of the 246 years of its history. In *Ramparts Magazine* (Vol. II, Part II), "Bertrand Russell's America: The Entire American People Are On Trial," Russell has very boldly proclaimed:

> Violence is not new to America. White men of European stock seized the lands of indigenous Indians with a ferocity which endured until our own times. The institution of slavery shaped the character of the nation and leaves its mark everywhere. Countless "local" wars were mounted throughout the twentieth century to protect commercial interests abroad. Finally, the United States

emerged at Hiroshima as the arbiter of world affairs and self-appointed policeman of the globe.[1]

American public opinion is constantly misled by propagating the idea that "We must fight against evil in all its form to promote democracy and preserve the Western way of life." In a nutshell, the U.S. military is destroying the lives of its own young men, ignoring the words of the Greek historian Herodotus, "In peace sons bury their father, but in war fathers bury their sons." According to Aldous Huxley (1894-1963), "What is absurd and monstrous about war is that men who have no personal quarrel should be trained to murder another in cold blood," which means war is a license to kill and murder merely to satisfy man's aggressive urge.

Sigmund Freud (1856-1838) knew that war has always been present. In 1915 he published an article "Thought for the Times on War and Death," arguing that war, though very dangerous, is an irresistible and dangerous temptation hidden in the human unconscious beings. He was of the view that humans need war when the burden of civilization becomes intolerable. In his opinion the alternative to war is neurosis, both for an individual and a group, which itself can become intolerably destructive. People cannot go on indefinitely acting as if they are civilized; they must be allowed an outlet for their unconscious murderous desires. This means killing is not an instinctive and conscious urge, but rather it is unconsciously desired by humans.

The classic just-war theory has its origins in Christian theology. Saint Augustine is usually identified as the first individual to offer a theory on war and justice. Augustine referred to the Bible and regarded some wars as necessary to amend an evil. Saint Thomas Aquinas revised Augustine's version, creating three criteria for a just war: *the war needed to be waged by a legitimate authority, have a just cause, and have the right intentions.* The moral justifications for a war are expressed in *jus ad bellum* (right to go to war), while the moral conduct of the war is expressed in *jus in bello* (right conduct in war). The just-war theory is a set of rules for military combat based on the idea that war, though always wrong, is sometimes necessary.

Gen Carl Von Clausewitz (1780-1831) whose world was the "world of men under arms" after Aristotle's saying, "Man is a political animal" presented his own explanation, "Man is a waring animal." Thus, in his book *On War* he presented his famous insight that "war is a continuation of politics by other means." But four centuries before Clausewitz, the Arab philosopher ibn Khaldun (1332-1406) in the *Prolegomena* (Introduction) to his *Universal History*, had remarked, "Conflict may stop if every person is clearly aware, *by the light of his reason*, that he has no right to oppress his neighbor. ... Oppression and strife might therefore cease, if men undertook to restrain themselves," which means that war embraces much more than politics.

Is Man Instinctively a Killer?

When we try to seek an answer to the big question of why we have war, we first ask ourselves, "Is man instinctively such a killer that he kills even his own fellow human beings or is that just a manly fancy?" Since man is also an animal, we are curious to know why he is homicidal since it is very rare that other animals, including most of the fiercest beasts, kill members of their own species. Animals do not make war; they kill other animals to eat or defend their territory. Regarding man, according to some anthropologists and psychologists, war is pre-civilizational phenomenon, which needs to be investigated: Is war embedded in man's nature or it is a learned behavior which can be unlearned? Do humans have a killer instinct which cannot be altered or is war just a "manly fancy"? By declaring that war is evil—even when it is considered justified—can humans unlearn their behavior of going to war?

Though the anthropologists and archeologists discover that man's uncivilized ancestors could be red in tooth and claw, sociologists and proponents of conventional wisdom believe, in the light of truism in human nature, that aggression is not inborn but results from imitation and suggestion. Regarding man being an aggressive animal, psychological and neuroscientific theories, relying on the science of evolution, profess that aggression as an instinct is a legacy of our ancestral past and an inbuilt tendency. But the novelty of this assertion is that human aggression was not wholly destructive; it had a positive, even constructive side which made possible "survival of the fittest."

Regarding man's being violent by nature or his tendency for violence through the operation of material factors, studies of individual and group behavior shows different directions. Thomas Hobbes (1588-1679) in his work *Leviathan* argues that human beings are instinctively ruthless and selfish, with everyone struggling for his own sustenance and preservation. He believed:

> In the nature of man, we find three principal causes of quarrel. First competition; secondly difference; thirdly glory. The first makes men invade for gain; the second for safety; and third for reputation. They first use violence, to make themselves masters of other men's persons, wives, children, and cattle; the second to defend them, the third for trifles, as a word, a smile, a different opinion, and any other sign, either direct in their persons of by reflection in their kindred, the friends, their nation, their profession, or their name.[2]

Here we can see the possibility that since Hobbes, from the age of four, was educated at Westport and received religious grooming, he could not have resisted the biblical tale of Abel's murder by his brother Cain and saw human beings as children of the surviving murderer. When we view the biblical narrative of the first man Adam and his two sons as a metaphoric way of presenting certain deep truths about man, the murder of one brother by the other throws light on man's homicidal instinct. Though Cain killed his brother out of jealousy, the issue of his sacrifice being unaccepted by God might have hurt his "self-esteem," or he lost his Hobbesian view of "glory." Self-esteem is confidence and respect in oneself which makes one experience a positive sense of one's worth. When one loses self-esteem, a severe reaction to this loss can create a negative effect.

Humans are the only species naturally born with distinctive "id," "self-esteem or self-respect," "ego," and "superego," which makes them responsible for their independent decisions. A human being's id, or his ego-instinct begins with the notion of "I" which very much remains an important part of his self-conscious being and distinctive personality. Thus, using "I" as a verbal symbol of his ego—defined by Descartes as man who thinks and proclaims, *"cogito ergo sum,"* or *"I think, therefore I am,"* or centuries before him as expressed by al-Ghazali, *"I will, therefore I am,"* or later promoted by Henri Bergson, William James, and John Dewy—man is the only creature that *wills* and *thinks*.

Here we can hypothesize that since man's "I" allows him to express this notion of *"I will, therefore I am,"* or *"I think, therefore I am,"* it can drive him to will or think to be a killer. When any one of the three parts of his personality—the id, the ego, or the superego—is hurt or challenged, he is perverted to think and act negatively. In other words, when no of his personality is disturbed and his "ego" is neither challenged nor hurt, he thinks and acts positively, and emerges as a compassionate and altruistic being displaying a dumbfounding kindness.

In response to the big question of how it's credible that we sacrifice ourselves for others when we see malice, greed, conflict, and war abound around us, Jean-Jacques Rousseau (1712-1778) in his *Discourse on the Origins of Inequality Among Men* (1754), renouncing Hobbes' view of "innate wicked human nature," proclaimed, "Man in a state of nature was a 'noble savage' who was naturally born good and by civilization or institutions is made bad."[3] Rousseau believed that the natural man was a greedless noble savage, a good husband and affectionate father who followed a faith of natural kindness. He professed that the natural man was a creature of good instincts and simple tastes who has been corrupted by civilization, particularly by urban life.

Rousseau's concept of the "noble savage" reflects a newborn child's natural bond of love and peace with its mother, and a mammalian mother's love for her baby and even grown-up children is like nothing else in the world. This bond of love and peace in human beings know no law or instruction, and crushes down remorselessly all that stands in its way. But does this mean that since human babies are unformed at birth and are helpless to *will* and *think* independently as "I," they become purely altruistic? As they grow, they learn, first by reflection, then by imitation, and later still by experience.

Regarding women, half of the human race have not typically been warriors, and fighting in warfare has always been a male activity; though there are some exceptions, such as Hazrat Ayesha in Islam, Razia Sultan in India, Joan of Arc in France, and a few more commanding an army, the combatants have generally been men. Today, however, when war is more based on technology than direct frontline combat, some women by their own choice are taking part in war-games. But the evolution of man as the more aggressive of the sexes has set a pattern of male-dominated warfare which is unlikely to be altered even by technological changes or ecological forces.

The Origins of War

Regarding the origin of war, we, first have to ask ourselves why we have war. It is a double-edged question. Naturalists find that conflict and war is embedded in human nature, while others believe that war is a learnt behavior which originates from external causes, and that war is always determinant and an expression of cultural forms. But it is an established fact that war is a predatory affair that began when hunter-gatherers started stealing the domesticated animals and food reserves of the pastoralists as an easy access to food. The pastoralists would join together into groups to defend their cattle and property; thus, arising from group conflicts, a culture of attackers and defenders appeared. Through the passage of time families with common lineages bonded together as a tribe or a race. For these tribes and races, the need for more resources led them to the institution of planned wars which developed into the world-wide wars of the modern age.

On May 16, 1986, the Spanish National Commission convened a meeting of international scientists at Seville, modelled on UNESCO's Statement on Race, and drafted the Seville Statement on Violence, which was subsequently adopted by UNESCO at the twenty-fifth session of the General Conference on November 16, 1989. The statement, which contains the five core ideas listed below, was designed to refute the notion that organized human violence is biologically determined.

1. It is scientifically incorrect to say that we have inherited a tendency to make war from our animal ancestors.
2. It is scientifically incorrect to say that war or any other violent behavior is genetically programmed into our human nature.
3. It is scientifically incorrect to say that in the course of human evolution there has been a selection for aggressive behavior more than for other kinds of behavior.
4. It is scientifically incorrect to say humans have a "violent brain."

5. It is scientifically incorrect to say that war is caused by "instinct" or any single motivation.

But John Kegan, in his book, *War and Our World*, writes, "There is much to be admired about the Seville Statement, since it seeks to liberate the human race from the deadening conviction that war is its natural lot. Unfortunately there is little that is scientific about it."[4] He further argues:

> Animals do not make war. They kill to eat, even if occasionally in a wasteful "feeding frenzy." War is too complex an activity for step-by-step genetic mutation to 'program' organisms for it; and geneticists lack the evidence to strike a balance between selection for this behavior or that within the vast human behavioral range. The Seville Statement, in short, is one step of hope, not objective truth. Objectively, all that science has been able to establish about human nature and war is the whereabouts in the human brain of what scientists call "the seat of aggression" and how it may be stimulated or physically altered to produce aggressive behavior.[4]

We know that friendship's opposite is enmity and that organized enmity takes the form of war. Whereas friendship reflects goodness, war is taken as an evil. Just as wars begin in the minds of men, peace also begins in our minds. The same species that invented war is capable of inventing peace. The responsibility lies with each of us. Edward O. Wilson, in his book *On Human Nature*, argues:

> Virtually all societies have invented elaborate sanctions against rape, extortion, and murder, while regulating their daily commerce through complex customs and laws designed to minimize the subtler but inevitable forms of conflicts. Most significantly of all, the human forms of aggressive behavior are species-specific: although basically primate in forms, they contain features that distinguish them from aggression in all other species. Only by redefining the words "innateness" and "aggression" to the point of uselessness might we correctly say that human aggressiveness is not innate. ... Innateness refers to the measurable probability that a trait will develop in a specified set of environments, not to the certainty that the trait will develop in all environments. By this criterion human beings have a marked hereditary predisposition to aggressive behavior.[5]

Human aggressive behavior as a structured pattern of interaction between genes and environments is consistent with the theory of evolution. Whereas it is true that man's aggressive behavior is learned, he also readily enters into an irrational and dangerous hostility. Regarding those who are the exponents of man being naturally a warmonger, John Kegan, in *War and Our World*, writes:

> If hard science will not show us the origins of war, we must look elsewhere, to the softer world of social science, particularly to anthropology. One of the earliest general explanations of group aggression was proposed by Sigmund Freud in 1913, who considered the patriarchal family was the most significant unit of the society. He suggested that sons resented father's sexual monopoly over the family's women and that this led to conflict, and eventually to the father's murder. The son's consequent guilt created revulsion against incest, and drove men first to take sexual partners only from beyond the family group and then to primitive warfare of wife-stealing.[6]

In spite of the fact that woman is not a warmonger, she is the one who pays the price. Wife-stealing was and is still a common cause of fighting. In wars from ancient time to the present day, women were raped, abducted, and taken as sex slaves.

Why do Wars Happen?

Throughout history, warfare, representing an organized technique of human aggression, is found from the earliest bands of hunter-gatherers to modern civilized societies. According to Pythagoras (271-496 BCE), *as long as men continue to be the ruthless destroyer of lower living beings, they will never know peace, and as long as they massacre animals, they will kill each other*. His statement leads us toward the male hunter-gatherers who had invented tools and used many new techniques to kill animals bigger and stronger than themselves to satisfy their hunger for meat. This tendency of the male hunter-gathers is evidence that even today all males are warriors.

Man as a power-monger throughout history, whether he evolved by aggressively fighting for his "survival as a fittest creature," or was created by God in his own image, has ever been emboldened to assert his Godlike desire for power. Supported by his aggressive instinct, man developed his desire for power into an ability to gain his desired outcome by the use of force. Our desire for power is so intense that most of us, irrespective of the fact that one believes or does not believe in God, would like to be as powerful as a god. For some it is difficult to admit the impossibility of being so powerful. When each one of us would like to be take the place of an omnipotent God with everyone else as our worshippers, social cooperation becomes difficult. This desire for godlike power creates an impulse to overpower other fellow beings, to down them and finish them, as God Himself would have done to punish the disobedient ones.[7]

Entangled in the cobweb of limitless desires and blinded by power, those who are sent to fight and kill fall prey to a ruthless and inhuman struggle, transgressing all moral and ethical limits. American singer-songwriter Bob Dylan (b.1941), in his song "Masters of War" wrote:

> *You fasten the triggers for others to fire,*
> *Then you sit back and watch,*
> *When the death count gets higher.*
> *You hide in your mansion*
> *As young people's blood*
> *Flows out of their bodies*
> *And is buried in mud.*[8]

The more intelligent and manipulative ones take action based on assorted mental aberrations. Their minds become an arena of strife and conflict. Their desires lead them to intense conflicts and frustrations, and consequently they are transformed into infernos. Inner disruptions, manifested both inwardly and outwardly, give rise not only to a ruthless and inhuman struggle for existence, but also to savage competition, unfair business and trade, greed and caprice, and false ostentation in knowledge. The impulse and craving for unbound power becomes one of the major factors of tyrannical oppression, war, and conflict. To harness such unbound and unlimited desires, ethics and morality based on reason needs to be an integral part of the social and cultural fabric of our life.

Today, a nuclear war machine with unlimited power capable of inflicting limitless destruction and countless loss of human life is produced by spending staggering amounts of money. It is estimated that trillions of dollars were spent on World War I, an amount which could have built a furnished home for every family in England, France, Belgium, Germany, Russia, the U.S.A., Canada, and Australia; for every population of two hundred thousand a library and a full-fledged university could have been erected; a hospital could have provided good pay for 150,000 doctors and 150,000 nurses for an unlimited period. Money could still have been left over to buy all the properties in Belgium and France at market price.

According to an April 25, 2022 report from the Stockholm International Peace Research Institute, global military spending in 2021 was estimated at $2.1 trillion, including $ 801 billion by the U.S. and $ 65.9 billion by Russia. This means, as argued by Bertrand Russell in his work, *Skeptical Essays* (1928) in the essay on "Freedom in Society," "In everything, power lies with those who control finance, not with those who know the matter upon which the money is to be spent. Thus the holders of power are, in general, ignorant and malevolent, and the less they exercise their power the better."[9] In spite of so much knowledge that war is a huge loss of life and property, the whole of mankind is under the threat of a horrible nuclear war, which can be averted only if a way could be found to tame man's lust for power and nurture peaceful behavior through education.

The Danger of Cyber War

Without noticing, we are fighting a cyber-war in which we are at every minute "preparing the battlefield." Cheap to develop and easy to hide, cyber-weapons are proving irresistible. Today, everyone, even those living in peace, is holding this weapon in the form of a "smart phone." Everyone is being hacked and at the same time freely hacking into others networks. Some hackers are stealing private information, while others are stealing money from bank accounts. But the most dangerous weapons are developed by a state's war and defense organization, as David E. Sanger has written in his book, *The Perfect Weapon* writes, "It would fry power grids, stop trains, silence phones, and overwhelm the Internet. In the worst case scenario, food and water would begin to run out; hospitals would turn people away. Separated from their electronics, and thus their connections, people would panic, or turn against each other." [10] Just as atomic technology, which was initially invented for peaceful use, but later developed into horrible atomic bomb, peaceful cyber-technology has led to cyber-weapons which are more dangerous than the atom bomb. Richard A. Clarke and Robert K. Knake, in their work *Cyber War,* have explained that there are five "take-aways" from cyber-incidents:

> **Cyber war is real.** What we have seen so far is far from indicative of what can be done. Most of the well-known skirmishes in cyberspace used only primitive weapons. It is a reasonable guess that the attackers did not want to reveal their more sophisticated capabilities yet.
>
> **Cyber war happens at the speed of light:** As the photons of the attack packets stream down fiber-optic cable, the time between the launch of an attack and its effect is barely measureable, thus creating risks for crisis decision makers.
>
> **Cyber war is global:** In any conflict, cyberattacks rapidly go global, as covertly acquired or hacked servers throughout the world are kicked into service. Many nations are quickly drawn in.
>
> **Cyber war skips the battlefield:** Systems that people rely upon, from banks to air defense radars, are accessible from cyberspace and can be quickly taken over or knocked out without first defeating a country's traditional defenses.
>
> **Cyber war has begun.** In anticipation of hostilities, nations are already "preparing the battlefield." They are hacking into each other's networks and infrastructure, laying in trap-doors and logic bombs, now, in peacetime. This ongoing nature of cyber war, the blurring of peace and war, adds a dangerous new dimension or instability.[11]

So far we have not experienced a full-scale cyber-war, but sophisticated cyber-weapons like unmanned drones have already been employed by air forces, while laser-guided weapons in the infantry and navies are in action in the wars being waged today.

Notes:

1. Russell's America: Ramparts Magazine, Volume II 1945–1970, Part II, p. 474.
2. Hobbes, *Leviathan*, Ch. 13, p. 91.
3. Rousseau, 1974.
4. Keegan, 1998 and 2001, p. 20.
5. Wilson, 1978, pp. 99-100.
6. Kegan, 1998, p. 22.
7. Russell, 1967, p. 8.
8. Dylan, 1941.
9. Russell, 1928, p. 153.
10. Sanger, 2018, p. ix.
11. Clarke and Knake, 2010, p. 30-31.

CHAPTER 14

The Origin of Democracy

Introduction

In the history of knowledge, much of what makes civilization existed in Egypt, Mesopotamia, India, and China, but nothing is so surprising as the appearance of the treasure of knowledge of philosophy, general science, medicine, history, art, and political science in Greece. What the Greeks achieved in art, literature, and the sciences might be similar to achievements made in some other regions of the world in one way or another, but what is mystical about the Greek genius is their unique polity of democracy that appeared in the fifth century BCE. Democracy, as we know today, was a form of government first established in the city-state of Athens, as well as in few other Greek city-states. The term originated from the Greek word *dēmokratía*, "rule of the people"— a composite of *demos*, meaning "people" and *krátos*, meaning "power" or "rule."

The democratic political system of the Athenians granted right of citizenship and participation in political affairs to an elite class of free men, excluding women and slaves from the political role. But still, the unique concept of people's rule through a democratic system as an alternative to an authoritarian and hereditary kingship was first invented and adopted by the Greeks. It is a subject of great interest—why was it the Ancient Greeks, or specifically the Athenians, who conceived of a democratic form of government when it remained unknown to many other regions where great intellectuals and sages had also appeared?

Genesis of the Athenian Democracy

Today, we associate democracy with progress, freedom, human rights, and the warrantor of a society's health and happiness, yet we generally do not consider why it was specifically ancient Greece which gave birth to the democratic form of government. Our study of the philosophical, social, political, and cultural life of the Athenians reveals that it was neither a political ideology nor a revealed religion that gave birth to the people's form of government we know as "democracy." Mark Chou in his article on "Democracy & Tragedy" argues:

> The performance of tragedies helped establish democracy. ... For the ancient Athenians, to whom we attribute both the birth of democracy and the creation of tragedy as an art form, democracy and tragedy shared intrinsic links. Born into a tragic world, democracy's story in Athens unfolded much like the tragic tales it inspired and then ensconced with the Greek city-state. ... Though of pre-democratic origins, tragic theater emerged as an alternate site of democratic politics in the wake of Athens' democratic revolution.[1]

Thus, the birth of democracy is linked with the art of tragic plays presented live on the stage. Tragic plays were so popular in Greece during the fifth century BCE that over a thousand tragedies were produced and presented in the theaters. Many of the Greek tragedies attempted to excite compassion by presenting the agonies of mental tortures and bodily pains inflicted by the tyrannical oppression of powerful authorities.

When human beings attend the presentation of a tragedy, it is natural they display empathizing struggle against the sorrow which the pathetic entertainment inspires in them. Today we know about Aeschylus, Sophocles, and Euripides as playwrights, and see them as protagonists of the ancient art. But when we view these tragedians as socio-political philosophers, we notice that they educated their theater audiences through the art of drama on issues of morality, politics, and philosophy. The most interesting subject of their plays was the misfortunes of the virtuous nobility, princes, and monarchs. The playwrites devised their plots around conflicts of mortal and divine, family and state, male and female, moral and immoral, and above all inside and outside of good and evil, by portraying the argumentative nature of human beings. By presenting such conflicts in an art form, the tragedians would teach their audience that life is transitory, and that the knowledge that motivates a search for certainty and eternity tempts the searcher to arrogance, conflict, and downfall.

Watching tragedies in the theaters, common people learned how to debate and argue, how to present their problems by speaking boldly and freely, how to say "no" to oppressors, and how to find solutions to their problems through consensus. Thus, the story of democracy, much like a tragic tale performed on stage in Athens, unfolded as a social and political order. In Greece, tragic theater of pre-democratic origin appeared as an alternate site of democratic politics in the wake of the Athenian democratic revolution. Commoners began to take center stage, projecting their views and presenting their problems before their fellow citizens as well as the ruling class. They were culturally and socially compelled to expand democratic ideals further to the courts, festivals, and marketplaces.

But in 399 BCE, after the verdict of the democratic jury which awarded the death penalty to Socrates—the greatest philosopher and exponent of freedom of speech—the symbiosis between democracy and tragedy was fractured. The theater and tragedy as its lifeline experienced a downfall and democracy died in the city-state of Athens. Democracies in other city-states of Greece did not last and were overthrown either by enemies from neighboring states or from outside Greece, but more frequently by the internal revolutions of the oligarchs. In Athens, Plato was disappointed by the democrats who condemned Socrates to death. By Aristotle's time, democracy seemed to be a failed experiment.

But though the democratic experience of Classical Greece, cultivated by the art of tragedy, was short-lived, its socio-political and cultural symbiosis helps us perceive that there is something deeper about democracy that makes it indispensable to politics and to life today. It promotes the importance of free voice and a passion for liberty. The art of tragedy, by dramatizing the spirit of democracy, has in the past helped develop it into an expansive worldview, displaying an understanding of proper political governance and more generally community life. It is a clear reminder of the Classical Greek society's belief that order could not and should not be tyrannically imposed, which is still an open message to modern societies. Democratic order in its true spirit is the only political system to prevent oppression, even with the risk that in some or even in many cases it can also become the source of oppression, as in the execution of the great philosopher Socrates.

Between the fourteenth and seventeenth centuries, with the appearance of the European Renaissance or re-birth of knowledge of Greek philosophy and literature, Greek tragedies were revived in French theaters. Though during the Italian Renaissance the economic freedom existed, no constitutional basis for people's rule could be found. Plots were taken by French authors from Classical Greek tragedies as well as from contemporary events. The tragic plays, just as in the Classical Greek period, helped provide a justification to the common man to say "no" to dictatorial and monarchial oppression. This instigated the spirit of the famous French Revolution (1789-1799) and opened a new chapter in the socio-political history of mankind. Thus, after the French Revolution, a constitutional form of democracy resurfaced. Once again, it was the art of presenting tragedy plays in the theaters that helped in establishing modern democracy, first in France and later transmitted to other regions. Today, though the world in its pursuit for democracy is indebted to the French Revolution, its seeds were sown in the Ancient Greece.

The Progress of Democracy

The symbiosis between democracy and tragedy, which played an important role in the perfection of morality and the emergence of democracy, has been socially and politically devalued in modern times. It is understandable that problems in our increasingly globalized society are vastly different from the problems faced by the societies that gave birth to democracy. Modern ways of reasoning, rationality, and scientific thinking have changed the concepts of morality and political outlook. However, because we are still humans, the art of tragedy is still alive. Despite our proclamations that we live in an age of unparalleled progress in equality and freedom, there exists a palpable sense of dread and doubt within all of us. Although separated by centuries of change from our past, our general condition is not so different; as rational sovereign agents, we are swept up by diverse irresistible social and economic forces.

Today, the fear of being annihilated by weapons of mass destruction, which in our past were epitomized by fate, gods, and religions, is constantly hanging over us. What is more troubling, in many cases, is that these fears have directly resulted from democratic processes as well as by the world-changing scientific revolution. Whereas this led to the creation of the modern secular world of liberal democracies, civil rights, liberties, equal justice under the law, religion-free political systems, and free economic, as well as a greater apprehension of the moral sphere to include people of all races, gender, color, and ethnic groups—and now even animals—as deserving ethical and moral consideration, this modern approach, while freeing us from the yokes of religion and the wrath of gods, is leading us toward the greater tragedy of nuclear war and the horror of the "day after."

The progress of democracy is based on three elements: the English decision in 1689 to erect a "government of laws, not men"; the declaration of the Founders of the United States of America in 1776 and 1789 that all men are equal and the people as a whole may ordain the law that stands superior to any man; and Abraham Lincoln's tripartite distinction, "Government of the people, by the people, for the people." Though democracy is understood by the world today, most of the countries of the world remained far behind in recognizing Abraham Lincoln's definition of democracy. After the two world wars of the twentieth century, a new light of universal suffrage over most of the globe spread—except for a few Middle Eastern monarchies—to the point that there is hardly a nation which does not constitutionally recognize the right of all citizens to vote for their representatives, or in many cases, leaders. The right to vote is protected, and there is an emphasis on governments existing for the general welfare of people. Though in some countries of the world people are denied the right to elect or choose their leaders, people everywhere in the world, in whatever circumstances they are living, desire democracy for a very good reason.

Democracy Today and Tomorrow

Today, the term "democracy" is defined to be a method of group decision-making, marked by a kind of equality among the participants at the stage of such collective decision-making. In this way democracy concerns decisions that are made by and for groups, and that are binding on all the members of the group—a form of collective decision-making. Epistemologically, democracy is viewed as the best decision-making method. Since it brings a lot of people into the process, it is generally more reliable in helping participants in finding the best possible decisions. Above all, in democracies, individuals are free and are encouraged to be more autonomous. The free and broad-based discussion mechanism typical of democracy enhances critical assessment of the different moral ideas helpful to the changing social environment.

The fundamental principle of democracy, that each individual has a right to liberty, helps each individual to be master of his or her life in the domain of collective decision making. Thus, whereas each person's life is deeply affected by the larger social, legal, and cultural environment in which he or she lives, each person having an equal voice and vote in the process of collective decision-making reflects that each one has control over this larger environment. We need institutions with society independent of the state authorities. In order to sustain democracy, civic education shared by independent educational and political institutions and promoted by the press and modern communication media, are the critical components in helping democracies in every state of the world to be compatible with contemporary situations.

However, one must also acknowledge that there is still no democracy as yet that is perfect in realizing the "liberal democratic ideal." Michael Shermer, in his book *The Moral Arc,* remarks:

> We are living in the most moral period of our species' history. Ever since the Age of Reason and the Enlightenment, thinkers consciously applied the methods of science to solve social and moral problems. The experimental methods and analytical reasoning of science helped create the modern world of liberal democracies, civil rights and civil liberties, equal justice under the law, open political and economic borders, free minds and free markets. More people in more places have greater rights, freedoms, liberties, literacy, educations, and prosperity—likes of which no human societies in history has ever enjoyed.[2]

But the most important implication today is the demand to expand democracy into the global realm. Freedom of speech helped by free and fast media is changing the world more rapidly than ever. It is unclear whether today's democracy will be able to keep up with the changes. The IT revolution is having unpredictable effects on the economy, society, and politics, both in positive and negative ways. Whereas inequality in the developed world is on the rise, millions in the developing world are rising out of poverty. Religious fundamentalism appearing in some parts of the world is posing a threat to the democratic world. In many regions there is also an increase in a non-ideological secular approach, while in some regions a religious revival is taking place. But the big question is, why have so few nations successfully adopted democracy, while most of the other nations and societies are reluctant to adopt it?

Today, as Moises Naim in his book *The End of Power* argues:

> We are on the verge of a revolutionary wave of positive and political institutional innovations in which power is changing in so many arenas that it will be impossible to avoid important transformations in the way humanity organizes itself to make the decisions it needs to survive and progress. That the institutions of representative democracy, the system of political parties, independent judiciaries, civil rights etc., were invented in the eighteenth century. ... The next set of political innovations will not be top-down, orderly, or quick, the product of summits or meetings, but messy, sprawling, and in fits and starts. Yet it is inevitable. Driven by the transformation in the acquisition, use and retention of power, humanity must, and will, find new ways of governing itself.[3]

It is an irony of modern man that humankind is thinking globally while it is still acting locally, making it difficult to answer the question "Does democracy guarantee peace and happiness?" Even as the modern perception of democracy enjoys almost universal appeal, democracy continues to face obstacles. The lives of citizens around the world are increasingly influenced by forces that lie beyond their sovereign borders. It is also important to note that many of the institutions working to shape global politics are neither transparent nor accountable to a democratic constituency. Therefore, it is still to be determined how to globally transplant democratic ideals when there is no universally institutionalized procedure of a dramatic debate, pragmatic decision-making, or system of accountability by an international forum of justice. Above all, failure to engage many different cultures' social and religious traditions in the democratic ideals may misrepresent the spirit and nature of those ideals.

So far, the modern liberal democratic system consists of a stable state and a sound political system, a strong rule of law, and justice and accountability. But the future of liberal democracies both intrinsically and consequentially depend upon the presence of the moral psychology of the citizens, meaning their manner, character, and proper behavior in terms of intentions and actions with regard to other moral agents. While a liberal democracy is regarded as the most popular and authentic form of government, its authenticity very much depends upon its performance. A democracy will continue to exist until the time the voters discover that they can vote themselves generous gifts from the public treasury. From that moment on, the majority always votes for the candidates who promise them the most wealth, with the result that every democracy will finally collapse over loose fiscal policy.

In a democratic state, society will not be stationary, but the impulse of the social body may be regulated and directed forward. Democracy, which in the past had to evolve out of a society's cultural and literary traditions, passing successfully through the spectrum of its environmental, traditional, historical, educational, and religious ethos, must now evolve through today's high-tech fields of the artificial intelligence. As the future rulership of the human race is predicted to be dominantly participated by the smart computers, human beings will have to accept them as both friends and foes.

Every day, our modern culture is projecting the increasing authority of science over cultural, religious, social, and political fields that fall under the jurisdiction of a socio-political order. Science and technology have succeeded on account of their practical utility, becoming more and more a series of easy techniques and less and less a complicated system. Our research and success in genetic engineering, neurobiology, and superfast communication systems are amazingly and progressively changing the levels of our socio-political spheres. Bill Gates remarked that his greatest fear was that someone sitting in his garage was devising something completely new, and likewise I can say that it is possible someone may invent a new political system.

Notes:

1. Chou, Mark: *Democracy & Tragedy*, Philosophy Now, Issue # 94, Jan-Feb 2013, p. 9.
2. Shermer, 215, p. 4 and 7.
3. Naim, 2013, pp. 243-244.

CHAPTER 15

The Progression of Knowledge in Western Civilization

The word "civilization," which is a relatively recent term from the eighteenth century when it came into currency, is generally invoked more with a rhetorical flourish than argued within philosophical perspective. But the history of knowledge considers its true object to be the study of the human mind—to know what his mind has believed, thought, and felt throughout the progression of human civilization. This also means, whereas it is important to understand today's world so that we can deal with its civilizational challenges, our understanding will be incomplete if we do not realize that modernity is born from the progress made by the past thinkers. But knowledge does not arrive fully formed; it requires many minds, specifically those minds which are free from a civilization's religious, cultural, and geophysical trappings.

In other words, no knowledge is complete without visiting the knowledge of the past, especially of the great Greek thinkers such as Thales, Homer, Pythagoras, Heraclitus, Democritus the Atomist, Socrates, Plato, Aristotle, Plotinus, and many more. In addition to the democratic political system, the knowledge of philosophy and sciences first appeared in the fifth century BCE in Greece, which is considered the foundation of Western civilization. It is interesting to note that such a treasure-trove of knowledge emerged in that region, becoming the foundation of voluminous works of literature in almost every field of knowledge, and how it flourished in the West making such an impact and spreading to every corner of the world.

Though Islamic theology stemmed from a different base from the Greek traditions, Greek philosophy, in what it could do and explain, proved a hard temptation to resist for the early Muslim theologians, philosophers, and scientific thinkers. Using the language and culture of their religion, Muslims started exploring and explaining the ideas and arguments of Greek thought which were agreeable to the Islamic view. When modern philosophical thought in the West began with Rene Descartes, the knowledge of Classical Greek philosophy and science, preserved and interpreted by the Muslims, had already penetrated deep into Europe. In the history of Western philosophy, there is sufficient evidence that most of the texts written in Arabic as well as in Hebrew during the golden era of Muslim rule had been translated into Latin and other languages and were made available to the European thinkers.

This essay postulates the hypothesis that it is due to the "civilizing of knowledge" rather than the traditionally abiding matrix of civilized practices that Western civilization is seen as universal. It is interesting to note that there were many special aspects about the Greeks or the region known as Greece for it to have produced such powerful knowledge that mankind even in the twenty-first century is indebted to them for their achievements in art, literature, philosophy, general science, medicine, history, politics, and ethics. At the same time, the progression of knowledge in Western civilization remains focused on the projection of free thought. With all its achievements in modern secular political theories and democratically republican systems, economic and social structures, scientific and technological developments, and its heritages of diverse cultures, Western civilization still considers the importance of religious traditions. Above all, a major role of Western civilization is to acquaint every new generation of students not only with the progress in human knowledge, but also that it is because of that knowledge's global appeal that this civilization remains universally alive.

Whereas some argue that Western civilization—complete with all its positive and negative features—indicates a decline in the moral values it inherited from its Greco Roman fount, yet Western civilization is neither shrinking nor being destroyed. Indeed, it is losing its original makeup and being diluted because of its interaction with diverse cultures as it spreads across the globe, and the impacts of modern technology, but it is still active and spreading by depositing seeds of knowledge of philosophies, sciences, and new technologies. In doing so, it is assisting mankind to develop a common global culture. Its progression is made possible by the erosion of distances enabled by research and developments in modern technology: new roads, bridges, ports, airplanes, massive container ships, fiber optic cables, and most importantly, cyber-net connectivity.[1]

The magnetism of modernity has remained humanity's perennial passion. A born thinker, philosopher, scientist, and discoverer, man has sought to define his identity by striving incessantly to shape it according to his contemporary ideals. Liberating himself from the deterministic modes of his existence and vowing to be no more at the mercy of biological and natural forces, he endeavors to weave himself like a tapestry by his own hands for himself. After the "First Explosion of Knowledge" which appeared in ancient Greece, and the "Second Explosion of Knowledge" during the European Renaissance, we are experiencing a "Third Explosion of Knowledge" engendered by information technology (IT) and artificial intelligence (AI). Today, a "Fourth Explosion of Knowledge" is well in sight which, with our stepping into "Digital Culture," will establish new perspectives of philosophical and intellectual outlook in the human imagination. The unique progression of knowledge in Western civilization established that today, what is much more important than human genius is the emerging power of digital technology and human intelligence's digital double, the artificial Intelligence.

Traditionally, knowledge has focused on the four basic subjects of religion, reason, logic, and ethics, while today, modern technology has taken over these four subjects in a unified "scientific form." However, today, the Western civilization's human legacy of geniuses is being overtaken by the Silicon Valley's geniuses." In place of the old institutions of knowledge, Western civilization has established a modern center, the "Silicon Valley of Geniuses," built on the foundation of contemporary culture and run by the algorithmically working and digitally cogitating Siliconian Geniuses, who do not fight against change but embrace it and empower the human quest for more inventions. But, by following the Silicon brain at an intoxicating level, we are plugging ourselves into the abyss of algorithmic consciousness, and for some thinkers, crippling our evolved brain's consciousness. It does appear to be true that in this era of the internet's instant connectedness, the intuitive mind is becoming sluggish in defining our own course. It may eventually become futile, unless the Siliconian Geniuses help us to make sense of the interplay between humans and digital technology, whose advances in the computing power of artificial intelligence threaten to overwhelm us with complexity.

Notes:

1. Kaplan, Robert D.: *The Return of Marco Polo's World,* Random House, New York, 2018: pp 6-7.
2. Attenborough, David: https://cnnespanol.cnn.com/2018/12/03/david-attenborough-el-colapso-de-nuestras- civilizaciones-esta-en-el-horizonte/

PART 2

Essays About The World Of Islam

CHAPTER 16

Ninth-Century Renaissance In Islamic World And Philosophical Tradition of Muslim Thinkers

A little philosophy inclines man's mind to atheism,
But depth in philosophy, brings men's minds about to religion.
(Francis Bacon: 1561-1626)

Introduction

The Arabs, carrying the light of spiritual experience and religious knowledge, marched out of the Arabian Peninsula to spread their new faith of Islam all over the world. But as they stepped into the civilized world with their mystical and spiritual lure to experience "unity of creation" the first thing they realized was that they needed to achieve knowledge which should have been far more than just spiritual consideration. Attracted by the glamour of the civilized world and the fruits of modernity, following the precept of their Prophet, "even if you have to go all the way to China, seek knowledge," they started seeking scientific and philosophical knowledge.

When the Arabs conquered the Persian and Roman empires, they interacted with Hellenistic, Greco-Roman, and Persian knowledge. Hungry for knowledge, they responded receptively to the modernizing influences of the sophisticated lifestyles and knowledge of the world beyond their rustic way of life as the people of the desert. Within a couple of centuries the towering and finely developed structure of an Islamic Civilization with a culture of modern knowledge appeared amongst the former illiterate and uncivilized pagan Bedouins. It was their concept of *deen* of Islam, a new way of life, which proved more inflammatory than their religion's prayers. Thus, the advent of the ninth century heralded an era of Muslim Renaissance, and the philosophical and scientific progress created a golden period in the World of Islam.

The Desert Bedouin and Urban Tribes of the Arabian Peninsula known as the Arabs, after conversion to Islam had already been united into a "Muslim Ummah," first mentioned in the Charter of Medina— also known the Constitution of Medina. But Prophet Muhammad's Last Sermon delivered on the Ninth Day of Dhul Hijjah, 10 A.H. in the Uranah valley of Mount Arafat in Mecca made an unforgettable impact upon the life of the Arabs when the Prophet emphasized:

> ... All mankind is from Adam and Eve, an Arab has no superiority over a non-Arab nor a non-Arab has any superiority over an Arab; also a white has no superiority over black nor does a black has any superiority over white except by piety and good action. Learn that every Muslim is a brother to every Muslim and that the Muslims constitute one brotherhood. Nothing shall be legitimate to a Muslim which belongs to a fellow Muslim unless it was given freely and willingly. Do not, therefore, do injustice to yourselves. ... All those who listen to me shall pass on my words to others and those to others again; and may the last ones understand my words better than those who listen to me directly. Be my witness, O ALLAH, that I have conveyed your message to your people.*

Religion, just like philosophy and science, is related with the present and the visible world. Its perception in many ways leads humans intellectually toward the same everyday life experiences that philosophy and science investigate and address rationally. According to Islam, the faculty of reason in human beings is an innate ability; it is the voice of God and submission to His voice is submission to reason. In addition to Divine invocations, many sayings of the Prophet of Islam have played an important role in inspiring intriguing discussions and complex intellectual debates by Muslim scholars and thinkers.

The History of Islamic philosophy

The quest for knowledge—philosophical and scientific—began in the time of the advent of Islam in 622 C.E. Revelations of Qur'anic injunctions, appealing to philosophical interests, like, "*My Lord! Increase me in knowledge*,"[1] inviting to God's mathematical universe, "*... and He has enumerated everything in numbers*,"[2] and emphasizing philosophy, "*Call [the mankind] onto the way of your Lord with wisdom and fair exhortation, and reason [argue] with them in the better way*,"[3] incited intellectual cognition, leading to philosophical discussions and scientific investigations. The famous twentieth-century Muslim philosopher M. M. Sharif argues in *A History of Muslim Philosophy* that in the light of the traditions of the Prophet of Islam, "God has given man the will to choose, decide, and resolve to do good and evil. He has endowed him with reason and various impulses so that by his own efforts he may strive and explore possibilities."[4] Muslim thinkers, finding no contradiction between Islamic faith and the philosophical quest, considered philosophy as a legitimate approach to understand and practice the way of Islam. Thus, soon after the advent of Islam, many philosophers, scientists, and literary scholars appeared in the world of Islam between the eighth and thirteenth centuries, which is known the "Golden Period" of Islamic history.

One key factor in facilitating the introduction of philosophical knowledge to Muslim believers, whose knowledge was based on revealed theology, was the perfection of the Arabic language. The Qur'an, which was collected around 633 CE, is the first book in Arabic prose and marked the beginning of literary composition in Arabic language. Its perfect grammar and faultless wording exercised a unique influence on Arabic language and literature that paved the way for the translation of philosophical and scientific terminology into Arabic. Oliver Leaman, in *A Short History of Islamic Philosophy*, remarks:

> Since the grammar of the Arabic language is the grammar of the language which God used in transmitting his final revelation, it was taken to represent formally the structure of what can be said and how it can be used. The miracle of the Qur'an lies in the language itself, and one of the proofs of Islam is taken to be the purity and beauty of the form of expression of the text itself. It is hardly surprising, therefore, that the grammar of that language is accorded high status as an explanatory vehicle.[5]

In Arabic vocabulary, a meaningful word initially from three Arabic alphabets known as the root or *makhraj*, with the help of its very articulate and systematic grammar, is capable of evolving and creating new words with great ease. Thus, the ease, fluency, and richness of Arabic language made it possible to coin new words, and translate Greek philosophical, scientific, and literary texts with complex terminology into Arabic. They were mostly available in Syriac which was an Aramaic dialect, a feature that made it easy to translate philosophy into Arabic

In 529 CE, the Roman Emperor Justinian declared Classical Greek philosophy a knowledge of the pagans and ordered the closing of Platonic schools all over his empire. Many scholars of Classical Greek philosophy along with their works moved to Persia. The Persian emperor Khusro-I Anushirwan welcomed them, but did not accept their philosophical achievements. When Alexander the Great conquered Persia, Greek knowledge was briefly introduced to Persia by the scholars accompanying him, as well as by those who were already settled there. This was virtually the first penetration of Greek philosophy in the east. But soon after the death of Alexander, Greek knowledge was considered the philosophy of enemies. Thus, finding an unfavorable attitude of the Zoroastrian Persians toward Greek learning, the Platonists turned to translate philosophical texts into Syriac.

Philosophy and revealed religion may appear for some thinkers so discrete in nature that there cannot be a philosophy of a particular religion. But regarding Islam and its linguistic suitability, this notion is not that serious. Arabic language during al-Kindi's time made it easy to construct and perfect most of the technical vocabulary of Greek scientific, medical, and philosophical words. Thus, philosophy in the Islamic world spread initially on account of the ease of the Arabic language. Its importance in the lives of Muslims seeking meaning helped them to standardize an articulate science of Arabic grammar and lexicography. Preserving the faultless and uncorrupted text of their Qur'an also helped Muslims to set a higher standard of speech and expression.

Philosophical thought in Islam, known as *falsafah*—the Arabic word for the Greek *philosophia*—emerged as a result of an intellectual discipline that matured from the philosophical appeal of the Greek, Persian, and Sanskrit texts translated into Arabic. Islamic scholars of the seventh century meditated on *falsafah,* which they defined as knowledge of all existing things, divine as well as human matters. They identified *falsafah* with the Qur'anic term *hikmah* (wisdom or organized thought), believing the origin of *hikmah* to be divine, and debated Qur'anic revelation and reason or *kalam*—a term used as a translation of the Greek *logos*. Above all, an ethical reverence for seeking knowledge was infused by the Qur'anic appeal to reasoning and its Prophet's traditions advising Muslims to pursue learning, even if one has to go as far as China to seek knowledge. This reverence and various other factors provided the impetus for knowledge-seeking. In order to understand why Muslim thinkers throughout the history of Islamic civilization have viewed philosophy as an important subject of Islamic tradition, it is important to understand the theological tradition of Islam. William Chittick, in *The Heart of Islamic Philosophy*, propounds:

> Like other religions, Islam addresses three basic levels of human existence: practice, understanding, and virtue; or body, mind, and heart; or, to use the well-known Koranic triad, *islam* (submission), *iman* (faith), and *ihsan* (doing what is beautiful). These concerns are patently obvious to anyone who has studied the Koran or the Hadith (the saying of the Prophet), and Muslims have always considered the "search for knowledge" that the Prophet made incumbent on the faithful to pertain to all three of these domains. ... Islamic virtue is grounded in the attempt to find God present at all times and in all places, just as the Prophet found Him present. Practice pertains to the domain of the body, understanding to the mind or "intelligence" or "intellect" or "reason" (*'aql*), and virtue to the heart (*qalb*), where one is able to experience the reality of God without any intermediary. [6]

In Islamic practice, it is important to first fully understand the Qur'an and the Hadith (the sayings of the Prophet) and investigate the objects of faith specified in its scripture. Some thinkers were doubtful of philosophy's compatibility with Islamic theology, but there is ample evidence that Muslim interpreters of Greek philosophy were sincere followers of the Qur'an and Hadith. At the same time, it is also worth considering that Islamic jurists and theologians who would criticize the philosophers, also attacked each other with rigorous criticism.

Muslim thinkers' philosophical and scientific achievements thus became a remarkable aspect of Islamic discourses. Whereas philosophical thought helped create a golden period of Islamic civilization, religious criticism amongst the believers led to the development of many factions, different sects, and disunity, with the consequence that philosophy and religion became separate subjects. Though Islamic theology had stemmed from a base different from the Greek traditions, the power of Greek philosophy, in what it could do and explain, proved a temptation hard to resist for Muslim thinkers. Thus, using the language and culture of their religion, Muslims started exploring and explaining the ideas and arguments of Greek thought which were agreeable to the Islamic view. For example, since the doctrine of Neoplatonism fitted neatly into Islamic theology, it made an overall impact on Muslim philosophy. Although Neoplatonism does not seriously affirm the idea of a God creating the world out of nothing, it does emphasize the existence of one Supreme Being out of which everything else emerges in such a way as not to tamper with the absolute unity of the One God in Islam.[7]

By the ninth century, what is known the "Islamic Golden Age," a "Renaissance in the World of Islam" began with the Abbasid Caliph al-Ma'mun who believed that reason and faith can be same; that by fully opening the mind and unleashing human creativity, many wonders can be unleashed. laid the foundation of *Bayt-ul-Hikma* meaning the "House of Wisdom" in Bagdad, the capital of his Empire. Thus, a great translation movement of Classical Greek philosophy and sciences, Persian literature, Indian mathematics, Chinese science, and Roman law, came to full swing in Baghdad. Many important philosophical, scientific, medical, mathematical, and literary texts were translated into Arabic. Muslim, Jewish, Christian, and Persian scholars, translating as well as writing in Arabic, interpreted the philosophical and scientific inheritance of the Greeks, especially of Plato and Aristotle. Introduction to philosophy and science was initiated by al-Kindi, al-Farabi, ibn Sina, and many more in Baghdad. In Arab Spain, philosophical and scientific knowledge came to its peak, with massive translations and commentaries on Aristotle by Averroes (1126-1198) and the Jewish thinker Maimonides (1135-1204).

Early Muslim Philosophers

Here, it is important to mention some of the early Muslim philosophers, and their views about philosophy and its compatibility with Islamic theology. Al-Kindi (801-873)—Alkindus in Latin—was the first great Muslim Arab philosopher to follow Neoplatonism. Generally he is considered an Arab philosopher, but with his strong theological inclination he was more than a philosopher. He differed from his contemporary, the Assyrian Christian Hunayn ibn Ishaq (809-873), in two things: his religion and his ignorance of the Syriac, Greek, and Latin languages. Hunayn, who had good knowledge of Latin, Arabic, Syriac, Greek, and Persian, played a pivotal role as a translator of Greek philosophical, scientific, and medical treatises. Though he was originally from southern Iraq, he had studied Greek and became known among the Arabs as the "Sheikh of the translators." He established such a method of translation that it was widely followed by all the later translators and rarely required any correction. The Abbasid Caliph al-Ma'mun, in recognition of his unique talent, put him in charge of the House of Wisdom, "*Bayt al Hikmah*" the famous institution where works of many foreign languages were translated into Arabic.

Whereas Hunayn and his students translated Syriac versions of Greek texts into Arabic, al-Kindi was one of the first benefactors of the translation movement that became the basic impetus for the Muslim philosophical tradition. Among al-Kindi's best-known philosophical works is *On First Philosophy* in which he has given his own definition of philosophy: "Philosophy is the knowledge of the reality of things within man's possibility, because the philosopher's end in his theoretical knowledge is to gain truth and in his practical knowledge to behave in accordance with truth." He maintained that the noblest part of philosophy is "first philosophy," which is knowledge of the "first truth" and the "first cause." Al-Kindi believed in the compatibility between philosophy and revelation and was firmly convinced that he could co-interpret literal Qur'anic religious doctrines and Greek philosophical concepts. He held that philosophy and religion correspond on the basis of three arguments: first, that theology is part of philosophy; second, that the revelations of the prophets and philosophical truth conform to each other; and third, that the theological pursuit is logically ordained. For al-Kindi, the supremacy of the revealed truth is the privilege of the prophets, who intrinsically possess this divine science that transcends human capability. He believed in revelations, the creation of the world *ex nihilo,* and finally its destruction.

Al-Kindi was followed by many philosophers in Baghdad which reached its highest point in Islamic literary, scientific, and philosophic spheres. Following the Greek philosophers, in Islamic tradition knowledge of science and philosophy—in some cases theology as well—were merged in a thinker's cognition. Al-Razi (865-925), in Latin Razes, a highly active physician and a passionate rationalist, believed in reason and reason alone. For him logical reason was the unique criterion of knowledge and conduct. Although he was a theist who believed in God, he was strongly against prophecy, revelation, and all irrational trends of thought. He argued that there was no sense in having some humans, like prophets, guiding the rest of humanity with dogmas. He believed, since God has given human beings reason in order to gain the utmost benefits that mankind can obtain, that reason is sufficient to guide one to God's presence. For him, instead of a prophet, reason is God's best gift to humankind. He held that human beings are born with an equal inclination toward knowledge, differing only in the cultivation of their dispositions. Some, inclined to learning them, are directed to everyday practical ways of life. He rejected al-Kindi's doctrine of creation *ex nihilo*, believing that the body is created from matter which has existed eternally and is made up of indivisible parts or atoms separated by the void.

After Aristotle, the "first teacher of philosophical sciences," Al-Farabi (870-950), known in Latin as Alpharabius, is generally referred to in Arabic sources as the "Second Teacher" of science and philosophy. Al-Farabi, remaining focused on philosophy, refined Arabic vocabulary to be used more subtly and with greater ease. Despite Greek philosophy's pagan identity, he successfully introduced Aristotle into Islamic thought, tradition, and culture, and cleared the way to make it compatible with Islamic theology.

Philosophy of al-Farabi is established on Aristotelianism, with a superstructure of Neoplatonic metaphysics. To this he added a political theory benefiting from his study of Plato's *Republic* and *Laws*. He is therefore regarded as the first Muslim thinker to have interpreted "Islamic Political Philosophy." However, the core of his philosophy is to be perceived in his conception of the "intellect." For al-Farabi, the only intellect entirely independent of matter is the "active intellect," which is actualized knowledge. For him the "active intellect" is to the potential intellect of man what the sun is to the eye.

Translation of Aristotelian logic became the center of great interest in the Arabic speaking world, mainly because it was useful in debates with non-Muslims for presenting the merits of Islam through rational argumentation. The distinctive feature of the development of philosophy in Islam is that Muslim thinkers within their theological preoccupation remained true to the Classical Greek ideal. According to William Chittick:

> The domain of practice came to be institutionalized in the Sharia (Islamic Law), whose experts, commonly called the "ulama" (*'ulama*)—the "knowers" or "scholars"—were trained in the science of jurisprudence (*fiqh*). The domain of understanding developed into three basic approaches to knowledge, which can be called "*Kalam*" (dogmatic theology), "theoretical Sufism," and philosophy (*falsafa*). The domain of virtue, the most inward of these domains, stayed for the most part hidden, but nonetheless it took on the broadest variety of manifestations. To it belong personal piety, devotion to God, love, sincerity, "god-wariness" (*taqwa*), and many human qualities bound with interior life.[8]

A genre of philosophical, scientific, literary, and religious knowledge with comprehensive meanings was introduced as *adab*. The word *adab*, though well known in the Arabic language, entered the Arabic lexicon loaded with new characteristics professing both theoretical and practical performances in diverse fields of knowledge. Chittick, explaining the word *adab*, writes:

> The word *adab*, for which we have no adequate English equivalent, refers to proper and beautiful deportment and correct behavior, both physical and verbal. It denotes a broad domain that includes all the little courtesies and politenesses, observance of propriety and good manners, elegant handling of social situations, accomplishment in belles letters and poetry recital, skill in calligraphy and music, care to observe one's social and professional duties, and perfect harmony between outward behavior and inward attitude.[8]

By the introduction of the new term *adab* in Islamic epistemology and religious knowledge, an "intellectual and cultural" uniqueness appeared.

Ibn Sina (980-1037), famously known in the West as Avicenna, a thinker of unique excellence, was a philosopher, a physician, and a man of science. He writes in his autobiography that he read Aristotle's *Metaphysics* forty times, exploring whether it dealt with Being or the principles of knowledge. It became clear to him only after he read al-Farabi's *Intentions of Aristotle's Metaphysics* that Aristotle was arguing on the subject of being. Ibn Sina conceived his original argument that universals enter human minds from outside, through the active intellect, and that reflection on specifics may prompt the mind for reception of the universal. He defined a thoughtful epistemology and psychology that formed his theory of prophecy, classifying prophethood at four levels: intellectual, imaginative, miraculous, and sociopolitical. His philosophy had a great impact in the East as well as the West. As Avicenna he was known to twelfth-century authors in Oxford and Paris. He attained new fame in modern political philosophy through Ernst Bloch's provocative book *Avicenna und die Aristotelische Linke.*

Introduction to philosophy in the Islamic tradition is incomplete without ibn Rushd (1126-1198) an Arab philosopher who appeared in Cordova, the capital and literary center of Arab Spain. He is known as Averroes in the Latin West. He produced voluminous and varied philosophical works as compared with other great philosophers of Muslim world. Three features distinguish him from al-Farabi and ibn Sina: his methodical commentaries on Aristotle's texts, his meticulous dealing with philosophy's relation to religion, and his composition of systematic treatises on *Islamic fiqah* (Islamic Jurisprudence). He declared philosophy the twin sister of religion, essentially subordinating religion to philosophy. However, his main contribution to Islamic philosophy, and to that of the Jewish and Christian worlds, is the message that there are three different routes to the same truth which are equally acceptable. His commentaries revived Aristotelianism in Western Europe and were fairly recognized by Jews and Christians. His impact on Latin philosophy is such that Western thought between the thirteenth and sixteenth centuries is inexplicable without considering his conceptual contribution. His rational and scientific discourses serve as a foundation for political freedom and religious tolerance in Western thought.

Muslims Transmitted Philosophy to the West

One of the interesting aspect of Muslim thinkers is that they were not merely the translators or followers of the Greek philosophers; as Oliver Leaman says, "They [the Muslim thinkers] created a metatheory, a theory about theories, which is even more radical than the theories themselves. This metatheory is sometimes called the 'theory of double truth,' and it argued that the truths of religion and philosophy are so distinct that there is no way that they can contradict each other."[9] The Arab philosophers understood that their Islamic faith and philosophy do not come into conflict; they are about the same truth, expressed in different ways.

In the history of world philosophies there is a well-recognized role of Muslim thinkers and philosophers in the successful transmission of Classical Greek philosophy to the West. They provided the foundation of the development of Western thought, the advancement of knowledge, the progression of empirical sciences. Muslim thinkers, philosophers, and scientists of the ninth-to-thirteenth-century era of Renaissance in the Islamic World played a great role in engendering the European Renaissance, and in delivering an impetus to philosophical speculation to the Western thinkers from Rene Descartes to modern-day philosophers and scientists. It is important to understand that Muslim philosophers not only played the role of translating Greek philosophies, but also made their own thoughtful contribution to philosophical and scientific knowledge. Peter Adamson and Richard C. Taylor, editors of *The Cambridge Companion to Arabic Philosophy* have argued in their work on Islamic philosophy:

> Certain philosophers of the formative period, like al-Kindi, al-Farabi, and Averroes, were interested primarily in coming to grips with the texts made available in the translation movement, rather than putting forward a properly "Islamic" philosophy. This is not to minimize the importance of Islam for any of the figures dealt with in this volume: even the Aristotelian commentator *par excellence* Averroes, who was after all a judge and expert on Islamic law, dealt explicitly with the relationship between *falsafa* and Islam. And once Avicenna's philosophy becomes absorbed into the Islamic *kalam* tradition, we can point to many self-consciously Islamic philosophers. Still, the term Arabic philosophy identifies a philosophical tradition from its origin in the translation movement.[10]

When modern philosophical thought in the West began with Rene Descartes, Muslim philosophy had already penetrated deep into Europe. In the history of Western philosophy, there is sufficient evidence that most of the texts written in Arabic as well as in Hebrew had been translated into Latin and other European languages. Adamson and Taylor further have argued, "Adelard of Bath (1116-50) speaks of his *studia Arabica/Arabum studia* (in reference to natural philosophy) and *magistri,* which he probably encountered in southern Italy and Sicily. Stephen of Pisa (1127), who wrote on cosmology in Antioch, expresses his debt to a certain Arab."[11] In the same book Adamson and Taylor have remarked,

> The Hebrew translation of al-Ghazali's *Tahafut al-Falasifa* was studied by the Dominican Raymond Martin. Descartes did not acknowledge it, but he came to conclude, "*I think, therefore, I am,*" based on al-Ghazali's view of being, "*I will, therefore, I am.*" Kamal al-Din ibn Yunus of Mosul (d. 1242), a great Muslim teacher of his time, upon becoming a household member of Frederick II Hohenstaufen's family wrote a book on logic for him. ... Andrea Alpago (d. before 1546) acquired knowledge of Avicenna's psychology from the Shiite scholar Muhammad ibn Makki Shams al-Din al-Dimashqi (d. 1531) in Damascus.[12]

Translations of Islamic literature and the philosophical works of al-Kindi, al-Farabi, ibn Sina, ibn Rushd, ibn Tufail, Maimonides, and many Muslim and Jewish thinkers helped in the birth of European Renaissance.

Today, students and researchers of Muslim philosophy question: What went wrong with the philosophical and scientific cultures of the Islamic civilization, which transmitted knowledge to Europe but failed to flourish further in its own home? Why did the Muslims put an end to ibn Rushd's threefold system of truth? While there are many factors related to the decline of Islam's inventive cultures of scientific and philosophical eminence, but a short answer is that the *Bayt al-Hikmah* in Baghdad and centers of knowledge in Egypt and Cordova sponsored by the Muslim caliphs, were in actuality a time and a milieu. They were not physical academies or universities, but rather were great centers of cross-cultural intellectual, philosophical, and scientific explorations. As the Arab patron-dynasties in Baghdad, Egypt, and Cordova lost power, their centers of learning were orphaned and finally died.

Notes:

* Extract from Prophet's Last Sermon.
1. The Glorious Qur'an, 20:114.
2. Ibid., 72:28.
3. Ibid., 16:125.
4. Sharif: 1961, p. 150.
5. Leaman: 1999, p. 6.
6. Chittick: 2001, p. 30.
7. Ashraf: 2007, p. 97.
8. Chittick: 2001, p. 31.
9. Leaman: 1999, p.
10. Adamson and Taylor: 2005, pp. 3-4.
11. ibid., p. 370.
12. ibid., p. 371.

CHAPTER 17

Scientific Research and Discoveries of the Muslims

Introduction

Regarding religion, it is often assumed that by its very nature it is difficult, or for some thinkers impossible, to interpret and investigate it philosophically or scientifically. At the same time, we find almost all great religious thinkers of prominent religions have also been philosophers, and many in Islam have also been scientists. They have interpreted and examined religions far more than a dogmatic or uncriticized faith, and have related their religious tenets to experiences and rational judgments. They have subjected even divinely revealed tenets to radical criticism. It is interesting to note that many philosophers and even scientists who have appeared in the history of knowledge at any time have also been believers in religion, and in some cases even theologians. This approach supports the fact that religion is not an abstract idealism but concrete and practical; that ideals are not only abstractly valid in the Platonic realm of ideas, but can be realized in the world of actual existence.

Science, medicine, technology, and philosophy in the newly Islamized societies of Syria, Iraq, Iran and Central Asia were influenced by the models presented in the early Islamic period. The Islamic Golden Age dating from the eighth to the fourteenth century was a period of cultural, economic, and scientific flourishing. This period is traditionally understood to have begun during the reign of the Abbasid caliphs Harun al-Rashid (786 to 809) and Ma'mun-ur-Rashid (813-833) with the inauguration of *Bayt al-Hikmah*, House of Wisdom in Baghdad.

Though for several reasons Muslims got seriously involved in scientific research in the fields of medicine, chemistry, physics, mathematics, and astronomy, it was still the magnetism of spirituality that attracted and absorbed within its mainstream the knowledge from diverse traditions.

Thus, their material and non-material culture soon became capable of setting knowledge in Islam on a historical path to modernity. Soon the intellectual achievement of Muslim scholars became the envy of the known world. In the magnificent centers of learning from Damascus to Baghdad and from Cairo to Cordova of Arab Spain, nineth-century mathematicians developed algebra, calculus, algorithms, and trigonometry—the foundations upon which modern technology is built. Inventors in the field of mechanical engineering devised early crankshaft versions of the torpedo and the parachute. In the field of medicine, physicians formulated the techniques of surgery and treatment ranging from orthodontia to tracheotomy.

Muslim astronomers successfully calculated the diameter and circumference of the planets to a remarkably degree of accuracy. Michael Hamilton in his work, *Lost History: The Enduring Legacy of Muslim Scientists, Thinkers, and Artists*, has detailed how Muslim achievements laid the cornerstone of the European Renaissance, Enlightenment, and modern Western civilization. As Hamilton chronicles the Golden Ages of Islam, he introduces great Muslim scholars and empirical thinkers, such as ibn al-Haytham, ibn Sina, al-Tusi, al-Khwarizmi, and Omar Khayyam who paved the way for Newton, Copernicus, Galileo, Einstein, and many others.[1] Within a few centuries, Islamic civilization was ready to transmit modern knowledge of philosophy and general sciences to the West. Unfortunately, at the dawn of the nineteenth century the glory of Islamic civilization faded, and its culture found itself stuck in the spiritual beliefs of its religion rather than the enlightening rationalism which they had learnt and adopted from the Classical Greek thinkers during the Muslim renaissance.[2]

Thinkers in Mathematics

In Baghdad, in the year 832, the Abbasid Caliph al-Ma'mun invited a Persian astronomer and mathematician Muhammad al-Khwarizmi (780-850) from Khorasan to assist in the search for God in the numerals. Searching through Indian mathematics at the House of Wisdom, al-Khwarizmi recognized the importance of a character shaped like a dot, later on known as zero. He fixed Arabic numerals by adding zero to them.

Modern numerals in the West are directly derived from this medieval Arabic-Indic number system.

Al-Khwarizmi also introduced "algebra" as an independent discipline, which was called *Hisab al-Jabr wa al-Muqabala,* or "calculus of transposition and simplification." He was followed by many more mathematicians, notably Abu Kamil (850-930), whose book on algebra appeared in 881. But another revolutionary achievement of al-Khwarizmi was a set of numerical calculations and instructions, which if carried out systematically produces a desired result. These calculations were coined after his name, "Alkhwarizm," and Latinized as "algorithm" in Europe,

Until about the sixteenth century, seven hundred years after al-Khwarizmi's death, Europeans would honor and dignify everything they postulate with the concluding footnote, *"dixit algoritmi,"* or "so says al-Khwarizmi," meaning that they have built their calculations on faith in the teachings of the Persian Muslim mathematician.[3] Today, algorithms are critical to software design, as well as much of modern science and engineering, enabling computers and smart electronics to sort out masses of digital data and text, calculate spatial relationships, encode and decode confidential information—all the basic processes of modern computing, supporting technology, commerce, and science. Facebook CEO Mark Zuckerberg can thank al-Khwarizmi pronouncing *"dixit algoritmi"* for the employment of hi system of "algorithm." In astronomy, al-Khwarizmi played a key role amongst other astronomers of his time who organized a major project to measure the length of a terrestrial degree, and developed tables for constructing horizontal sundials that were precisely adjusted to latitude.[4]

Late in the 900s, ibn al-Haytham (965-1040), born in Iraq, authored almost two hundred books on various subjects, building on the discoveries of al-Khwarizmi and his contemporaries, and laid the foundation of mathematics and optical theories. In his famous work, the *Book of Optics,* one of the best of his time, he gave a detailed explanation of how the eyeball works. Thus, five hundred years before Leonardo da Vinci, al-Haytham had delved into things that were later attributed to the great Italian and to Kepler and Descartes. They, like other Renaissance and post-Renaissance thinkers, were merely replicating or building on what the great Muslim scientists had established long ago.[5]

Merging his interest in empirical science, optics, light, and the skies to create perhaps the most scientific and accurate view of the physical universe, al-Haytham's research helped Galileo and Copernicus to understand the true relationship of the Earth to other heavenly bodies. His fame led him to the "House of Knowledge" in Egypt established by the Caliph of Cairo, Al-Hakim Bi-Amr Allah (996-1021) al-Haytham experimented with light and vision, the laying foundation for modern optics. His greatest discovery was that light rays do not emanate from the eyeball of the viewer, and his research on how light passes through various media—water, glass, paper, and smoke—ranks him with Archimedes, and ranks him alongside Kepler and Newton as a great mathematical scientist. Voluminous writings of al-Haytham, Latinized as Alhazen, were translated into Latin and printed by Friedrich Risner in 1572. Many great scholars of empirical science followed al-Haytham at the "House of Knowledge" in Egypt.

Astronomical Science

At the House of Wisdom, Abu Abdullah al-Battani (858-929) an Arab mathematician and astronomer born in Turkey, later known to the Europeans as Albategnius, introduced a number of trigonometric relations. He computed his own *Zij*, an Islamic astronomical book that tabulates parameters used for astronomical calculations of the positions of the sun, moon, stars, and planets, which made their way into Latin and Spanish in the twelfth and thirteenth centuries. His book, *Kitab Az-Zij* made a greater impact on the astronomical studies of al-Biruni, while in Europe it was greeted with wide acclaim. Almost seven hundred years after him, Copernicus referred to al-Battani's *Zij* twenty-three times in his work, *On the Revolutions of the Heavenly Spheres.*

After al-Battani, in the World of Islam in Central Asia, a great polymath Abu Rayhan al-Biruni (973-1048)—a mathematician, astronomer, and geographer—was born in what is today Uzbekistan. He produced some 146 works including ninety-five books written and devoted to astronomy, mathematics, and other related subjects like "mathematical geography." In discussing speculation by other Muslim writers on the possible motion of the planet Earth, al-Biruni commented favorably on the idea that the Earth rotates. He wrote an extensive commentary on Indian astronomy in the

Kitab ta'rikh al-Hind—History Book of Hind—in which he claims to have resolved the matter of Earth's rotation in a treatise on astronomy. In his *Miftah-ilm-alhai'a—Key to Astronomy*—he claims to have surpassed the works of his predecessors. He held that the rotation of the Earth does in no way impair the value of astronomy, as all appearances of an astronomic character can be explained quite as well according to this theory as to the other.

Al-Biruni carried on a lengthy correspondence and sometimes heated debate with ibn Sina repeatedly attacking Aristotle's celestial physics. He argued by simple experiment that vacuum must exist. In his astronomical work, the *Mas'ud Canon*, al-Biruni utilizes his observational data to disprove Ptolemy's immobile solar apogee. His eclipse data was used by Dunthorne in 1749 to help determine the acceleration of the moon and his observational data has entered the larger astronomical historical record which is used today in geophysics and astronomy. Four hundred years before Galileo, al-Biruni had proved that the Earth is round and rotates on its axis. He showed through a diagram how a lunar eclipse occurs when the Earth blocks the sun's light from reaching the moon. His works were translated into Latin and reached Europe in the second millennia.

Maslama al-Majriti (950-1007), Latinized as Methilem, an Arab Muslim astronomer, chemist, mathematician, economist and a scholar of fame beyond the Pyrenees, was born in Majrit what is today Madrid, in Andalusia, Arab Spain. He was among the most brilliant of Spanish Muslims and was the best mathematician and astronomer of his time. Al-Majriti took part in the translation of Ptolemy's *Planispherium*, improved the existing translations of his *Almagest*, and introduced and improved the astronomical tables of al-Khwarizmi. He assisted in working out tables to convert Persian dates to Islamic lunar dates. Al-Majriti was one of the earliest alchemists to record the usage and experimentation of mercuric oxide. He also introduced new surveying methods by working closely with his colleague Ibn al-Saffar. Al-Majriti translated his own works into Latin, which triggered a European hunger for the ideas of his predecessors, from Ptolemy to al-Khwarizmi and al-Battani.

During the eleventh century, a Spanish Arab astronomer, Abu Ishaq al-Zarqali (1029-1087), Latinized as Arzachel, was born to a family of artisan-mechanics who made instruments and devices at the directions of contemporary scientists and scholars. As a self-educated astronomer, he was advised to go to school, which he did at the age of thirty-one. In the year 1062, after completing his education, he joined the group of astronomers. He also designed and built the legendary water clock of Toledo which told the hours of the day and night and also the days of the lunar calendar. Al-Zarqali built a sophisticated astrolabe and wrote essays on the astrolabe, which, almost two hundred years later were personally translated by the Castilian King Alfonso X.

Omar Khayyam (1048-1131), a well-known Persian poet throughout the West whose quatrains were translated in English by Fitzgerald, was originally an astronomer and a mathematician of great fame. He perfected the Gregorian calendar by adding a day in the month of February every four years, creating the "leap year." He is widely considered to be one of the most influential scientists of the middle ages. He wrote numerous treatises on the subjects of mechanics, geography, mineralogy, and astronomy. Khayyam wrote an influential *Treatise on Demonstration of Problems of Algebra* (1070), which laid down the principles of algebra, part of the body of mathematics that was eventually transmitted to Europe. In particular, he derived general methods for solving cubic equations and even some higher orders. He wrote on the triangular array of binomial coefficients known as "Pascal's triangle." His philosophical view of mathematics had a significant impact on his celebrated approach and method in geometric algebra, particularly in solving cubic equations. His solution is not a direct path to a numerical solution; in fact, his solutions are not numbers but rather line segments. In this regard, Khayyam's work can be considered the first systematic study and the first exact method of solving cubic equations.

Islamic astronomy reached its zenith in the thirteenth and fourteenth centuries when Nasir al-Din Tusi (1201-1274), a Persian astronomer, and his successors surpassed the limits of the Ptolemaic world view that had ruled for a millennium. Al-Tusi's work on ethics, astronomy, mathematics, and philosophy marked him as one of the great intellectuals of his age. Halagu Khan, the grandson of Genghis Khan, built an observatory for him at Margha, in what is today Iran. The road to modern astronomy leads through the work that he and his followers performed at the observatory of Margha. Al-Tusi found a way to restore most of the symmetry to Ptolemy's model by adding pairs of cleverly designed epicycles to each orbit.

Following the footsteps of al-Tusi in the fourteenth century Abul-Hassan ibn al-Shatter managed to go further and constructed a completely symmetrical model of Ptolemy's universe. In the year 1420, astronomers at the Samarkand observatory measured star positions to a fraction of a degree. Though their works were not translated, Dr. Owen Gingrich, an American historian of astronomy, wrote in the magazine *Scientific American* that the whole idea of criticizing Ptolemy and reforming his model was part of "the climate of opinion inherited by the Latin West from Islam."

The Science of Medicine and Surgery

Works of Greek physicians, particularly Hippocrates and Galen, had been translated into Arabic early on. A Zoroastrian who converted to Islam, Ali ibn Sahl Rabban al-Tabari (c.783–858) was a scholar, physician, and psychologist, whose work *Firdous al-Hikmah,* one of the oldest encyclopedias of Islamic medicine, was based on Syriac translations of Greek sources specified by Hippocrates, Galen, and others. His stature, however, was eclipsed by his more famous pupil, Muhammad ibn Zakariyya al-Razi (865-925), Latinized as Rhazes. Al-Razi, a Persian Jew who converted to Islam, was an active physician and a rationalist who believed in reason and reason alone. He authored some two hundred major books on nearly every known aspect of medicine, as well as on philosophy and alchemy. He was the first physician to have clinically and scientifically described the scourge of smallpox and the less dire measles, and showed that they are separate afflictions. He wrote a book on this subject, *Kitab al-Jadari wa'l Hasbah,* or *The Book of Smallpox and Measles.* He viewed that disease has scientifically based physical causes and that the old belief that it is punishment on humans by God is wrong.

Another great name in the field of medicine and surgery is that of Abul al-Qasim Ibn Al-Abbas Al-Zahrawi (936-1013), also spelled Abul Kasim, Latinized as Albucasis. He was an Andalusian Arab Muslim physician born in the town of Al Zahra, located six miles northwest of Cordoba, Spain. He has been considered one of the fathers of modern surgery. His greatest contribution to medicine is the *Kitab al-Tasrif,* a thirty-volume encyclopedia of medical practices. The surgery chapter of this work was later translated into Latin where it received popular acclaim and became the standard textbook in Europe for the next five hundred years. He was the first physician to identify the hereditary nature of hemophilia, as well as to describe an abdominal pregnancy—a subtype of ectopic pregnancy which in those days was fatal. Al-Zahrawi's pioneering contributions to the field of surgical procedures and instruments had such an enormous impact in the East and West that some of his discoveries are still applied in medicine to this day. His comprehensive medical texts shaped both Islamic and European surgical procedures up until the Renaissance.

The most towering figure in the fields of philosophy, medicine, science, mathematics, logic, grammar, law, and theology, was the Persian physician Abu Ali ibn Sina (980-1037) known in the West as Avicenna. His great book on medicine, *al-Qanun fi al-Tibb* (Canon Medicinae) was counted as a key text in both Islamic and Western medical traditions for many centuries. His philosophical work *Kitab al-Shifa* (*The Book of Healing*) is sometimes confused with his *Canon Medicinae* because of its reference to healing, but in fact it reflects philosophy as remedial against the illness of false opinions. His books were widely translated in the Eastern regions and the Western world.

In Arab Spain, Abu Bakr Muhammad ibn Bajjah (1070-1138) Avempace in Latin, was a major figure in the history of philosophy whose specialty was the science of medicine. He was also proficient in the theory and practice of mathematical sciences. Another famous physician in Granada was Abu Bakr Muhammad ibn Tufail (1105-1185), Latinized as Abubacer. He was a private physician of the Caliph and rose to the rank of a vazier. He wrote many books on medicine, philosophy, and astronomy. In 1182, ibn Tufail resigned from his position as physician of Caliph Abu Yaqub Yusuf, allowing ibn Rushd, Latinized as Averroes, to succeed him.

Ibn Rushd (1126-1198) was born in Cordoba in Arab Spain. Though he had full knowledge of Greek philosophy and sciences, for a short time he remained with ibn Tufail as a physician at the Caliph's court. After the death of ibn Tufail, ibn Rushd emerged as a great figure in the fields of medicine, mathematics, astronomy, philosophy, and Islamic jurisprudence. As many of his books on medicine, mathematics, astronomy, and philosophy were translated into Latin, he had even more influence in the Christian West than in the Islamic world. His impact on the Latin tradition is such that Western thought between the thirteenth and sixteenth centuries is inexplicable without considering his conceptual contribution. His presentation of scientific and rational discourses, serve as a modern foundation to Western thought.

Notes:

1. Morgan, inside cover, 2007
2. Lewis, Bernard, 2004, p. 44.
3. Morgan, 2007, p 91.
4. Starr, 2013, p. 8.
5. Morgan, 2007, p 104

CHAPTER 18

Ibn Khaldun: The First Muslim Social Scientist

Introduction

Abu Zayd Abd ar-Rahman ibn Muhammad ibn Khaldun al-Hadrami, better known ibn Khaldun (1332-1406), was born in Tunis and died in Cairo, Egypt. In the Islamic world he was an amazing scholar, inventor of social sciences, and a protagonist of philosophy of history. His famous work, *Muqaddimah* (*Prolegomena*)—the introduction to his *Universal History*— is the best-known work on medieval historiography of the philosophy of history and social sciences. He was actively involved in the politics of his time, and traveled widely across Spain, North Africa, and the Middle East.

Ibn Khaldun came from an influential North African Arab family that had settled in Andalusia at the beginning of the Muslim conquest of the Iberian Peninsula. His father was a famous scholar of Islamic jurisprudence who worked primarily as a jurist. He made it possible for ibn Khaldun to attain the best education from the most famous scholars. In the mid-fourteenth century, the western Berber Marinid tribe invaded Tunis and established a short-lived dynasty which left its mark on the young scholar. He saw the Marinid tribe's period as a model for the historical development and decline of Islamic societies.

Ibn Khaldun was a Muslim thinker of the philosophy of history, political science, sociology, economics, and human affairs. He devoted his life to a systematic study of human sciences and civilizations. He was the first great historian-philosopher whose research provided a rational and scientific basis for history to be classified as type of philosophy. Ibn Khaldun's *Muqaddimah* (*Prolegomena*) to his *Universal History* (*Kitab al-Ibar*) is the most comprehensive synthesis of the human sciences achieved by the Arabs. For him, history is not mere chronicle of events but is sociology. Other Muslim thinkers who had an impact on Western thought, such as al-Farabi, ibn Sina, ibn Rushd, and al-Ghazali, had inquisitive insight into metaphysical, philosophical, and religious disciplines, but ibn Khaldun, profiting from the philosophical cognitions of these thinkers, surpassed them in his approach to mankind's socio-political affairs and the many problems of the social sciences.

An Abstract of the *Muqaddimah*

The *Muqaddimah* or *Prolegomena*, an introduction to ibn Khaldun's *Universal History* (*Kitab al-Ibar*) is the most significant and challenging account of Islamic history in the pre-modern world. An abridged English version translated by the eminent Islamist and interpreter of Arabic literature Franz Rosenthal was published by the Princeton University Press in 1967, condensing the three volumes published in 1958 for the Bollingen Foundation into one. In the *Muqaddimah,* ibn Khaldun praises the excellence of historiographical approaches to history, offering glimpse of different kinds of errors to which historians are liable and arguing why these errors occur. Throwing light on the nature of civilization, he starts from the homeless Bedouins roaming in the deserts, to those living a settled life, enjoying gainful occupations and livelihoods through science, crafts, and many other professions. He explains various issues that affect civilization. Reflecting upon human civilization in general, he discusses parts of the earth where it is found, providing information about oceans, rivers, and zones, defining temperate and intemperate zones.

Starting from the influence of the air and atmosphere upon the color of human beings and upon many other aspects of their condition, ibn Khaldun argues about the influence of climate upon human character. He writes about abundance and scarcity of food in the various inhabited regions of the world and specifies how they affect the human body and character. Explicating various types of human beings, he reflects upon those who have supernatural perception either through natural disposition or through practice, preceded by a very thoughtful discussion of inspiration and dream visions. He gives an account of Bedouin civilization, and the conditions of life of the savage nations and tribes with basic and explanatory statements.

Discussing political philosophy, ibn Khaldun writes on dynasties, royal authority, the Islamic Caliphate, ranks of government, and all that goes with basic and supplementary propositions. He writes about countries and cities and all other forms of sedentary civilization's conditions, how they occur in particular regions, with consideration of their primary and secondary connections. He gives an account of various aspects of people making a living, such as many crafts for profits and various problems connected with them.

Ibn Khaldun in his *Muqaddimah* discusses kinds of sciences, methods of instruction, and conditions that impel human beings to obtain education. He takes a philosophical approach to the human ability to think, which distinguishes him from the animals and enables him to obtain his livelihood, helps him to cooperate with his fellow beings and study the Master whom he serves. Ibn Khaldun writes about people who follow the revelations that the Messenger transmits to them. He conveys that God has caused all animals to obey man and to be in the grip of his power. Through man's ability to think, God has given him superiority over many of His creatures.

According to the twentieth-century famous British historian Arnold J. Toynbee, "Ibn Khaldun's star shines the more brightly by contrast with the foil of darkness against which it flashes out; for while Thucydides and Machiavelli and Clarendon are all brilliant representatives of brilliant times and places, ibn Khaldun is the sole point of light in his quarter of the firmament."[1] The *Muqaddimah* is undoubtedly the greatest work of the philosophy of history and social sciences. Neither the classical nor the medieval Western world can show one nearly of same brightness and intellectual depth.

Ibn Khaldun as a Theorist of Socio-political Sciences

Ibn Khaldun was a towering figure in the fields of philosophy of history and social sciences during the time between Aristotle and Machiavelli or any political philosopher of the modern age. Charles Issawi in his work *An Arab Philosophy of History* introduced ibn Khaldun by accrediting a remarkable passage from Toynbee's *A Study of History* vol. III, in the following words:

An Arab genius who achieved in a single 'acquiescence' of less than four years' length, out of fifty-four years' span of adult working life, life-work in the shape of a piece of literature which can bear comparison with the work of Thucydides or the work of a Machiavelli for both breadth and profundity of vision as well as for sheer intellect power. ... He is indeed the one outstanding personality in the history of a civilization. In his chosen field of intellectual activity he appears to have been inspired by predecessors, and to have found no kindred souls among his contemporaries, and to have kindled no answering spark of inspiration in any successor; and yet, in the Prolegomena (*Muqaddimah*) to his *Universal History* he has conceived and formulated a philosophy of history which is undoubtedly the greatest work of its kind that has ever yet been created by any mind in any time or place.[1]

In the *Muqaddimah*, ibn Khaldun sets forth a clear exposition of his theory of the social and historical development and decline of a society. This monumental work in three volumes laid the foundations of several fields of knowledge, particularly the philosophy of history, remaining focused on how historical events should be interpreted. The *Muqaddimah* provides historians with a criterion by which they can judge recorded events and social changes. As a great thinker in social science, he introduced a tradition of scientific method with a positive outlook and matter-of-fact style. This renders him a congenial figure to the modern world, particularly to the World of Islam, which is in search of a political system compatible with its faith.

The greatest merit of ibn Khaldun appears prominently in his methodological thinking, which established him as the first "social scientist." As a philosopher of human affairs, ibn Khaldun analyzed the past of mankind in order to understand and shape its present and its future. He did not follow Islamic philosophy's tendency to debate old themes of the relation between revealed theology and rationalistic Greek philosophy. He believed that the intellect should not be engaged in such issues as the oneness of God, the other world, the truth of prophecy, the real character of divine attributes, or matters that lay beyond the level of human intellect. He therefore construed a fresh and novel philosophical approach in the form of "natural science." While remaining connected with his contemporary genre of philosophical thought, he explored a uniquely new perspective which set him apart.

With a legacy of Greek science and philosophy, it was not easy for ibn Khaldun to draw a line between the natural sciences and the positive sciences or that of divine law. As a result, he introduced a "science of culture" anchored in natural philosophy. He was convinced that his science of culture was based on natural science and was an entirely original social science newly introduced to the Islamic traditions. It relates the study of human society and the causes of its rise and fall. Arguing about the importance of history, he stated, "Water is not so like to water as the future to the past." He was the first thinker to have introduced sociology as an important part of social sciences. To him, sociology is the study of the present, which throws light on the study of past in the same way that history provides materials for it. Sociology is basically a study of the various forms of human society, conducted by investigating the nature and characteristics of each of these forms and analyzing the laws governing its evolution.

The Stepfather of Economics

Ibn Khaldun's thinking in the field of economics regards the division of labor serves as the basis for any civilized society, and identifies division of labor not only on the factory level but in a social and international context as well. He was the first thinker who explained that if one has to obtain food it creates surplus value with a combination of many hands from among his fellow beings. Thus, through cooperation the needs of a number of persons, many times greater than their own number, can be satisfied.

Hundreds of years before the Western philosopher Adam Smith, ibn Khaldun had presented similar ideas. Believing that there is no distinction between productive and unproductive work, his economic philosophy of the division of the production process is more expressive than Smith's explication. Philosophizing further about the economy, ibn Khaldun analyzed markets which arise based on the division of labor and examined market forces in a simple, didactic way. Emphasizing the role of inventories and merchandise trade, he described the relationship of demand and supply, which was made known by Western economists in the nineteenth century. He divided the economy into three parts—production, trade, and the public sector—since according to his theory market prices include wages, profits, and taxes. He analyzed markets for goods, labor, and land as well. This approach led ibn Khaldun to invent the labor theory of value, which made him a pre-Marxian classical thinker. His idea that the produced value is zero if the labor input is zero seems surprisingly classical, far ahead of his time.

Ibn Khaldun's Theory of *Asabiyah*

According to ibn Khaldun, while man is the center of his world, he is fully dependent on his physical environment, and in his capacity as an individual he cannot secure all the things required for his livelihood. Thus man, the individual, must cooperate with others and live as a family, tribe or a nation. This act of cooperation is basically enabled by man's natural ability to think as a social being. According to Charles Issawi:

> The core of ibn Khaldun's political and general sociology is his concept of *asabiyah*, or Social Solidarity. Society is natural and necessary, since the isolated individual could neither defend himself against the more powerful beasts nor provide for his economic wants. But individual aggressiveness would make social life impossible unless curbed by some sanction. This sanction may be provided by a powerful individual's imposing his will on the rest—in this Ibn Khaldun anticipates Hobbes—or—and here he shows deeper insight than Hobbes—it may be provided by Social Solidarity. Ibn Khaldun traces the origin of this Solidarity to the blood ties uniting the smaller societies, but is careful to point out that blood ties mean nothing unless accompanied by proximity and a common life, and that living together may generate as powerful a solidarity as kinship. Moreover, the relations between allies, between clients and patrons, and between slaves and masters, may all lead eventually to a wider solidarity.[2]

Human beings, insofar as they display *asabiyah*, or socio-political cohesion, form into more or less stable social groups. It is not by accident that human beings live together; rather, society is natural and necessary.

For ibn Khaldun, to establish an organized political society, it is necessary to band together for defense, for agricultural, and industrial fulfillment. An abundance of resources in a particular region leads to the emergence of a group. Then a need arises for the distribution of resources and introduction of cultures, which is possible only by living together. Ibn Khaldun also points out the effect of climate and atmosphere on various cultures and their influence on character. He argued that earlier Islamic societies, which mostly originated from the desert lands, *asabiyah* became the foundation for all social relations. It provided fundamental motives for cultural, intellectual, and economic development. Over time, however, the sense of group solidarity breaks down, followed by a slow period of decline until a new group asserts itself into a society and brings with it a new sense of *asabiyah*. For him, *asabiyah* is an essential attribute of humanity more basic even than religion. Ibn Khaldun's concept of *asabiyah* is similar to what we know today as "secularism."

Rejecting Divine Political Order

Addressing the issue of prophecy in a society, ibn Khaldun maintained that "divine political science" is not natural. Unlike Aristotle, he believed that man by nature is a political being, naturally capable of observing natural constituents. He daringly argued that for the formation of a society and the survival or continued existence of man, there is no need to follow revelation and introduce divine rules to establish divine government. His other argument was that the premises and conclusions of divine political science are not rationally demonstrable, as unaided reason cannot achieve certainty of divine law. Divine laws only command but do not demonstrate rationally the need to hold opinions and perform actions. For human reason, divine commands remain undemonstrated. However, they continue to hold the status of belief or religious opinion. Ibn Khaldun's naturalistic approach is the forerunner of modern social science, history, secularism, and economics.

But while preferring rationalism to theological views, ibn Khaldun was a passionate believer of the religion of Islam. He lived an agitated life which took him into the huts of savages and into the palaces of kings, into dungeons with criminals and into the highest courts of justices; into the companionship of the illiterate and into the academies of scholars; into the treasure houses of the past and into the activities of the present; into deprivation and sorrow and into affluence and joy. It led him into the depths where the spirit broods over the meaning of life. His constant intrigues and naturalistic views led him to changes of allegiance to different rulers and regions from Arab Spain to Syria, which give modern critics the impression of a lack of patriotism. But this great genius and scholar has remained true to one fatherland known as *Dar al Islam* and Muslim civilization.

Ibn Khaldun believed that the differences between people arise out of variances in their occupations. His psychology of education is built on the notion of aptitude or skill. Every thought and action necessarily leaves its imprint on the mind of the agent, so a continued or a prolonged repetition of the same action indisposes the mind to acquiring a different occupation. He explains the effect of supply and demand factors on prices and wages, supports free competition, and condemns monopoly. As civilization progresses the importance of agriculture declines, while that of services increases. His views on "pure economics" earned him the title of "Pioneer Economist." He visualized ahead of many modern economists and sociologists the interrelation of political, social, economic, and demographic factors. He describes various social sciences, their development, and the process of professionalization that scholars had to endure to become certified by their contemporaries as qualified academics. According to ibn Khaldun, this process of professional certification, which had become so extensive during the Islamic medieval period that it prevented scholars of in-depth knowledge in any one field, was one of the factors that led Muslim societies to decline. His theories about the decline of Muslim society would influence Muslim scholars, who embraced ibn Khaldun's theories as evidence of the need for renewal of Islamic culture and thought.

Regarding God's existence, ibn Khaldun believed that all objects in the created world, whether they are things or acts (human or animal) presuppose prior causes which bring them into being. Each of these causes is in its turn an event that presupposes prior causes. Hence the series of causes ascend until it culminates in the Cause of causes, their Maker and Creator. He held that man is made up of two parts: one corporeal and the other spiritual, fused together, but each with its own particular power of apprehension. The spirit sometimes apprehends spiritual matters and other times corporeal, but whereas it apprehends spiritual matters by its own essence, without using any medium, it apprehends corporeal objects only through the instrument of the body, such as the brain and the sense organs.

Notes:

1.   Issawi, 1987, p. ix.
2.   Ibid. pp. 10-11.

CHAPTER 19

Islamic Political Philosophy

Introduction

Political Islam, rooted in the belief of its revealed scripture the Qur'an, the precepts of its Prophet Muhammad, its successful implementation by the Prophet and his Rightly Guided Caliphs, has remained active for more than a millennium. It never died out to find resurrection, unlike the Greek city-state democracy; rather it remained dormant in the Islamic regions even under Western colonial rule. Islamic political philosophy is distinctive and phenomenal in the political history of the world. With a logic of its own, it comprises an intelligible system founded on the interplay of faith and reason. Presenting a concept significantly different from that of other political systems—one based on the harmony of revelation and rational application—Islam initiated a new beginning in the history of political thought. Comprising a coherent, ongoing tradition, separate from the conceptions of Greek and even modern liberal democracies or the words of Jesus, "My kingdom is not of this world," Islam introduced a vertically horizontal form of political philosophy that bridged the yawning gap between religion and politics to be recognized as a this-worldly discipline with spiritual freedom.

Condemning Socrates to death by the democrats of Athens had already created a wide gulf in the history of democratic thought. It was resurrected after more than two millennia and also after the bloody terrorist-sponsored French Revolution. But some four hundred years after the death of Socrates, the crucifixion of Jesus created another gulf—this time between religion and politics, when Jesus proclaimed, "Render unto Caesar the things which are Caesar's; and unto God the things that are God's." He was saying, decide who your god is—the prince of this world or the God of Abraham? Jesus thus separated religion from state politics. But six hundred and twenty-two years after Christ, a new form of political outlook presented by Prophet Muhammad, grounded in a revealed religious faith but entwined with the matters and affairs that appear to be this-worldly, emerged as Islamic political philosophy within the ideology of *Islam deen-wa-dawla*, Islam as a way of life and state.

From Religion, Morality, Law, to Statecraft

Since Islamic political ideology has been conducted in terms of religious politics, it is important to know how it started. The first revelation occurred to Muhammad in the year 610, in the town of Mecca, while he was meditating in a cave on Mount Hira. When the Prophet began to convey to the citizens of Mecca the message that "*there is no god but only Allah, and Muhammad is His messenger,*" it seemed unlikely that this would affect the political life of the tribal leaders or merchants of Mecca. His early messages did not seem to have political relevance or pose a threat to Meccans' tribal traditions. The verses revealed to Muhammad as Prophet in the Meccan period were oracular utterances on the unity, glory, and omnipotence of God and the moral responsibilities of human beings. Early verses were mostly directed toward many erratic religious perversions, unethical and immoral practices of the decadent contemporary Meccan and Arab tribes.

The *Hijra*, the migration of Prophet Muhammad to the city of Medina in 622, marks the beginning of his political activity and the hypotheses that led to an Islamic political philosophy. In Medina, there was neither any political system nor any legal discipline. The Prophet did not suddenly look for political power. He kept preaching the new religion and inviting people to believe in one transcendent monotheistic God until a sizable community of Muslims had grown. With their firm faith in Prophet Muhammad as a true messenger of God, and with strong religious ties and an ideal message in hand, a social structure of a society of believers in the faith of Islam, the *Muslim ummah,* emerged. Consequently, there was a need to adopt a course that would protect the rights of this new Muslim ummah.

The Prophet first entered into agreements with prominent clans, the most important of them being the affluent Jews of Medina. Thus, he laid the foundation of a new body politic, an Islamic city-state without precise geographical landmarks. Actualized within the scope of this body politic were the political potentialities projected in the Qur'an, resulting in an Islamic Constitution. Apart from the Qur'an, among the early chronicles of Prophet Muhammad's career as a leader, there is a well-documented Charter called the "Constitution of Medina." The main political feature of this Charter was that for the first time in the history of the Arabs, a political unity of different factions and tribes was formed under the leadership of Prophet Muhammad. In the Constitution of Medina, he did not render pre-Islamic concepts irrelevant, which proved to be a wise political move. It was part of his diplomatic activity to create a federation of Arab tribes to live together peacefully, which also legitimized his leadership not only politically but also religiously. As a leader of the Islamic Ummah, Prophet Muhammad, authorized by divine revelations, managed to integrate religious tenets with political interests to form a new political philosophy. The Qur'anic verses revealed during this period were directed at the general conduct of life, at legal, social, financial, and political matters, and at issues of war and peace.

The Constitution of Medina proved a steppingstone for the Prophet in constructing from tribal confederacies the edifice of a new community driven by a sense of moral mission. He was now comfortable preaching spiritual brotherhood plus an all-embracing law and universal control to be achieved, if necessary, by military power. The religion he introduced fulfilled the social needs of Arab tribal society. Politically, tribal identity continued to have meaning in the mainstream of the Islamic Ummah, and the space left by Islam for clans and tribes helped absorb newcomers, such as the North Africans, Persians, Central Asians, Turko-Mongols, Indians, and Southeast Asian peoples. The social solidarity of Muslim Ummah, later defined by ibn Khaldun as *asabiyah*, is the central point of Islamic political philosophy and proved to be a major contribution to Islamic political discipline.

Muslim Ummah laid the foundation of a state on certain clear-cut principles revealed in the Qur'an and the traditions construed by its Prophet. Islamic ideology was a starting point of its political philosophy, which after the life of the Prophet developed under the influence of Greek philosophy and the political outlook in Islamic theology. Arabic translations of the Persian-Sasanian ethical traditions, which were corroborated by the political philosophy and wise sayings of Greek philosophers, provided a new vision in Islamic political thought. Byzantine literature on warfare and administration, which included texts from the classical and later Hellenistic periods, was translated from Greek into Arabic. This gave birth to a very mature ethical literature aimed at the moral education of man as ruler and ruled. In Islamic history it is classified to this day as *adab*—a comprehensive term for sociopolitical order, philosophy, sciences, art, and literature. Greek thought and philosophy prominently became integrated into Arabic texts and served as guidelines for the philosophical, political, and ethical prospectus of the Islamic adab. Such ethical traditions, carefully integrated with Islamic theology and not violating Qur'anic message and Shari'ah, firstly became a central point and later formed a background of Islamic political philosophy.

Although the Qur'an is generally concerned with ethics and morality within the religious sphere, with little to say about political and governmental rules, it reflects a guideline from which political inferences can be taken. According to Muhsin Mahdi, in his work *Al-Farabi and the Foundation of Islamic Political Philosophy*:

> There are a number of striking resemblances between many of the fundamental features of Islam and the good regime envisaged by classical political philosophy in general, and by Plato in his work *Laws* in particular. Both begin with god as the ultimate cause of legislation and consider correct beliefs about divine beings and the world of nature as essential for the constitution of a good political regime. In both, these beliefs should reflect an adequate image of the cosmos, make accessible to citizens at large (and in a form they can grasp) the truth about divine things and about the highest principles of the world, be conducive to virtuous actions, and form part of the equipment necessary for the attainment of ultimate happiness.[1]

Al-Farabi (870-950), further reflecting upon the comparative approach of Plato and Islamic political thought, argues:

> Both [the Prophet and Plato] are concerned with the giving and the preserving of divine laws. Both are opposed to the view that mind or soul is derivative from body or is itself bodily—a view that undermines human virtue and communal life—and to the timorous piety that condemns man to despair of the possibility

of ever understanding the rational meaning of the beliefs he is called upon to accept or of the activities he is called upon to perform. Both direct the eyes of the citizens to happiness beyond their worldly concerns. Finally, both relegate the art of the jurist and that of the apologetic theologian to the secondary position of preserving the intention of the founder and of his law, and of erecting a shield against attacks.[1]

However, between the ideal state of the Prophet of Islam and that of Plato there is a big difference. The Prophet of Islam was a practical idealist for whom the ideal and the practicable converged. Khalifa Hakeem, in his work *Ideology of Islam* writes, "He [the Prophet] thought it of no use placing ideals before humanity which by its nature, with all its limitations, was incapable of embodying in actual life. He said, "God imposes no duties on men which are beyond their capacities and He knows what the inescapable demands of human nature are."[2] Another difference is that the Prophet visualized the whole of humanity as one body, as a multitude of single souls. Plato, on the other hand, addressed only the citizens of a city. The Prophet guided by the Qur'an, which addresses all of mankind and not the citizens of any one city, would not be satisfied with setting up just the city-state of Medina or Mecca.

A New Political System

With the Jewish, Christian, and Arab tribal traditions already in place, Prophet Muhammad introduced a new political pattern founded upon a powerful social solidarity—the Khaldunian *asabiyah*—in the light of Qur'anic revelations. Following a coherent ongoing tradition endorsed by the spiritual and rational appeal embedded in the ethos of society, the Prophet of Islam introduced new ways to explain human life by giving practical meaning to human beings' ideologies. Through a unique system based on its own theo-political ideology, Islam motivated individuals and groups to integrate into an ummah. Graham E. Fuller, in *The Future of Political Islam*, argues:

> The spiritual inspiration of Islam and its vision of society and the
> state obviously explains much about its permanent acceptance

by such diverse cultures and peoples over so long an expanse of time …. Indeed, it is not just the conquest but its very durability that is also striking; it did not melt away in a generation or two, as did Mongol power. Vast numbers of adherents of different religious cultures—Christian Byzantium, Zoroastrian Persia, Buddhist Central Asia, large parts of the Hindu subcontinent, Hindu/Buddhist Java, and animist Africa—after the Muslim conquest ended up permanently accepting the spiritual, ethical, and legal principles of Islam …. Whatever Westerners may think about Islam, we cannot ignore the reality that in a political and social sense, Islam has in fact prevailed more widely, longer, and over more diverse cultures than any other religion.[3]

Since in Islam politics and the affairs of state were not considered separate from religion, morality, law, or clan values, it is important to study its political thought with reference to the context of the Qur'an, the Hadith (precepts of its Prophet), and the tribal traditions of the Arabs. Although the Arabs initially understood only metaphysics, after conquering the Roman and Persian Empires, they studied logic, mathematics, astrology, medicine and classical Greek philosophy of the pagan Greek thinkers with full interest, but showed little interest in the democratic system of the Athenian city-state.

The search for the ideal man has been a perennial quest in the world's cultures, each using different words for this end goal. In Hinduism they are known as *avatars* (divine incarnates) while the followers of the Abrahamic tradition revered them as *prophets*. In his *Dialogues*, Plato speaks of philosopher-kings or king-philosophers—that is, the ideal man as a ruler. The early Arabs were among the last to join this search for the ideal man. The Bedouins of the Arabian Peninsula had their own distinctly nomadic, self-contained, coherent, and ongoing traditional culture. They needed a reformer of a much higher order than a philosopher-king, someone who would relieve their contemporary malaise and set them on the right path from everyday life to a higher art of statecraft.

Of all the spiritual guides of mankind, Muhammad, the Prophet of Islam and the ideal man of the Muslims, presented the most practical realization of an ideal society and an ideal state. He came as a practical idealist, the Prophet King, the man with high ideals of ethics, justice, and character. He was equipped with the wisdom and power to put those ideals into practice and see their actualization with his own eyes during his lifetime. The *deen* of Islam (meaning way of life) as revealed to him and compiled in a single sacred volume, the Qur'an, presented a complete social and political system, covering the exercise of power (who should exercise it and how much he should have); justice in relationships between people (particularly between those in power and those they rule); just distribution of wealth; and enquiries and solutions as to why states exist and what they should try to achieve.

Islamic Political Thought

Islam presents an all-embracing system of life comprising a distinct self-contained culture and a coherent, ongoing tradition, separate from the West and with a logic of its own. Islam's capacity to assimilate other cultures into its system, including Central Asian, Persian, Egyptian, Indian, Mongolian, Chinese, European, and Far Eastern peoples, is based on its appeal to *humanitarian theism* which demands of its followers much more than mere spiritual commitment. Its concept of *humanitarian theism,* based on an intertwined commitment of *haqooq-ul-ebaad* (rights of the people) and *haqooq-Allah* (rights of God), obligates Muslims to comply with a political and moral framework of law and governance that falls strictly within the teachings of the Qur'an and the precepts of the Prophet. Politics is not a subsidiary set of rules and regulations; it is the central component of Islamic discipline. The Qur'an, however, does not dictate a specific political system or form of government; rather, it gives believers discretion to establish a suitable system in the light of Qur'anic injunctions and the practice of the Prophet. Muslims may adopt any form of government—be it democratic or republican, presidential or parliamentary, federal or unitary, or even monarchic—as long as the leadership pursues justice through social cooperation and mutual assistance by strictly following the Qur'anic decree of sovereignty, it is accepted as an Islamic way of rulership. The Qur'an says, "*Unto Allah belongs the Sovereignty of the heavens and the earth. Allah is able to do all things.*"[4] The Islamic conception of sovereignty stipulates that man is not all-powerful but is God's viceroy on earth—a concept that has been exploited and misused by many rulers in Muslim history.

The true mission of Prophet Muhammad was not just to preach but to reform and enforce the message contained in the Qur'an about the natural religion of humanity, "submission" to the will of God: *Unto Allah belongs the East and the West, and whithersoever you turn, there is Allah's countenance. Lo! Allah is All-Embracing, All-Knowing.*[5] In Islam, though man can frame laws according to the needs of contemporary society, he cannot frame or implement laws repugnant to what is revealed in the Qur'an. In Islam, only God has knowledge of the perfect, eternal, and just laws that preceded both society and state. Both divine and natural laws are designed for all times and are characterized as universally applicable to the whole of mankind. These laws existed prior to mankind's existence. As the norms of natural law exist in nature to be discovered by reason, so the norms of Islamic law were revealed to be defined rationally by its Prophet.

Islam aspires to be a universal faith, subsuming any society, culture, or tradition into its discipline. The complexity of its political thought goes beyond its theological or philosophical context. G. E. Von Grunebaum, in *Classical Islam: A History 600-1258,* defines:

> The structure of Islam arose on a foundation which derived its survival and its greatness from its ability to transform itself from a religious community possessed of a national political character into a commonwealth of culture which was both religious and supranational, while yet retaining its existence and validity as a state. The political history of Islam contains a paradox peculiar to this religion alone: it is the history of the transformation of an Arab sect into a community dominating an empire, and furthermore a universal religious community which was primarily non-political, yet was the determining factor in political events and imposed its own qualities on whole cultures. In other words, it was not the physical domination but the cultural power of the new teaching, not its origin in a particular geographical and intellectual zone but its immanent universality, which proved the deciding factors in its development.[6]

Today there is a major concern that some of the ways in which political Islam manifests itself are anti-Western, anti-secular, anti-modern and undemocratic. What is feared and being challenged in Islam is its doctrine of immanent universality. Yet Islam's appellations of peace and submission to the will of God mean serving a universal authority above any human being. In Islam, when mankind acts in accordance with his nature of peace and submission, this leads him to seek peace in this world. The religion of Islam—a driving force in Muslim civilization—has been and is still politically misunderstood, misinterpreted, and exploited both within and beyond Islam. But the Islamic political system is meant to be studied and analyzed within the injunction of "*to God belongs Sovereignty.*" Just as the belief in God is universal, so is the idea of divine sovereignty. However, the core of submitting to Divine sovereignty is "*striving after righteousness.*" It also implies surrender to the sovereignty of a person, dynasty, or majority of persons acting as God's vice regents striving for righteousness. It is not a personal dictatorship, monarchy, or ideology of one who is vice regent of God; rather, it is the sovereignty of a superpower above man, of a God who is closer to every person than his jugular vein. The Qur'an exemplifies this by saying, "*Now God be exalted, the True King! There is no god save Him, the Lord of the Throne of Grace.*"[7]

The concept of divine sovereignty in Islamic political thought helps to foster reciprocity among different peoples, nations, and cultures. For the Muslims, be they Arabs, Persians, Africans, Indians, Mongols, Turks, Europeans, or Americans, it is not a matter of submitting just to a temporal authority, but to a universal Sovereign Divine authority which is close to everyone. It is not a black race submitting to a white ruler or a white race submitting to an Indian or Chinese ruler; rather, it is submitting to a non-physical entity symbolically identified as God. It was a universal transcendent vision of Abrahamic monotheism, the belief in a unique and final revelation by God to humankind which was revealed to the Prophet of Islam. Such a vision neither destroys nor desecrates the spirit of diverse cultures but allows their integration into a globalized universal Islamic socio-political system. Islam has accepted such diversity to the extent that it is not against the basic teachings of the Qur'an. Moreover, it was reciprocity between temporal cultures and the values of Islamic discipline which proudly espouses its vocation of universality. Cultural reciprocity is a boost to Islamic universality, but it also presents a problem in the practice of many fundamental principles of Islam, given the traditions remaining within Islam's spiritual appeal.

One of the best features of Islamic political thought is its new economic strategy. The Prophet established the dignity of the laborer, asserting that the wage-earner is the friend of God. He said, "Pay the laborer before his sweat dries up."[8] He held that, "Who has a land should cultivate it himself or give it to his (Muslim) brother gratis rather than charge a certain amount for it."[9] The Prophet founded a state of merchants, seekers of knowledge, workers, and peasants. An outstanding feature of the Arab economy was agriculture, particularly the skillful use of irrigation, which the people had learned from living where water was scarce. Prophet Muhammad was the first economist in the world to levy a tax on surplus capital, abolishing usury, which is unearned income representing parasitism. Islam believes in hard-earned income which is known as *rizq-e-halal*, or income gained by hard labor or through running capital.

It is related in *Sahih al-Bukhari,* a collection of the Prophet's precepts, that "Allah's Apostle said: 'Nobody has ever eaten a better meal than that which he has earned by working with his own hands [efforts].' David, the Prophet of Allah used to eat [only] from the earning of his manual labour."[10] Instead of seeking interest through usury on investing capital, Islam levied *zakat,* a certain amount of compulsory tax on surplus capital to spread out wealth. Zakat could be distributed directly to the needy, the poor, orphans, widows, and the disabled, who are incapable of earning their livelihood; or it could be collected by the state to be spent for general public welfare. The Qur'an enjoins Muslims to spread out wealth so that it does not remain hoarded by the rich.

Islam is often misunderstood as founding a theocratic state, trifling with politics and legislative enterprises. A theocratic state is one that derives the authority for its sanctions from a divine figure, or from religious principles that act as regulative forces. Theocracy, in its real form, is a state that has an overt or covert religious basis. It may be a government run by priests or according to religiously sanctioned customs. In a theocracy, somehow, the "Invisible must be the basis of the Visible." Theocracies are defenders of specific metaphysical beliefs. Other great religions of the world are mostly concerned with metaphysics or with preaching morality. Islam is a *deen,* a way of life, and it does not confine itself to morality, spirituality, or salvation of the individual as an isolated entity. Islam does not follow the biblical principle, *"render unto Caesar the things that are*

Caesar's," but, maintains that not to stand up or protest against evil is equal to committing evil. Those who do not rise to eliminate evil are the slavish sufferers and they would rather help in giving birth to tyrants who prove to be a greater evil for the whole society.

According to the views of Khalifa A. Hakim in his work *Islamic Ideology,* the Prophet of Islam preached as did "Plato and Aristotle that a just man can live justly only in a just state; therefore, the founding of a just state is the sine-qua-non-of social justice and the life of well-being for an individual."[11] For Islam, implementation of justice is the foundation of a society. Justice must be achieved and executed at all levels—within the family, the social hierarchy, and the political system. God says in a well-known sacred hadith, "*My servants, I have forbidden myself injustice and made injustice forbidden to you. Therefore, do not act unjustly to one another.*"[12] Islam is, thus, not a mere belief in God; its aim is the betterment of life by conducting all human affairs practically and just fully. Islam values human beings as social and political animals whose welfare is bound up with the welfare of their society.

Islam emerged in the seventh century with an ultimate idea of a global community living in *dar al-Islam,* or the "abode of peace." In Islam *dar al-Islam,* therefore, is a worldwide state or a geographic area in which a majority of Muslims live. Seyyed Hossein Nasr, in his work, *The Heart of Islam: Enduring Values for Humanity,* stated that: "Classically, *dar al-Islam* was juxtaposed with *dar al-harb,* or the 'abode of war,' in which Muslims could not live and practice their religion easily because the Shari'ah was not the law of the land, although there were in practice always Muslim minorities living in various parts of it."[13] Some Muslim jurists later introduced a third category—*dar al-sulh*—also known as *dar al-aman* ("territory of truce or at peace with Islam.") *Dar al-sulh* means a country that is not part of the region of *dar al-Islam* but is either a protectorate of or at peace with *dar al-Islam,* where Muslims could live in freedom to practice their faith.

In the Islamic state, rulers and the ruled follow a political system along the guidelines of Qur'anic revelation, practiced by the Prophet of Islam and later implemented by the first four Caliphs, the successors of the Prophet. Muslims rigorously adhere to the Qur'anic admonition, "*So set thy purpose (O Muhammad) for religion as a man by nature upright—the* nature *(framed) by God, in which He has created man.*"[14] Islamic political discipline, thus inspired by divine commandments, had no problem being influenced by the Aristotelian and Neoplatonic trends of natural ethics. Plato's ideal state and Islamic divine ethics converged into the practical state of *dar al-Islam.*

What is remarkable in the Islamic concept is its universalistic attitude, an appeal that leads to *asabiyah,* or social solidarity, the central point propounded by ibn Khaldun in his political philosophy. Social solidarity, or unity of the people, is the fundamental social norm in which people, regardless of race or color, share the same rights and obligations. It is further strengthened by the Qur'anic injunction related to the basic right to live "*that whosoever kills a human being for other than manslaughter or corruption in the earth, it shall be as if he killed all mankind, and whoso saves the life of one, it shall be as if he had saved the life of all mankind.*"[15] In Islam only knowledge and piety form the basis of a person's superiority in the community. Thus, Islam instituted a flexible constitution that reflected a divinely natural code of ethics and justice, and above all emphasized human rights and obligations. It applied control over the power of rulers by rendering them subordinate to the law—one based on religious sanctions and natural moral order.

The glorious days of Islam were, therefore, the days when there was an eagerness to learn among peoples and their sponsors. Lenn E. Goodman, in *Islamic Humanism,* propounded that:

> What made for [their] greatness—a greatness whose spiritual and intellectual achievements are still appropriable and worthy of appropriation today—was the way in which those resources were integrated, cultivated, put to work. That is, what gave greatness to Islamic civilization in its heyday was its self-confident openness to what was of genuine value in the achievements of predecessors and contemporaries. What makes Islamic culture a lesser presence in the world today is a lesser openness, a loss of confidence, a crabbed defensiveness and chafing chauvinism grounded in insecutiry."[16]

The decline of the world of Islam and its breakup into various small Muslim states started when eagerness to learn and interchange of knowledge diminished. But the overall predicament of the Islamic world is that after the two world wars, Western colonialism divided much of the Muslim world into so-called nation-states. The Arab world was divided into artificial units that reflected neither traditional nor logical boundaries. The main cause of the fall of the Islamic world is that Muslims have lost their legacy, which political historian Antony Black describes:

> The unity of the People emerges as the fundamental social norm. Within the People, all adult males share the same rights and duties. The only basis for human superiority is piety and knowledge; even then (according to a hadith of uncertain date), "a man shall not lead another man in prayer in a place where the latter is in authority, and no-one shall occupy the place of honor in another's home except with his permission." There was a religious duty to provide for the needy (especially orphans) by charity (zakat: alms). This was the ideology which overthrew empires.[17]

Politics and religion in Islam are so intricately integrated that it is impossible for Muslims to replace their allegiance to faith and Shari'ah with nationalism and secular law.

Notes:

1. Mahdi, 2001, p. 126
2. Hakim, 1951, p. 191.
3. Fuller, 2003, p. 3-4.
4. Pickthall, the Qur'an, 3:189.
5. Ibid. 2:115.
6. Von Grunebaum, 1960, p. 13.
7. Pickthall, the Qur'an, 23:116.
8. Karim, Al-Hadith, 2006, vol. II, 299.
9. Matraji, Sahih al-Bukhari, vol. III, # 2341-42.
10. Ibid. # 2072.
11. Hakim, 1951, p. 194.
12. Hadith (Unanimous)
13. Nasr, 2004, p. 163.
14. Pickthall, the Qur'an.
15. Ibid. 5:32.
16. Goodman, 2003, p. 7
17. Black, 2001, p.14

CHAPTER 20

Liberal Democracy
and Islam

Introduction

There are many views for and against the compatibility of democracy and Islam. In spite of some thinkers pointing to the fact that a disposition to democracy is present in the spirit of Islam, it is still a big question: why it is difficult for the followers of the Islamic faith to accept democracy? Even in the light of the waves of revolt launched as the "Arab Spring," it seems uncertain that the Western form of secular liberal democracy will take hold in Islamic regions of the world. However, it is often assumed that the first four Caliphs who succeeded the Prophet of Islam during the seventh century were elected in Medina, showing that the seeds of democracy exist in Islamic system, and need proper nourishment to flourish. But although the first four Caliphs were elected by a group of elites of the city-state of Medina, they were not elected by the general population, nor were the members of this elite group elected by the people. In fact, it was a political system similar to the Roman Republic, which allowed the elite class only to elect a head of the state. Later traditions reveal that just like the Roman Republic, the Muslim Caliphate became monarchic, hereditary, and authoritarian in its rulership.

The democratic system which emerged and died in Greece was almost unknown to the early Muslims. They were only familiar with the political system of two empires warring with each other: the Romans and the Persians. This is because soon after Socrates was condemned to death by the democrats, Greek democracy died. Plato, Socrates' pupil, put a final nail in the coffin of democracy by proclaiming:

> Until philosophers are kings, or the kings and princes of this world
> have the spirit and power of philosophy, and political greatness
> and wisdom meet in one, and those commoner natures who

pursue either to the exclusion of the other are compelled to stand aside, cities will never have rest from their evils—no, nor the human race, as I believe—and then only will this our State have a possibility of life and behold the light of day.[1]

However, democracy resurrected in Europe after the American and French Revolutions. Later on, liberal democracy emerged from secularism, the free market, and the natural moral values of a society or a nation in which its citizens, irrespective of faith and ethnicity, are sovereign and can express their free will by electing representatives of their own choice. Generally, liberal democracy requires not only a secular political system but also a liberal cultural, free intellectual outlook, and rational societal resources at the disposal of the democrats. In addition to these resources, liberal democracy must be properly understood within the perspective of humanism and secularism, rather than religion.

Islam and Democracy

So far there are no signs that the future of democracy in the Muslim world is bright. The only exception was the movement known as the "Arab Spring," which helped the Arabs to understand their position between a fading authoritarian rule and the need for a democratic order. In spite of the Arab Spring apparently smashing the myth of the political passivity of the Arabs, there still exists in all Muslim societies an Islamist-utopia—a religious idealism—which stands as an impediment to political modernity as well as to democracy. Another significant reason is that Islam presents itself as a public religion—revealed in the Qur'an as a way of life rather than only as a religion—that gets easily involved in the legitimization of political power by religious rules. In Islam, both the public aspect of religion and its utopia of religious idealism aim at retaining its society's communal structure.

Democracy is a political system that demands the singularity of a political discipline, implying a human-to-human horizontal relationship among the individuals in a society. On the other hand, religion is primarily a vertical relationship between an individual and his God, where Divine sovereignty is imposed from top-down. The emergence of liberal democracy is impossible when the political system is imposed top-down. It succeeds when the system based on democratic consensus emerges bottom-up. Within such a frame of thought, Islam's vertical belief of Divine sovereignty clashing with the democracy's horizontal concept of people's sovereignty, raises a key question: Is Islam, particularly in the Arab world, compatible with democracy?

Democracy depends upon the presence of the natural moral psychology of its citizens which has to evolve from a society's cultural, literary, and educational impetus. It has to pass through the channels of its cultural, environmental, social, historical, and religious ethos. Therefore, first of all we have to know the ethos of the literary, cultural, moral, and traditional etymology which was inherited by the Arabian people who were first to embrace Islam and establish an Islamic civilization. In the literary genre we find only poetically based literature in the traditions of the peoples of the Arabian Peninsula. Poetry presents human emotions and feelings in the form of love poems, odes, and long poems interwoven with stories focused on spiritual values. Its emotional appeal is aesthetic rather than a free voice of reason and rational thinking. In prose form we find only short stories, teaching lessons of ethics and morality that place greater emphasis on obedience to family, social, political, and divine order. To make people feel safe, these stories mostly instruct them to obey and be faithful to the traditional truth or the given order. In religious tradition there is very little—or rather, no—room to say "no" openly or to be disobedient to a traditional institution, to disagree with a teacher, mullah, or imam, who enforces unquestionable obedience to divine order.

The most important aspect in pre as well as post-Islamic culture is that we do not find the genre of fine art, theatre, or drama—as we saw in Ancient Greek society and the European Renaissance—which is undoubtedly the root of free speech. The art of theater was not only absent in pre-Islamic societies of the Arabian Peninsula, but has not found a place in the Islamic discipline until today. The kind of fine art admissible in Islamic discipline is "art for God's sake," promoted through the calligraphy of Qur'anic verses, the ninety-nine attributes of God, His Prophet, or in the Sufi tradition of Islam, the names of the first four Caliphs. Art for God's sake is baroquely displayed in mosques, tombs of the saints, and other religious structures as a prominent form of Islamic architecture. But art that reflects the insight of a person, freely expressed on canvas or presented on stage, away from the pressures of everyday existence and limitations of reality, is missing in the Islamic way of life. The natural inclination to express inner thoughts and feelings through the art of theatrical performance is so powerful that it urges the performers and the audiences to express their free will, raise their voice, emphasize their interests and speak about their imperfections. This is missing in Islamic tradition. We, therefore, do not find the ingredients of democratic discipline in the Arabian or Islamic literary, cultural, and moral traditions, reflected in the "Deen or Way of Islam" and inherited by the Muslims all over the globe.

The Fault Line in the Way of Islam

Human rights and democracy emerge from the contention between politics and religion. Today, instead of struggle for liberal democracy, we find the emergence of a wave of fundamentalism and a reversion to an extreme form of Islam in some regions of the Muslim world. Psychologists affirm that more extreme a person's views are the more he thinks he is right. Hard-line religious fundamentalists have a staunch belief of superiority with disdain for all those who do not share their views. On account of this approach, despotism rather than free thought takes control of the political system, demanding submission, both to God and to those who rule in His name. Within these situations, it is not possible for Muslims to recognize a separation between religion and politics, and thus, a theo-totalitarian system becomes the state of affairs. Bernard Lewis in *The Middle East and West* argues:

> One reason for the absence of liberal democracy in the Muslim world is that Islam discouraged the formation of independent groups that might have challenged despotic rule. In what is today a standard Oriental trope, the problems of contemporary Muslim societies can be located in medieval Muslim history. Islamic law knows no corporate legal persons; Islamic history shows no councils or communes, no synods or parliaments, nor any other kind of elective or representative assembly. It is interesting that the jurists never accepted the principle of the majority decision— there was no point, since the need for a procedure of corporate decision never arose. Delving deeper into the history of medieval Islam to explain contemporary absence of democracy, the political experience of the Middle East under the caliphs and sultans

was one of almost unrelieved autocracy, in which obedience to the sovereign was a religious and a political obligation, and disobedience a sin as well as crime.[2]

Today there are two types of cultures in Islamic societies: the high culture and the low culture. The high culture is that of the urban bourgeoisie and *ulama* (religious scholars), characterized as scriptural and puritanical, which is normative for the urban life of the Islamic world. The high culture is to be contrasted with the low culture of common-folk followers of Islam, which is comparatively more tolerant and flexible.

Under the current situation, scriptural puritanism is appropriated on a mass level through education of Islamic political centralization and urbanization. Within this perspective, Islamic fundamentalism is the demand for the realization of this norm which, assisted by popular support, enjoys the aspiration of the higher culture. If in Islamic society political organization is not applied top-down, and the religious groups reconcile themselves to a concept of politics that separates religion from state, a religious-based theory of political secularism could possibly be a practicable solution. Muslims need to realize that the Charter of Medina, also known as the Constitution of Medina, drafted and implemented by the Prophet during his life, was a secular charter based on pre-Islamic customs and traditions of the Arabian tribes, devised and implied bottom-up in the light of requirements by the Prophet of Islam.

For the believers in "Islamic exceptionalism," the modern term secularism is negatively associated with the ravages of post-colonialism in the Islamic world. But political secularism is fine if we accept it within the perspective of ibn Khaldun's ideology of political and general sociology's core concept of *asabiyah*, or "social solidarity." Human beings, insofar as they display *asabiyah* or political cohesion, form into more or less stable social groups. The end of social solidarity, according to ibn Khaldun is societal-sovereignty. Nader Hashemi in his book, *Islam. Secularism, and Liberal Democracy* is of the view that:

> Secularism is the study of promoting human welfare by material means; measuring human welfare by the utilitarian rule and making the service of others a duty of life. Secularism relates to the present existence of man, and to action, the issues of which can be tested by the experience of this life—having for its objects the

development of the physical, moral, and intellectual nature of man to the highest perceivable point, as the immediate duty of society: inculcating the practical sufficiency of natural morality apart from Atheism, Theism, or Christianity: engaging its adherents in the promotion of human improvement by material means, and making these agreements the ground of common unity for all who would regulate life by reason and ennoble it by service.[3]

I have abridged the definition of secularism, particularly for Muslims, after reviewing many definitions and picking up some points which are relative to Muslim societies. I believe secularism is not anti-religion—it is in fact warranting an ideology, a faith, or a religion as a personal belief of an individual, a group, or a majority of citizens. Societies become secular not when they dispense with a faith or religion altogether, but when they are no longer agitated by it.

We know that political Islam took a start from the Constitution of Medina, which in spirit is a secular charter, or in ibn Khaldun's concept of *asabiyah* projecting a secular social solidarity. It also laid a new tradition of first four successors of the Prophet as elected Caliphs by the elites of the city-state of Medina. They all, the elected and the electors, strictly believed in the faith of Islam. Today, Muslims need to understand the remark of French political scientist Alexis Tocqueville that the first political institution of American democracy is religion, which seems odd when considering secularism. For Tocqueville the main reason to see religion as the primary political institution of democracy is religion's powerful conviction that human liberty is central to the entire purpose of the universe. He argues that a religion adds to the morality of reason, an acute sense of acting in the presence of an Undeceivable Judge- Omnipresent God, who sees and knows even acts performed in secret.

Islam's Possible Way to Liberal Democracy

Today, in some countries of the Islamic world, a non-ideological, secular-political, and free-market understanding is on the increase. IT technology is having far-reaching impacts on vital aspects of democracy, such as freedom of speech and media. In some respects, Facebook, Twitter, and other internet technology is silently infusing the importance of the free voice and the need for democracy, even under authoritarian rulership and absolute monarchies. Thus, the polity of liberal democracy can be learned and instituted by sharing new ideas about democratic values. In order to prepare a ground for the emergence of a liberal democracy, an educational system must be introduced to help produce a generation of free and moderate thinking.

During the Golden Era of Islamic historym free thinking allowed the knowledge of scientific and philosophical reasoning to stay dominant, and Islamic civilization flourished. But no nation or civilization basking in past glory can give its present a revival of its past. It has to shape its present by adapting the four fundamental dimensions of its contemporary period: educational, cultural, economic, and political. Since humans are naturally spiritual and by cognitive experiences rational beings, the educational dimension can establish a harmony between spirituality and reason. Within the cultural dimension, there is freedom in Islam to adapt to different cultures and environments, to experiment, to change, and to develop. As regards the economic dimension, the Prophet himself being a merchant is a guide for today's Muslims in adopting modern economics.

The political dimension, which is founded on four universal liberties, is critical today. These liberties are already an essential part of Islamic discipline: liberty of worship, liberty of speech, liberty from poverty, and liberty from tyranny. Islam's interpretation of human rights and liberty are clearly reflected by its greater emphasis of *Haquq-ul-Abad*—rights of the people—which is over and above *Haquq Allah*—rights of God. Islam's concept of *Haquq-ul-Abad* is egalitarian and a close interpretation of the Islamic view of humanism that began in the late ninth century. Islamic humanism attempts to reconcile individuality with community, responsibility with liberty, originality with tradition, art with experience, knowledge with understanding.

In order to resolve the economic, cultural, and political crisis in Islam, an awakening, a renewal, and a rejuvenation both in the literal sense and in the way of thinking is the need of the hour. This cannot be achieved by a breeze like the Arab Spring; it is the work of a political as well as an intellectual revolution, like the French Revolution that drastically changed the European world. The concept of minimal boundaries of freedom of action must somehow be crafted for political institutions *vis-a-vis* religious authorities, and for religious individuals and groups *vis-a-vis* political institutions, intertwining liberal democracy with the belief of the religiously oriented masses. Political leaders need to indigenize a form of democracy based on the Islamic concept that "the rights of the people are more venerable than the rights of God."

Religious traditions, liberal democracies, and political ideologies are not present inherently in a society. They appear out of the orientation of a social culture which provides a ground for the development and construction of these ideas. Democracy is a political system, which is neither revealed nor can be imposed by force upon the people. It emerges from the grass roots of the masses, based on the philosophy of libertarianism—a philosophy of freedom that throughout history has inspired people to fight for human dignity and individual rights. It is not a movement that would end with elections in some countries, or with a promise of elections in many others. Democracy requires more than elections. It must incorporate fundamental rights of the citizens, equality of race and gender, freedom of conscience and religious practices, and above all freedom of speech. Liberal democracy is not practicable without the concept of "secular faith and spiritual freedom."

Muslims need to understand that secularism is a political term, not a godless or anti-religion concept. It is in fact the privatization of religion—particularly that there should be no religion in politics and no politics in religion. Human societies are distinguished and identified on the basis of their cultures. Culture is defined as a sum total of the quality in a person, a society, or a nation that arises from excellence in ethics and morality, art and literature, the quest for knowledge and philosophical pursuits, behaviors and characteristics, religious belief and political systems, and social discipline and intellectual credentials, all achieved and developed by education and training. Culture is a way of living built up by a group of human beings and is transmitted from one generation to another as a form of civilization. Islamic civilization is founded on diverse cultures and traditions of many ethnic groups and races from different regions of the world, which in the modern age can flourish better under a liberal democracy rather than a theocratic caliphate.

Notes:

1. Plato: The Republic, V: 473.
2. Lewis: 1964, p. 48.
3. Hashemi: 2009, pp. 104-105.

CHAPTER 21

Islam: A Faith of Peace

*Islamic ideology, by its name and the spirit of
its teaching, is a proponent of peace.
The conflict and violence we see today in Islamic world do not countenance
the teachings of its Qur'an and the sayings of its Prophet.*

Introduction

The ideological spirit of Islam, by its name and the essence of its teaching,
is a proponent of peace. The conflict and violence we see today within
the world of Islam do not countenance the teachings of its Qur'an. Islam
considers mankind's existence in this world to be affected by an unstable
balance between its dispositions toward peace and aggression. Recognizing
both peace and a tendency toward aggression as instinctive and natural
in human affairs, Islam emphasizes altering aggressiveness through moral
conduct. It presents a code of ethics and a systematic way of cultivating
human habits to unlearn what is bad and to learn what is good and
necessary for existence. The Qur'an explains: *"O mankind! We created you
from a single (pair) of a male and a female, and made you into nations and
tribes, that you may know each other (not that you may despise each other)."*[1]
Focusing greater attention on moral values, it advises that: *"The good deed
and the evil deed are not alike. Repel the evil deed with one which is better,
then lo! he between whom and you there was enmity (will become) as though
he was a bosom friend."*[2] Since existence is impossible without peace, every
living being naturally craves peace. Islam by definition means "peace" and
"surrender," presenting it as a universal ideology for all time.

Prophet Muhammad appeared among a people steeped in bloody
feuds and barbarous wars, familiar only with an eye for an eye, a tooth for
a tooth, and a life for a life. They proudly eulogized horrible acts of war,
conflict, and violence as supreme objects of their lives. To these people,
with few moral or ethical values, Prophet Muhammad gave the message

of one God of truth and purity, of self-restraint and love. The religion he presented had a distinctive appellation—that is, Islam. His message of faith in one transcendent God was supported by reason. The rationality of his message was so powerful that people far from the humanized world, who were fighting and killing each other, on embracing the faith of Islam were instilled with a feeling of being at peace with themselves.

For thirteen years the Prophet preached peace and tolerance to his followers. In his life he peacefully resisted extreme persecution and oppression. The Qur'an did not give him any mandate to fight back against such persecution. He took up arms only when the Muslims were attacked by an army led by the Meccans. Thus, he fought defensive wars to safeguard his religion and his followers. His final expedition was his march into the city of Mecca, his birthplace, from which he had been forced by his bloodthirsty enemies to flee to Medina. He entered Mecca without shedding a drop of blood and forgave his enemies, displaying in practical terms that Islam was for peace. The amnesty and forgiveness he granted to his former deadly enemies and persecutors may well have been unparalleled in history.

Reflecting on the literal and religious interpretation of the Arabic word "*islam*," Khalifa A. Hakim explains in his work, *Islamic Ideology*:

> The very word "islam" means "peace," the second meaning being "surrender to the will of God" and the two meanings fuse together into the essence of all morality and spirituality which is the attainment of peace and harmony by surrendering the individual will to the universal will, whereby the finite participates in the life of the infinite.[3]

Peace is enlightened by submission, and one cannot be at peace with oneself or the surrounding humanity unless one voluntarily surrenders his will to the universal will. Hakeem interpreting the conception of "harmony" in the Qur'an explains:

> Harmony which is the spirit and goal of existence is called peace in the terminology of the Qur'an. In peace the contending individuals and elements do not cease to exist; they get reconciled retaining their individuality but realizing their identity of purpose. Natural beauty and art are expressions of this peace we call harmony.

Intellectual understanding is peace, aesthetic contemplation is peace, and virtue and happiness is peace.[3]

According to Islamic philosophy, man is in himself a "miniature universe" and as such his consciousness reflects the entire cosmos. External and environmental happenings influence the mind of every man; and it is equally true that man, this "microcosmic universe," also influences the macrocosmic physical universe. He affects and brings about changes in the vast expanses of the material cosmos. Inner tranquility and peace enjoyed by man makes its impression on the outer world. This external manifestation of inner peace takes the form of an attitude toward life known as Islam. For Islam, world peace is unthinkable without the perfection of inner peace among its people.

The Way of Peace in Islam

A study of the Islamic way in the context of its religious and social order reveals that Islam endorses the unity of all monotheistic religions for a lasting and durable peace. Islamic ideology, countenanced by its name and the spirit of its teaching, is originally a proponent of peace. Karen Armstrong in *Muhammad: A Biography of the Prophet*, has remarked:

> Far from being the father of jihad, Muhammad was a peacemaker, who risked his life and nearly lost the loyalty of his closest companions, because he was so determined to effect reconciliation with Mecca .... We need new solutions for our unprecedented situation, and can learn much from the Prophet's restraint. But above all, we can learn from Muhammad how to make peace. His whole career shows that the first priority must be to extirpate greed, hatred, and contempt from our own hearts and to reform our own society. Only then is it possible to build a safe, stable world, where people can live together in harmony, and respect each other's differences.[4]

For Islam the purpose of life is to live it in a progressively purified, harmonized, and strengthened way with inner and outer peace. The spirit of Islam lies in its harmonious interaction of faith and reason. It does not command beliefs that are not based on reason; rather, it incites intelligent faith, beginning with nature and what is all around mankind, stemming from observation, reflection, and contemplation. There is no conflict amongst religion, philosophy, and science in its teachings or practices. Rather, it endorses ways to explore by seeking knowledge of all sciences. On account of its harmony of faith and reason, Islamic civilization absorbed philosophical knowledge from ancient Greece, and political and natural science from Persia, India, and the Orient. Islam transmitted this knowledge, not by the sword, but peacefully to Europe, laying the foundation of European Renaissance that enabled Europe to emerge out of Dark Ages and create a spirit of enlightenment in the Western world.

Prophet Muhammad preached the message of a natural religion of humanity, though revealed in the Qur'an as a *deen* or a way of life. The Qur'an defines human beings as naturally both peaceful and violent, but proposes peace as the primary feature. It is because of this primary characteristic of peace that, in spite of their violent tendency, humans do not cease to exist. The peaceful aspect of their nature, reacting to their violent tendencies, leads to harmony. In Qur'anic terminology, this harmony, which is the spirit and true purpose of existence, is recognized as *al-Islam* or a "faith of peace." According to Islam, natural beauty and art are expressions of peace, intellectual understanding is peace, aesthetic contemplation is peace, and virtue and happiness are peace. So the Qur'an calls paradise an *"Abode of Peace,"* where residents are greeted with *"Peace, peace."* In Islam, peace is a supreme ethic that reflects the divine attributes, and harmony is a supreme virtue, a moral characteristic of human beings.

Behavioral ecologists believe that the gregarious and pro-social aspect of human behavior is generally a reciprocal altruism based on a general conviction that "I'm being nice to you only because you are also nice to me." The Qur'an elevates this notion by advising, *"When you are greeted with a greeting, respond with better than it or return it."*[5] It emphasizes this further with an injunction to *"Repel evil with that which is better."*[6] Imam Bukhari reported in his voluminous collection of *hadith, Sahih Al-Bukhari,* the words of Prophet Muhammad: "No one of you will become faithful till he wishes for his brother what he likes for himself,"[7] and "The Prophet of God said, 'Help your brother Muslim, be he the oppressor or oppressed.' People asked, 'O Messenger of God, if he is oppressed we shall help him, but what if he be the oppressor?' Prophet replied: 'Prevent him from oppressing.'"[8]

Since this universe is believed by religions to be a creation of God, it must reflect the attributes of its Creator. Compassion, Love, Beauty, Forgiveness, and *Al-Islam* are some of the ninety-nine names of God in Islam. The Qur'an says that God has made man in the nature of God: "*So set thy purpose (O Muhammad) for religion as a man by nature upright—the nature (framed) of Allah, in which He hath created man. There is no altering (the laws of) Allah's creation. That is the right religion, but most men know not.*"[9] "*So, when I have made him (man) and have breathed unto him of My spirit, do ye (angels) fall down, prostrating yourselves unto him.*"[10] Although human beings are endowed with a divine nature, whereby the finite participates in the life of the infinite, they also are gifted with free will which allows them to discern what is right or wrong in thought and action. Islam maintains that, unlike other creatures, everyone is born "*muslim*" (in Arabic, "one who is a clean slate and peacefully submits to instruction and to his Creator") and is naturally bound and constantly obedient to his Sustainer. Bestowed with free will and a rational approach to life, he is free to become or not to become a Muslim in the sense of a believer in the religion of Islam. Naturally blessed with reason and intelligence, with the power to think and make judgments between right and wrong, man's freedom of choice becomes operative. Since everyone is born "*muslim,*" peace and harmony is natural in humans.

Peace in Islamic View is not Pacifism

According to Islam it is the aggressive tendency of human beings that entices them to conflict and war. Whereas the Qur'an says, "*And that you slay not the life which Allah has made sacred, save in the course of justice,*"[11] it also says, "*Fight in the way of Allah against those who fight against you, but begin not hostilities.*"[12] This injunction clearly explains that Islam does not believe in pacifism. Muslims have been oppressed, persecuted, and attacked on account of religious and ideological differences by other nations. They were attacked and persecuted by the Mongols, who had empire-building ambitions. In the present time they are going through economic as well as ideological oppression. Therefore, the Qur'an permits them to take up arms: "*And fight them until persecution is no more, and religion is all for*

Allah. But if they cease, then lo! Allah is Seer of what they do. And if they turn away, then know that Allah is your Befriender—a Transcendent Patron, a Transcendent Helper!"[13] The Qur'an has made it clear: "*O you who believe! When ye go forth (to fight) in the way of Allah, be careful to discriminate, and say not unto one who offers you peace: 'You are not a believer,' seeking the chance profits of this life (so that ye may despoil him).... Therefore take care to discriminate. Allah is ever informed of what ye do.*"[14]

Human beings are wired for more than mere survival. Whereas the activities of other animals are actuated by their primary needs to feed and reproduce for survival, human beings' survival also depends on their impulses for peace and aggression. Greatest among the intellectual and emotional differences between humans and other animals is the fact that humans have boundless desires. Since humans first became civilized their desires have been triggering dynamic forces for peace and war. These forces may be imperialistic, ideological, religious, economic, or nationalistic. Such pressures, along with complexes of fear, hate, and revenge, are intertwined in the infrastructure of civilization, creating an unstable balance in man's temperament toward peace and aggression. All major religions and ideologies cover many of the same themes; each has its own particular insights and interpretations. Generally, all people by nature are the same, but in practices they are deeply divided.

The message of Islam is not that of a dynamic imperialism that permits movement of races or peoples over their established boundaries. The traits of traditional imperialism, such as lust for power, nationalism, economic gains, and feeding upon another's resources, are to be abhorred by the true believers of Islam. Islam did not make its start by building an empire as did the Greeks, Romans, Mongols, British, Germans, Soviets, and other nations. It did not permit dominance by the sword, but focused on explaining the peaceful theses of Islam. Prophet Muhammad inherited the nobility of the Quraish, a powerful tribe of Mecca, and he had the leadership qualities and the vigor to lead his tribe beyond Mecca if he wanted to. Islam was not a state with a pre-established polity, a people of solidarity, or a specific boundary of land. The perfection of the Arabic language of the Qur'an and the message of peace—a natural code of ethics prescribing a way of life and religion—is persuasive evidence to many that the Qur'an is indeed a miracle and the Word of God.

Concept of *dar-al-Islam* and *dar-al-Harb*

Islam is not imperialistic, and all that is part of the Islamic world is *dar al-Islam*, or the abode of peace. *Dar al-Islam* is a worldwide state. It is any area in which a majority of Muslims live, and the rest of the world is *dar al-harb*, or the abode of war. The concept of *dar al-Islam* is not that of an Islamic state and it does not mean that Islam has to fight with it, but rather that *dar al-Islam* is in danger of being attacked and subdued. According to Muhammad Asad—a Jewish man born Leopold Weiss and a convert to Islam:

> *Dar al-Islam* is not a goal or an end in itself but only a means: the goal being the growth of a community of people who stand up for equity and justice, for right and against wrong—or to put it more precisely, a community of people who work for the creation and maintenance of such social conditions as would enable the greatest possible number of human beings to live, morally as well as physically, in accordance with the natural Law of God, Islam.[15]

Prophet Muhammad's glorious successes in his lifetime at religious, social, moral, economic, and political endeavors shaped a universal Islam that tempted his critics to view such achievements as the result of some militant injunctions cited in the Qur'an. It cannot be ruled out that ideas involving human belief and faith inherently contain aggressiveness and are colored with militant spirit. Believers in Judaism, Christianity, Islam, and other great religions, as well as supporters of the Protestant Reformation and the Divine Right of Kings, and even revolutionary Liberalists, have in their time carried swords. Followers of the modern ideologies of Communism, Fascism, Nazism, and Maoism have gone on fierce warpaths. But Islam first carried the message of *al-Islam*, a message of peace and submission to the will of a transcendent monotheistic God. Although the message of Abraham's one transcendent monotheistic God was spoken by all the Jewish prophets, it was not ordered to be spread to all mankind. Islam, however, promoted this message through *da'wah,* a call to embrace Islam, and carried the sword wherever its religious beliefs and the security of Muslim *ummah* were in danger of persecution. It is true that there are many instances where Muslim rulers waged wars to extend their territories, but these are not considered Islamic wars by Islam itself, but rather political wars.

Although the spirit of Islam is strictly against imperialism and monarchy, examples of Islamic empires do exist, such as the Safavid Empire in Iran, the Moghul Empire in India, and the Ottoman Empire in Anatolia, Syria, North Africa, and Arabia. These imperial states were influenced by the Mongol tradition of the army ruling the state. Even the Abbasid caliphates, however famous, were not completely subject to the laws of Islamic *Shari'ah* and therefore did not conform to the true spirit of Islam. After the death of the Prophet, the rule of the first four elected caliphs, known as the Rightly-Guided Caliphs, represented an exemplary fulfillment of Islamic religious, social, and political concepts. Since the message of Islam is eternal, the Qur'an and the Prophet's traditions permit adaptation, recognizing that as knowledge of the world progresses, the wisdom of Islamic Law can be better understood. To believe that people in modern times of great scientific progress should blindly follow the system implemented by the Rightly-Guided Caliphs is to reject the right of independent judgment granted by the Qur'an and Sunnah. Independent judgment is mandated in matters on which the *Shari'ah* is silent regarding modern society's needs.

With regard to Islam in the dynamic of religious ideology, the Qur'an clearly instructs, "*There is no compulsion in religion. The right direction is henceforth distinct from error.*"[16] Prophet Muhammad was, thus, the first leader to strengthen the conviction that ideology can be used to foster peace. This is what led Bernard Lewis to comment in *Cultures in Conflict* that "Islamic society did, however, grant toleration; there was a willingness to coexist with people of other religions who, in return for the acceptance of a few restrictions and disabilities could enjoy the free exercise of their religions and the free conduct of their own affairs."[17] It is recorded that "The Syrians, who were largely Nestorians, suffered persecution at the hands of the Catholics, whereas Mohammedans tolerated all sects of Christians in return for the payment of tribute."[17] In preaching Islam to the people of conquered territories, the Qur'anic injunction that "*there is no compulsion in religion*" was strictly observed. History tells that whereas it might take a decade to conquer a region and establish settlements, it generally took three hundred years for the majority of people in a conquered area to convert to

Islam. Muslims ruled India for close to a millennium until the British took over the Indian subcontinent, but they remained a minority.

Islam's View of Peaceful Economy

Islamic *jihad* for war in the earlier period of its history was never waged with the motive of attaining economic gain. Muslims are not permitted by Qur'anic command or by that of their Prophet to fight to enrich themselves at the cost of a conquered people. The most important aspect of what are known as the Islamic conquests is that they were defined as *futuhat*, or "opening the doors," not as encroaching on the resources of the conquered nations. Muslim jurists are in full consensus that fighting for the extension of territory, financial gain, or to convert subdued people forcibly is against Islamic *Shari'ah*. The Prophet was determined to liberate people, irrespective of race, color, or creed, from economic oppression. He ordered that throughout new areas under Muslim control, agricultural or urban property would stay with the original owners. However, non-Muslims had to pay *jazia*, a tax much lower in percentage than that of their previous rulers. Those who willingly converted to Islam were free from *jazia*, as they were obligated to pay *zakat* two and a half percent annually on surplus capital.

Islam encouraged free initiative to acquire wealth, and the Jewish community took full benefit of this freedom. But unlawful means of acquiring and accumulating wealth were stopped by legal sanctions and moral injunctions. Since usury in all forms, personal or in market, is prohibited by the Qur'anic order, it was abolished with the conviction that money must not "breed" without effort. According to Khalifa Hakim:

> The Prophet was fully conscious of the fact that economic life reacts very intimately on the advancement or retardation of spiritual or non-economic values. He realized that the dignity of human life cannot be preserved without economic security, and social justice is, to a very large extent, based on economic justice. He devised a system [in the light of Qur'anic injunctions] that could prevent society from splitting up into classes of haves and have-nots.[18]

Armstrong writes in *Muhammad: A Biography of the Prophet,*

> The inaccurate image of Islam became one of the received ideas of Europe and it continues to affect our perceptions of the Muslim world. ... It is a mistake to imagine that Islam is an inherently violent or fanatical faith, as is sometimes ascribed through a worldwide propaganda. Islam is a universal religion and there is nothing aggressively oriental or anti-Western about it.[19]

Conflict between Islam and the West has arisen today in great part because of the encroachment of Western powers on oil, gas, and other natural resources of the Muslim world.

Nationalism and Peace

The dynamic of nationalism has evolved from deep-rooted primitive tribal instincts intermixed with strong human emotional forces. The Arabs of the pre-Islamic period had divided the world into two spheres on the basis of linguistic differences; one was Arabic and the other was *Ajumi,* which in Arabic means "dumb." Islam, in a continuation of Biblical traditions—namely, that since the fall of Adam there have lived two ideologically opposed nations of believers and nonbelievers, monotheists and polytheists, pious and impious representatives, good and evil—divided the world into believers and nonbelievers. Islam did not divide the world according to language in the Arabic tradition, but on the basis of belief, which could encompass people of any language, color, or creed. With the establishment of the Muslim state and its further expansion, this notion of believers and nonbelievers evolved into *dar al-Islam,* the abode of peace under universal Islam, and *dar al-harb,* areas beyond the world of Islam. The concept of nationalism in its modern sense has no place in Islamic discipline.

The decline of the world of Islam and its break-up into various small nation-states started with the fall of the Ottoman Empire. The present state of conflict is evidence that the decline of a universal *dar al-Islam* coupled with the rise of nationalism, based on ethnic or racial groups, is one of the most potent reasons behind violation of peace. Islam strictly denounces nationalistic assertions and actions such as those that were imposed on the Muslim world by the Western theory of divide and rule. Although this theory serves the purpose of Western interests by making it easy to encroach on oil and other resources in Muslim regions, its dynamic is a leading cause of terrorism and is dangerously challenging to world peace.

The dynamic of fear, hate, and revenge is another complex that leads to conflict, violence, and war. Age-old hatreds based on previous wrongs, rivalries, and oppression are psycho-biological complexes of victimhood that remain engrained in the minds and hearts of peoples who have suffered over many generations. The defeated are the most deeply affected by the complex of victimhood because they have been humiliated and impoverished. It is strictly forbidden in Islam to massacre and enslave the conquered, and above all, to humiliate them or to strip them of their rights or property. The Prophet of Islam has shown two choices to humanity: the way of ignorance, which triggers a lust for worldly increase which in turn leads to a moral error and a kind of intellectual sickness; or the way of *al-Islam* or submission, which follows the Qur'anic order. According to the Qur'an, the way of ignorance, of life outside *al-Islam*, multiplies a kind of sickness. *"In their hearts is a disease (of doubt and hypocrisy), and Allah increases their disease. A painful doom is theirs because they lie."*[21] The way of ignorance can lead to a life described by Hobbes as "solitary, poor, nasty, brutish, and short." To avoid such a state, human beings have only to make a covenant, and that covenant in Islam is with a Supreme Authority above all human beings. This means a submission to the will of God, which leads to peace by establishing a just social order.

Negating the dynamic of fear, hate, and revenge, the Prophet of Islam repeatedly instructed the commanders of the Muslim army to adhere to a long list of restraints. This was also practiced by his immediate successors. Majid Khadduri, translator of *The Islamic Law of Nations,* by Shaybani Siyar, writes that the Prophet said:

> Do not act treacherously; do not act disloyally; do not act neglectfully. Do not mutilate; do not kill little children or old men, or women; do not cut off the heads of the palm trees or burn them; do not cut down the fruit trees; do not slaughter a sheep or a cow or a camel, except for food. You will pass by people who devote their lives in cloisters; leave them and their devotions alone.

> You will come upon people who bring you platters in which are
> various sorts of food; if you eat any of it, mention the name of
> God over it.[22]

The actions of the Prophet and his successors, guided by the Qur'an,
established the rules of government proportionately and justly so that the
conquered peoples would not fall into the complexes of fear, hate, and
revenge. Moreover, the ultimate end of Islamic *futuhat* was the opening
of the world to the Islamic faith, not material gain or territorial conquest
for any ruler or emperor.

Among the dynamic forces responsible for creating the current crisis
of violence, conflict, and war, the most important element is the will to
peace. Muslims believe that human beings are naturally blessed with an
undying stimulus to strive for peace. They approve peace as a supreme
ethic that reflects the divine attributes. Islam recognizes harmony as one of
the highest virtues and moral dispositions of mankind. This recognition is
based on a humanism transmitted in the Qur'an that says, *"You (mankind)
are truly of noble creation."* This is exemplified by its Prophet, in the claim,
"Man has in the messenger of God (Muhammad) a good example." In his
book, *Islam: Beliefs and Observances,* Caesar E. Farah defined Islamic
humanism this way:

> The underlying premise of Islamic humanism is common to all
> that treats human relations in terms of reciprocation by individuals
> of serenity and affection in the spirit of mutual tolerance and
> understanding. It presupposes an atmosphere of well-being and
> fraternization, of flexibility and sufferance, and the elevation of
> conscience of the collective body to the level of calling for the
> well-being of the individual as the cornerstone of the well-being
> of society."[23]

The Prophet of Islam displayed in his relationship with his followers,
who are addressed in the Qur'an as *Yaaa-'ayyuh-allaziina 'aamanuu* (O
ye who believe), and in his interaction with other peoples, *Yaa-'ayyuh-
annaas* (O mankind), the model example of Islamic humanism, founded
on affection, love, and tolerance for all. At the time of the conquest of
Mecca—the city of his birth where he and his companions had been
persecuted and oppressed—the Prophet entered with humility instead of

pride. Zakaria Bashier describes this in *War and Peace in the Life of the Prophet Muhammad*:

> Standing there, at the door of Ka'ba, the people of Makkah converged to him, anxious to know their fate, and the Prophet's decision .... "What do you think I am going to do to you?" he asked. They replied: "Good! You are but a noble brother, and son of a noble brother!" He said: "Go your way in peace and freedom, for you are the freed ones."... He forgave his fiercest enemies which is unparalleled in the annals of history to this day.[24]

The elements of fear, hate, and revenge have always been outside of the Prophet's context. He was a perfect example of the merciful man. God addresses him thus in many places in the Qur'an: *"We have sent you only as [an act] of mercy to mankind,"* to *"call to the good and refrain from that which is objectionable [in the sight of God]."* The only fear Islam recognizes is the fear of God, who is watching human beings and who is as close to them as their jugular vein.

Islamic Humanism

Islam recognizes the universally acknowledged human values based on the Qur'anic declaration that, *"Surely We created man of the best stature (with the noblest image)."*[25] With such powerful assertions, Islam stands for a strong will to peace. Describing the spirit of Islamic humanism, brotherhood, and love for universal peace, Lenn E. Goodman states in *Islamic Humanism* that during the twelfth century the Brethren of Purity (*Ikhwan al-Safa*), a society of Muslim philosophers in Iraq, would describe their ideal man as:

> Persian by breeding, Arabian in faith, Hanafite [thus, moderate] in his Islam, Iraqi in culture, Hebrew in lore, Christian in manners, Damascene in piety, Greek in the sciences, Indian in contemplation, Sufi in intimations, regal in character, masterful in thought, and divine in insight. I see a cosmopolitan spirit here that is authentically Islamic.[26]

Throughout history the pressures of the dynamic forces of religion and ideology, economic problems, imperialism and nationalism, fear, hate, revenge, and the will to peace, have shaped the balance of war and peace in the world. Islam has provided solutions to meet these great pressures before they are exploited and violate world peace. But history has often witnessed ideologies and religions that, once in practice, get distracted from their original convictions or faith for reasons beyond their true spirit. Armstrong, reflecting upon spiritual and worldly lives in *Islam: A Short History,* says:

> The spiritual quest is an interior journey; it is a psychic rather than a political drama. It is preoccupied with liturgy, doctrine, contemplative disciplines and an exploration of the heart, not with the clash of current events. Religions certainly have life outside the soul. Their leaders have to contend with the state and affairs of the world, and often relish doing so. They fight with members of other faiths, who seem to challenge their claim to a monopoly of absolute truth; they also persecute their co-religionists for interpreting a tradition differently or for holding heterodox beliefs. ... These power struggles are not what religion is really about, but an unworthy distraction from the spirit of life, which is conducted far from the madding crowd, unseen, silent and unobtrusive.[27]

Since Islam considers itself a complete way of life, its inner spirituality is fused with its outer practice as inseparably as a kernel's core with its crust. Thus, in the sociopolitical life of the Muslims, when Western materialistic standards are forced upon them, they appear incidental to their faith. The militant trend in Islam springs from the determination of Muslims to apply Islam in every sphere of communal and state affairs.

Notes:

1. Ali, Abdullah Yusuf, the Qur'an, 49:13.
2. Pickthall, the Qur'an, 41:34.
3. Hakim, 1965, p. 135.
4. Armstrong, 1992, 5-6.
5. Pickthall, the Qur'an, 4:86.

6. Ibid., 23:96
7. Matraji, Sahih al-Bukhari, vol. I, no. 13.
8. Ibid., 2444.
9. Pickthall, the Qur'an, 30:30
10. Ibid., 15:29.
11. Ibid., 6:151.
12. Ibid., 2:190.
13. Ibid., 8:39-40
14. Ibid., 4:94
15. Asad, 1961, 30
16. Pickthall, the Qur'an, 2:256.
17. Lewis, Bernard, 1995, 17
18. Hakim, 336.
19. Armstrong, 1992, p. 11.
20. Lewis, Bernard, 1995, 10.
21. Pickthall, the Qur'an, 2:10.
22. Khadduri, 1966, 101-102.
23. Farah, 412.
24. Bashier, 232-233.
25. Pickthall, the Qur'an, 95:4.
26. Goodman, 24.
27. Armstrong, 2000, ix.

CHAPTER 22

The Islamic Philosophy of Jihad

*Jihad means exertion of will and power to repel
an internal or external enemy
to one's best ability by words or deeds.*

Introduction

The literal meaning of the word *jihad* in Arabic is "exertion," or "struggle," which has a very wide application in Islamic philosophy, literature, and theology. *Jihad*, within the context of belief and practice is the "élan vital" of Islamic civilization. It can be applied to myriad situations, including striving to recognize the Creator, loving Him, staying on the straight path, cleansing oneself of evil whims and avoiding evil acts, conveying the message of Islam and defending the *ummah*, helping the poor and paying alms, seeking knowledge and educating people, freeing people from tyranny, preserving peace in society, fighting wherever necessary, and overall, striving to perform righteous deeds. After embracing Islam, the Arabs, through the ideology of multiple forms of *jihad*, declared themselves Muslims instead of Arabs. Semantically, the word *jihad* is not associated with conflict, war, or holy war, since according to Islam, it is unholy to instigate or start a conflict or war. There is no reference in the Qur'an to *jihad* as holy war.

In the Qur'an, the word *jihad*, which is derived from the Arabic *jahadun*, appears in many forms: "*And whosoever strives [jahada] strives only for himself, for lo! Allah is altogether Independent of (His) creatures.*"[1] "*As for those who strive [jahadu] in Us, We surely guide them to Our paths, and lo! Allah is with the good.*"[2] "*And strive [jahidu] for Allah with the endeavor [jihadih] which is His right.*"[3] The word has numerous connotations, but where *jihad* is a form of struggle with an external enemy posing a challenge to fight, it is interpreted as "*jihad* for war," meaning "struggle to fight war." The juridical-theological meaning of *jihad* is exertion of one's power in the way prescribed by God, which is the way of righteousness. The reward for *jihad* is salvation, since it is Allah's promised way to paradise. The Qur'an says;

> *O you who believe! Shall I show you a commerce that will save you from a painful doom? Ye shall believe in Allah and His messenger, and should strive [jahadu] for the cause of Allah with your wealth and with your lives. That is better for you, if you did but know. He will forgive your sins and bring you into Gardens underneath which rivers flow, and pleasant dwellings in the Garden of Eden. That is the Supreme triumph. And (He will give you) another blessing which you love: help from Allah and present victory. Give good tidings (O Muhammad) to believers.*[4]

Jihad, in the general sense, does not mean war or fighting; rather, fighting is a sub-subject of *jihad*. Abul Ala Maudoodi, a scholar of Islamic studies is of the view that:

> The Arabic word "jihad" means to exert one's utmost for the achievement of an object. And a "mujahid" is one who is always after the achievement of his ideal, plans for it, propagates it with his tongue and pen and struggles for it with all his heart and body. In short, he spends all his efforts and resources for its achievement and fights against all those forces that oppose it; so much so that he does not hesitate to put even his very life in danger for his ideal. The struggle and fight of such a person will be technically "jihad."... Thus it is clear that the jihad of a Muslim is not "general war of extermination against infidels."[5]

The complexities of *jihad* and its connotations of holy war are a result of the challenge faced by Muslims looking for precedents in the *Shari'ah* that would provide direction on how to overcome their diminished power. In the current scenario, a Muslim's fight to repel aggression and defend the sanctity of the religion reflects the notion of *jihad* for war as sacred. It is the same as for any nation struggling to repel an enemy that is attacking its life, religion, or ideology, in which case war is not only justified but becomes a sacred struggle.

Concept of Jihad

The concept of *jihad* is pluralistic—a struggle for existence by peaceful means, and by fighting when the natural right of existence is endangered. It subsumes various activities that lead toward the divinely defined *siratal-mustaqim*, or "straight path." God's path may be achieved by peaceful means; it may be regarded as a form of religious preaching by way of persuasion, a struggle against one's own sinful temptations, or of speaking truth and shunning evil. The Prophet of Islam has said,

> Every prophet sent by God to a nation (*ummah*) before me has had disciples and followers who followed his ways (*sunna*) and obeyed his commands. But after them came successors who preached what they did not practice and practiced what they were not commanded. Whoever strives (*jahada*) against them with one's hand is a believer; whoever strives against them with one's tongue is a believer; whoever strives against them with one's heart is a believer. There is nothing greater than a mustard seed beyond that in the way of faith.[6]

Jihad, as explained by Muslim philosophers, jurists, and scholars, has two classifications: greater *jihad* and lesser *jihad*. Greater *jihad* comprises the acts, deeds, and functions of a person who strives (*jahidu*) throughout his life to fulfill all the requisites of his faith in Islam and struggles to achieve the "excellence of *jihad*," which is the conquest of a person's self. Islam puts great emphasis on the cultivation and perfection of the self. Lesser *jihad* is basically a community function, and thus becomes a matter of fulfilling obligations. Since war is a community affair, it is considered lesser *jihad*. The Qur'an does not pronounce the obligation of war as an article of faith. However, in the hadith, the Prophet's collected sayings, lesser *jihad* is presented as a form of active struggle, which invariably inclines it toward its widely understood militant interpretation.

Muslim jurists have explained that *jihad* of the sword, or *jihad al sayf*, as a classification of religiously grounded war, is only authorized to defend Islam and promote the teaching of Islam under the safe haven of *dar al-Islam*. According to a commonly cited hadith, the Prophet said to a people returned from a war, "Welcome to you all, you have returned from little fight [the lesser *jihad*] to the greatest fight [greater *jihad*]." Someone questioned him, saying, "O Messenger of Allah! What is the greatest fight?" He answered, "Fighting with passion [struggle against the self is the greater *jihad*]."[7] Following these precepts, Muslim thinkers, mystics, and ascetics started differentiating between greater *jihad* and lesser *jihad*. "A true ascetic is he who fights with his evil forces in obedience to Allah." The Qur'an says, *"Have you seen him who takes his low passion for God?"*[8]

Philosophy of Jihad

Philosophically, the greater and lesser *jihads* are intertwined. Greater *jihad* is not a substitute for lesser *jihad*. David Cook, in his work, *Understanding Jihad*, argues:

> Ascetics were among the earliest converts to Islam and among the most enthusiastic fighters in the jihad [for war]. Probably the best known [ascetic] is 'Abdalla ibn al-Mubarak, who wrote the early *Kitab al-jihad*. Ibn al-Mubarak was originally from the region of eastern Iran; he immigrated to Syria in order to fight the Byzantines, whom he viewed as Islam's most dangerous enemies. During the course of his career, he became known as a popular figure who could (and did on occasion) challenge the caliph for not applying himself energetically enough to waging jihad. A tradition cited in the *Kitab al-jihad*, Ibn al-Mubarak makes it clear that he saw no contradiction between being a warrior and an ascetic: "Every community has a form of asceticism (*rahbaniyya*), and the asceticism of this community is jihad in the path of Allah."[9]

In the eyes of ascetics, one who does well with greater *jihad* is better able to perform lesser *jihad*, since he has already fought with his passion and is thus well prepared to fight the enemy not for any personal cause or out of hatred, but exclusively for *jihad fi sabil Allah*. Rumi relates an incident reflecting the true spirit of *jihad*:

> Ali, the "Lion of God," was once engaged in conflict with a Magian chief, and in the midst of the struggle the Magian spat in Ali's face. Ali, instead of taking vengeance on him, at once dropped his sword, to the Magian's great astonishment. On his

inquiring the reason of such forbearance, Ali informed him that the "Lion of God" did not destroy life for the satisfaction of his own vengeance, but simply to carry out God's will, and that whenever he saw just cause, he held his hand in the midst of the strife, and spared the foe.[10]

Fundamentally, the true spirit of *jihad* is nonviolent, as revealed in the Qur'an: "*So obey not the disbelievers, but strive [jahid-hum] against them herewith with a great endeavour* [in Arabic it is mentioned as *jihadan kabira*, that is, greater *jihad*]."[11] Ibn Hazm, a renowned Muslim jurist, in distinguishing between types of *jihad*, maintained that Prophet Muhammad showed a preference for *jihad* of reason over the sword.

Four Ways to Fulfill Jihad

Muslim jurists have distinguished four different ways in which the believer may fulfill his *jihad* obligation: by his heart, his tongue, his hands, and the sword. The first is concerned with combating the devil to escape his persuasion toward evil; or, according to the Prophet, the greater *jihad* is the fight against one's own evil passions. This type of *jihad* is a struggle of the soul to suppress an evil or sinful inclination within one's heart and mind.

The second, which is *jihad* of the tongue, is speaking truth in support of what is good, and proscribing evil. "Traditions indicate that the best type of jihad was to speak openly and honestly to a ruler: 'The best type of jihad is the word of justice in the presence of an iniquitous ruler.'"[12] The ascetic *jihadists* following the Qur'anic injunction, "*So obey not the disbelievers, but strive against them herewith [by preaching] with a great endeavor [jihadan kabira]*,"[13] believed that, whereas the highest form of *jihad* was speaking out truthfully before an unjust and tyrannical ruler, being killed for it was martyrdom.

The third is *jihad* by one's hands, which is mainly fulfilled by supporting what is right and correcting what is wrong with righteous acts and deeds. This type of *jihad* can also be interpreted as *jihad* to eradicate ignorance, poverty, illness, or epidemic diseases. The search for knowledge is one of the highest forms of *jihad*. The Prophet said, "Whoso goes out in search of knowledge, he is in the path of Allah."[14]

The fourth is armed *jihad*, which is concerned with fighting unbelievers and enemies of the faith. The Prophet said, "War is a stratagem."[15] But he also advised, "O you men do not wish an encounter with the enemy. Pray Allah to grant you security; (but) when you (have to) encounter them, exercise patience, and you should know that paradise is under the shadows of the swords."[16] Armed *jihad* is the struggle to root out oppression and persecution by the sword. In the early Meccan revelations, the emphasis of *jihad* was mainly on persuasion. This is evidenced by the Qur'anic definition that "*he who exerts himself, exerts only for his own soul,*" which expresses *jihad* in terms of the salvation of the soul rather than as a struggle for conversion. In the revelations of the Medina period, *jihad* is often expressed in terms of strife, but there is no doubt that in certain verses the concept of *jihad* is synonymous with war and fighting, testifying to the Prophet's words that war is a stratagem.

The concept of military *jihad*, with its emphasis on the notion of continuous struggle against nonbelievers in God, tended to keep alive the spirit of solidarity in the Muslim community over and against outsiders. The incentive for *jihad* as war lies in its twofold benefits: booty in this life, and martyrdom, with its promise of an immediate, blissful, eternal hereafter for those killed in battle. God promises to the martyrs, "*And those who fought in the way of Allah, He renders not their actions vain. He will guide them and improve their state. And bring them [those who are slain] in unto the Garden which He has made known to them.*"[17] It has been recorded that a nomad addressed the Holy Prophet on this issue:

> O Messenger of Allah, one man fights for the spoils of war; another fights that he may be remembered, and another fights that he may see his (high) position (achieved as a result of his valor in fighting). Which of these is fighting in the cause of God? The Messenger of Allah said, "Who fights so that the word of Allah is exalted, is fighting in the cause of Allah."[18]

Although *jihad* for war is regarded by Muslim jurists as a collective obligation of the Muslim community and not of the individual, it does not mean that all believers are obligated to fight if the community is attacked. At least two important considerations are involved. In the first place, the duty need not necessarily be fulfilled by all the believers. The Qur'an says, "*And the believers should not all go out to fight. Of every troop of them a party only should go forth, that they (who are left behind) may gain sound knowledge in religion and that they may warn their folk when they return to them, so that they may beware.*"[19] The Qur'an exempts those who are old, sick, and handicapped. Women and children are excused from combat, although many women have contributed indirectly to war efforts. In the second place, since it is a community obligation, declaring *jihad* for war is a state affair. Accordingly, it is to be controlled and managed by the state, not by any individual civilian; only the head of a Muslim state or someone of equivalent stature can declare *jihad* for war. A non-Muslim ruler of an Islamic state or community is not authorized to issue a *fatwa* for *jihad*.

The Conduct of Jihad for War

Al-Shaybani, a renowned Muslim jurist, describes in his *Kitab al-Siyar*, translated into English by Majid Khadduri, the conduct of *jihad* for war, conditions for peace, diplomacy, and rules for treatment of the enemy.

> Whenever the Apostle of God sent forth an army or detachment, he charged its commander personally to fear God, the Most High, and enjoined the Muslims who were with him to do good [to conduct themselves properly]. And [the Apostle] said: "Fight in the name of God and in the path of God [truth]. Combat [only] those who disbelieve in God. Do not cheat or commit treachery, nor should you mutilate anyone or kill children. Whenever you meet your polytheist enemies, invite them [first] to adopt Islam. If they do so, accept it, and let them alone. You should then invite them to move from their territory to the territory of the émigrés [Medina]. If they do so, accept it and let them alone. Otherwise, they should be informed that they would be like the Muslim nomads in that they are subject to God's orders as [other] Muslims, but that they will receive no share in either the *ghanima* (spoil of war) or in the fray. If they refuse [to accept Islam], then call upon them to pay *jizya* (poll tax); if they do, accept it and leave them alone. If you besiege the inhabitants of a fortress or a town and they try to get you to let them surrender on the basis of God's judgment, do not do so, since you do not know what God's judgment is, but make them surrender to your judgment and then decide their case

according to your own views. But if the besieged inhabitants of a
fortress or a town asked you to give them a pledge [of security] in
God's name or in the name of His Apostle, you should not do so,
but give the pledge in your names or in the names of your fathers;
for, if you should ever break it, it would be an easier matter if it
were in the names of you or your fathers."[20]

Jihad in its militant context does not affect a state's non-Muslim subjects
and residents. All non-Muslims are exempt from direct participation in the
jihad for war. However, non-Muslims can indirectly support *jihad* for war
by providing financial, logistic, or technical needs. Jews under Muslim rule
liberally provided finances to Muslims during the Crusades. However, in
a *jihad* for war with non-Muslim soldiers, participating and fighting side
by side with Muslim soldiers does not fulfill the Islamic tenets of *jihad*.

Concept of Jihad as Justified War

Since the dawn of history, and for any number of reasons, people have
fought people different from themselves; but the Arabs unlike many other
tribes also warred amongst themselves. Since tribes were the basic political
units, these war took the form of raids, mainly for robbery or revenge. Ibn
Khaldun, in his discussion of war in *The Muqaddimah: An Introduction to
History*, distinguishes four types of wars:

> The first usually occurs between neighboring tribes and competing
> families. The second—war caused by hostility—is usually found
> among savage nations living in the desert, such as the Arabs, the
> Turks, the Turkomans, the Kurds, and similar people .... The
> third is the (kind) the religious law calls "the holy war" [not jihad
> for war]. The fourth, finally, is dynastic war against seceders and
> those who refuse obedience. These are four kinds of war. The first
> two are unjust and lawless; the other two are holy and just wars.[21]

Wars in the Arabian Peninsula were usually fought for plunder between
hostile neighboring tribes or competing families. The concept of just war
was outside their frame of reference and beyond their experience.

With the advent of Islam, Arab allegiances shifted from tribes and
their leaders to submission to Allah as the one ultimate sovereign God for

all. The introduction of *jihad* as war in the way of Allah shifted the focus of conflict from personal and intertribal warfare to the outside world. Islam thus elevated the traditional tribal militancy and rapacity into a supreme hierarchy of religious virtue by strictly outlawing all forms of war except the *jihad* for war in the way of Allah, with its greater objective of replacing non-Muslim religious cults and ideologies with the belief that "there is no other God except Allah and Muhammad is the messenger of Allah." It would, indeed, have been very difficult for the Islamic state to survive had it not been for the doctrine of the *jihad*, which replaced unjustified tribal raids and wars with just wars against the outside world in the name of the new faith and Allah as its supreme power. Islam regulated war on moral and ethical grounds and made such a virtue of *jihad* as war for the believers in Islam that this enabled believers to achieve a smooth, progressive transition from tribalism to an Arab nationhood and to an international *ummah*. This concept allows the Muslims to understand that *jihad* for war in the way of Allah is only against the polytheists; war against the people of the book is not considered *jihad*.

Terry Nardin, a professor of Political Science at the University of Wisconsin-Milwaukee, and editor of the book, *The Ethics of War and Peace*, has elaborated:

> According to the Sunni legal schools, jihad, properly speaking, was war waged against unbelievers. Because all Muslims were understood to constitute a single community of believers, wars between Muslim parties were usually classed in a separate category, or *fitna* (literally, a "trial" or "test"). Like Plato, who has Socrates declare that Greeks do not make war on one another, the Muslim jurists viewed intra-Muslim disputes as internal strife that should be resolved quickly by the ruling authorities.[22]

The salient characteristic of *jihad* is that it is not a war fought for a ruler, even if he is a Muslim, but a war in the path or way of Allah. Therefore, a *jihadi*—one who struggles in the way of God—fights with the spirit of his own pledge to Allah and his commitment to the religion of Islam. He does not fight for personal glory or any imperial design of the caliph or the ruler under whose command he fights.

Since the Islamic State is an important instrument in universalizing the religion of Islam and God's sovereignty, in its pursuit to establish Islam as a universal ideology of Islam, the state sought to expand and thus came into conflict with the non-Muslim communities. Muslims divided the world into *dar al-Islam* (the abode of Islam)—*"And Allah summons to the abode of Peace [dar al-Salam], and leads whom He will to a straight path"*[23]—and *dar al-harb* (world of war). Soon after Islam became supreme in Arabia, the Prophet's successors conducted a series of wars in the name of Islam. The concept of *jihad fi sabil Allah* as a concept of justified war was applied to universalize the message of Islam and to extend the domain of *dar al-Islam* to the farthest corners of the known world.

Islamic discipline used the state not as a territory of a political community, but as an instrument to achieve a doctrinal and religious objective—the proselytization of mankind. Since its borderless region of *dar al-Islam* is identified with *dar al-Salam*—the abode of peace—it becomes inevitable that the peaceful sector of the world should eventually expand at the expense of the rest of the world, which is in the eyes of Islam *dar al-harb*. This expansion, according to Islam, is a just cause, since it is for the benefit of not only believers, but also of nonbelievers, whose rights are all protected under Islamic rule.

The doctrine of *jihad* as a justified war is not one of continuous fighting but of a permanent state of preparedness. According to Muslim jurists, even to be in a state of preparedness for *jihad* is a fulfillment of its obligation. This means that an Islamic state must be prepared militarily not only to repel aggression or attack but also to be fully capable of offensive purposes when the ruler finds it necessary to make a call for *jihad* to fight.

During the course of Islamic history, the concept of *jihad* as a justified state of war went through various changes suitable to the changing circumstances of Muslim life and cultural diversity. One major change placed this obligation into a dormant status, which could be revived at times of necessity only by the Muslim head of an Islamic state or an *imam* of high authority. This relaxed state of *jihad*, as noted by ibn Khaldun, signified a change in the character of the Muslim *ummah* from warlike *jihadists* to civilized rationalists who aided the emergence of intellectual and philosophical schools of thought. However, this did not change the basic concept of the *jihad* for justified war, nor was it an apology for failure to apply its doctrine, but simply a dictate of Islam's evolving interests and social conditions. Thus, *jihad* for war, in its capacity as a lesser *jihad*, began to be interpreted and implemented according to the circumstances and requirements of different factions of the Muslim *ummah*.

Sunni and Shi'ite Concepts of Jihad as Justified War

According to Sunni theorists—who represent the majority of the Islamic *ummah*—*jihad* is just war if it is in conformation with God's command to follow what is good and avoid evil in the quest to establish peace and justice on earth. They find the mandate for nonviolence in the Qur'an, and in the Prophet's way of nonviolent resistance and protection of his people during his early years in Mecca. They follow Prophet Muhammad's reluctant endorsement of limited warfare after his migration to Medina, taking it as strong evidence in support of the view that fighting is undesirable for Muslims, and that it is permitted only if all other effective means to resist aggression against the faith have been exhausted. Terry Nardin, a professor of Political Science at the University of Wisconsin-Milwaukee, remarked that:

> In Islam, constraints on the conduct of war can be traced back to the pre-Islamic "rules of the game" of intertribal warfare. These rules forbade fighting during certain periods of the year and condemned excessive destruction, reflecting both a code of honor that protected the weak—women, children, the aged, and prisoners—and the view that fighting is instrumental to an end. But these rules of war are reinforced by the morality of the Qur'an and the Sunnah (practice of the Prophet). If the purpose of war is to order the world on Islamic principles, then indiscriminate killing and destruction are forbidden because they neither respect nor further this end. Despite many differences, then, the idea of jihad resembles the Western idea of just war not only in presuming that peace is the end of war but also in insisting that the values of peace govern conduct of war.[24]

The concept of *jihad* as justified war in the Shi'ite sect of Islam is linked with its doctrine of *walaya*, or "allegiance to the imam." Majid Khadduri explains,

In Shi'i legal theory, not only would the failure of a non-Muslim to believe in Allah justify waging a jihad, but the failure of a Muslim to obey the imam would make him liable for punishment by jihad. While to a Sunni the jihad is the sure way to Heaven, a jihad without an allegiance to the imam would not constitute an imam (a necessary requirement for salvation) in the Shi'i creed.[25]

In Shi'ism the *jihad* is regarded as one of the major responsibilities of the imamate. The imam is revered as an infallible ruler, and he is the only one to judge and decide when to declare *jihad* for war. The disappearance of the twelfth imam, according to Shi'ite creed, has rendered the obligation of declaring the *jihad* unable to be fulfilled. Therefore, according to Shi'ite ideology, the obligation of *jihad* for war is dormant or in a state of suspension. Whereas Sunni doctrine permits the resumption of *jihad* when Muslim power is regained, the Shi'ite view of *jihad* is dependent on the return of the twelfth imam, who will appear as a Mehdi, or "Guided one," and will revive the obligation of *jihad* for war to combat evil forces and reestablish justice and righteousness. Islamic discipline abolished all kinds of warfare except the *jihad* for war. Majid Khadduri holds that, "Only a war which has an ultimate religious purpose, that is, to enforce God's law or to check transgression against it, is a just war. No other form of fighting is permitted within or without the Muslim brotherhood. All secular wars are prohibited in Islam."[25]

According to Islam any war against nonbelievers to establish the law of Allah is a *jihad fi sabil Allah* and is morally justified war. Terry Nardin is of the view that "When Muslims wage war for the dissemination of Islam, it is just war (futuhat, literally 'opening,' in the sense of opening the world, through the use of force, to the call of Islam); when non-Muslims attack Muslims, it is an unjust war (*idhan.*)"[26] Because the Qur'an asks Muslims not to be aggressors and only to *"Fight in the way of Allah against those who fight against you, but begin not hostilities. Lo! Allah loves not aggressors,"*[27] war is basically a mission of peace, and it lays greater stress on the peaceful call for *da'wah*, though this can involve fighting if the *da'wah* is hindered by force or aggression, which would be an unjust war against Islam. There is great stress on avoiding war, but when it becomes necessary it is to be conducted with full conviction as a *jihad fi sabil Allah* so that the enemy may learn a lesson and come to a permanent peace: *"And fight them until persecution is no more, and religion is for Allah. But if they desist, then let there be no hostility except against the wrongdoers.*"[28]

Islamic Jihad as Just War Different from Others

The Islamic concept of *jihad* as just war is not exactly the same as the modern Western notion of just war. War has historically been viewed as just when it is fought under a certain system of law or is waged for justifiable reasons. In his *Politics*, Aristotle referred to certain wars that are regarded as just by nature. Cicero, the Roman philosopher, discussed the rules and formalities of a just war. Islam followed the ancient concepts of justified war and social vendetta that conformed to its religious articles of faith. Thus, a pattern of war developed into the Islamic concept of *jihad* as just war, assuming a special position in its juridical order, where natural law and religion formed a unity. The ultimate objective of Islam was to establish peace and order in accordance with Islamic justice within its territory, and to expand that territory to include the whole world.

Prophet Muhammad is reported to have said, "I am ordered to fight polytheists until they say: 'there is no God but Allah.'"[29] This permission to fight polytheists is validated by the Qur'anic invocation, "*Slay the idolaters [polytheists] wherever you find them.*"[30] Islam justifies war sanctioned by its religion and the commands of God as *jihad* to fight against polytheism only when they do not accept the message of Islam for peace and submission to One God. War against the people of the book—that is, the Jews, Christians, and all those who do not worship idols and believe in One God—is not *jihad*, but is considered a political war. For an example, the Crusades by the Christians were never justified by the Muslims as *jihad* or a holy war for them. For Islam, as in Christendom's Augustinian *bellum justum*, the *jihad* for war is a just war when it fulfills the condition laid by the Qur'an mentioned above. Thomas Aquinas (1225-1274), who was acquainted with Muslim thought and philosophy, devised his theory of the just war along lines similar to the Islamic doctrine of *jihad*.

In Islam, waging a *jihad* to establish Islam's supremacy and the sovereignty of Allah's word according to its scriptural conditions, is vested with an Islamic state's authority only, and to be the *raison d'état*, it must be implemented by the state under Muslim rule. A non-Muslim ruler of a

Muslim state, an individual Muslim, a religious sect, or a group without rulership authorities, is not authorized to wage *jihad*. *Jihad* is strictly rule-bound, protecting non-combatants, women, children, animals, trees, fields, and gardens. People who are old, sick, or a student, scholar, teacher, a sole breadwinner for his family, and women are not obligated to participate in *jihad*. Therefore, for all its importance, *jihad* is not included in the five obligatory pillars of Islam.

With regard to war, the Abrahamic faiths are nearly on the same page of history. The Islamic approach to war had much in common with ancient Jewish traditions and with the works of St. Augustine (354-450), who wrote in *The City of God* that "War—when conducted in a manner that limits harm and shows mercy to the vanquished—can be justified by the overarching need of a legitimate authority to preserve peace, protect the innocent, repulse invasion, or reclaim territory."[31] In the eighth century, hundreds of years before the codification of international law in Europe by Hugo Grotius and others, Muhammad ibn al-Hassan al-Shaybani (750-806), an eminent Muslim jurist of the Hanafite School and advisor to Caliph Harun al-Rashid, wrote the first major Islamic treatise on the law of nations, *Kitab al-Siyar al-Kabir*. This treatise describes in detail the conditions and principles of *jihad* for war and peace, the conduct of military action and diplomacy, and rules and regulations for the treatment of non-Muslims in Muslim *dar al-Salam*. It provides an insight into the rules of relationship between Muslims and the rest of the world from the earliest times to the present. Muslim jurists codified the traditions and Qur'anic injunctions to form the *Shari'ah*—defined as Divine Law. To regulate the Islamic concept of warfare, they also provided a legal definition of *jihad* for war, which was not addressed in detail in the Qur'an or the *hadith*. David Cook has mentioned in his work, *Understanding Jihad:*

> One of the bases for this type of regulation was defining the manner in which war should be declared and what its limits were. The Messenger of Allah, when he would send a commander with a raid or an army would enjoin upon him the fear of Allah, especially with regard to himself, but also with regard to the Muslims, and say: When you meet your polytheist enemy, call to him [to choose] between three possibilities—accept whichever one they accept, and desist from them…. Call them to Islam; if they

211

accept, then accept it from them and desist from them…. If they refuse, then call them to pay the *jizya* [poll tax]…. If they refuse, then ask Allah for aid against them, and fight them.[32]

The Prophet outlined a procedure that established the concept of a just war for his followers. Although the Islamic concept of *jihad* for war and the modern Western theory of just war are not identical, the similarities between them are numerous. Terry Nardin is of the view that:

> Jihad, like just war, is grounded in the belief that inter-societal relations should be peaceful, not marred by constant and destructive warfare. The surest way for human beings to realize this peace is for them to obey the divine law that is imprinted on the human conscience and therefore accessible to everyone, believers and unbelievers. According to the medieval view, Muslims are obliged to propagate this divine law, through peaceful means if possible, through violent means if necessary. No war was jihad unless it was undertaken with right intent and as a last resort, and declared by right authority. Most Muslims today disavow the duty to propagate Islam by force and limit jihad to self-defense. And finally, jihad, like just war, places strict limitations on legitimate targets during war and demands that belligerents use the least amount of force necessary to achieve the swift cessation of hostilities. Both jihad and just war are dynamic concepts, still evolving and adapting to changing international realities.[33]

The core of the Islamic concept of *jihad* in the way of God is to exert one's efforts to bring about that state of affairs "when the word of Allah is supreme," which is basically embedded in the Qur'anic injunction, *"And fight them [unbelievers] until persecution is no more, and religion is all for Allah. But if they cease, then lo! Allah is Seer of what they do."*[34] In the light of these interpretations, *jihad* for war against a non-Muslim state would be justified if it resorts to oppression (implying persecution) upon its people. War would be justified if a state attempts to impose an ideology or religion by force against the will of the people, since for Islam *"there is no compulsion in religion."*

Notes:

1. Pickthall, the Qur'an, 29:6.
2. Ibid., 29:69.
3. Ibid., 22:78.
4. Ibid., 61:10-13.
5. Chaudhry, 419-420.
6. Siddiqui, Sahih Muslim, vol. I, no. 69-70
7. Karim, Al-Hadith, vol. I, 555-556.
8. Ibid., 553.
9. Cook, 33.
10. Whinfield, Rumi, Book 1, Story 16.
11. Pickthall, the Qur'an, 25:52.
12. Cook, 33-34.
13. Pickthall, the Qur'an, 25:52.
14. Karim, Al-Hadith, vol. I, 354.
15. Siddiqui, Sahih Muslim, vol. III, no. 1739.
16. Ibid., vol. III, no. 1742.
17. Pickthall, the Qur'an, 47:4-6.
18. Siddiqui, Sahih Muslim, vol. III, no. 1904.
19. Pickthall, the Qur'an, 9:122.
20. Khadduri, 1966, 75-77.
21. Rosenthal, 224.
22. Nardin, 156.
23. Pickthall, the Quran, 10:25.
24. Nardin, 259.
25. Khadduri, 1955, 69.
26. Nardin, 131.
27. Pickthall, the Quran, 2:190.
28. Ibid., 2:193.
29. Matraji, Sahih al-Bukhari, vol. IX, no. 6924.
30. Pickthall, the Quran, 9:5.
31. St. Augustine.
32. Cook, 19-20.
33. Nardin, 164-165.
34. Pickthall, the Quran, 8:39.

CHAPTER 23

Diversity and Unity in Islamic Civilization

From the Perspective of Philosophy of History

Introduction

In our search through the history of humankind, we find a period about 900 to 200 BCE that German philosopher Karl Jaspers (1883-1969) called the Axial Age—the age in which the spiritual foundations of humanity were laid simultaneously but independently in Egypt, Greece, Babylon, Judea, Persia, India, and China. These foundations, according to philosophers, were laid by great sages within their contemporary social environments, upon which humanity subsists today. According to Karen Armstrong, a modern thinker on religious affairs, "The final flowering of the Axial Age occurred in seventh-century Arabia, when Prophet Muhammad brought the Qur'an."[1] This final flowering of the axial age developed from a revealed *deen* of Islam into an Islamic civilization, but modern observers of socio-political affairs are critical of the surprising civilizational importance of Islam—a holistic sum of religion, polity, culture, and modernity, whose demise has been predicted many times throughout history.

However, held together in the common bonds of a shared tradition and a way of life despite many ethnic differences, in religious interpretation and socio-political matters, *deen-e-Islam* (the way of Islam) is still a powerful consensus of its friendly as well as conflicting nations, self-assertive ethnic groups, and religious factions. From Morocco in the west to Indonesia in the east, and from central Asia to central Africa, all see themselves spiritually united in their obedience to Allah, the Qur'an, the Prophet, and the sacred Arabic language of the Qur'an. Today, beyond the regions of Islamic countries, Muslims are present in Europe, America, Australia, and almost everywhere in the world. Wherever they are, and in whatever conditions they are living, all take pride in a common inheritance and view themselves as part of a great Islamic civilization. They gather in millions from every corner of the world, irrespective of color, race, and regional identities, all clad in white circling the black-robed Ka'ba, taking pride in a common civilization. Prophet Muhammad in his "Final Sermon" at Mina addressed the Muslim Ummah, witnessed by those performing the obligation of Hajj:

> *All mankind is from Adam and Eve. An Arab has no superiority over a non-Arab, nor does a non-Arab have any superiority over an Arab; a white has no superiority over a black, nor does a black have any superiority over a white; [none have superiority over another] except by piety and good action. Preference is only through righteousness. Learn that every Muslim is a brother to every Muslim and that the Muslims constitute one brotherhood. Nothing shall be legitimate to a Muslim which belongs to a fellow Muslim unless it was given freely and willingly. Do not, therefore, do injustice to yourselves. (From the Final Sermon of the Prophet).*

However, what is meant by the term "Islamic civilization," and what lies at the root of the present-day clash of civilizations? How does Islam stand in the contemporary battle of faiths, ideologies, and globalization? Islam, initially revealed as a religion, marching from the concept of Muslim *Ummah's dar-al-Islam* developed into an Islamic Civilization. As after the First World War the world of Islam was divided into small states, its civilizational unity remained dormant under the colonial rule of the Europeans. But after the Second World War, Hitler who on the one hand had weakened and devastated some of the European colonizing nations, on the other hand had paradoxically proved a blessing for the colonized nations by paving the way of freedom for the nations subjected by the Europeans. Another great event of history unfolded soon after the fall of the Soviet Empire which was made possible by the vigor of Islamic ideology of *jihad* for war when Muslim countries of Central Asia were declared free from the yoke of Soviet Union. When we study history of the Muslim peoples, we find that one of the hallmarks of Islamic civilization is its universality, diversity, and unity.

Birth of a Universal Civilization

The great twentieth-century philosopher Bertrand Russell remarked in his *History of Western Philosophy* that the "Mohammedans developed an important civilization of their own." Islamic civilization realized the greatest level of interracial and interethnic integration that existed in the world. It offered every nationality and ethnic group the chance to participate fully in the development and cultivation of the civilization that they shared. This can be verified by looking at the great people in Muslim history who represent excellence and achievement in the arts, sciences, and vocations that give a civilization its character. There are great thinkers, leaders, artists, and achievers from every ethnicity, religion, and nationality that came into the fold of Islam, including Turks, Kurds, Arabs, Persians, Berbers, Europeans, Africans, Indians, and Central Asians, all equally represented. The religion which united these people into a civilization, though its Prophet was an Arab, is not a religion for the Arabs alone. The concept of nationalism in its modern sense has no place in Islam. Bernard Lewis, in the *Cultures in Conflict*, argues:

> Islamic civilization, in contrast [to other civilizations], was the first that can be called universal, in the sense that it comprised people of many different races and cultures, on three continents. It was European, having flourished for a long time in Spain and southern Italy, on the Russian steppes, and in the Balkan Peninsula. It was self-evidently Asian and also African. It included people who were white, black, brown, and yellow. Territorially, it extended from southern Europe into the heart of Africa and into Asia as far as and eventually beyond the frontiers of India and China.[2]

Before arguing the paradigm of Islamic civilization's internal dynamics and the diversity of its cultures, it is important to understand the complex historical subject of the interconnections, fluid transitions, mutual enrichment, and co-existence that made a nomadic race of the Arabian Peninsula evolve into a universal civilization grounded in a revealed religion. The philosophy of history—a concept first described by ibn-Khaldun (1332-1406) in the fourteenth century and later followed by many Eastern and Western historians—is a study of how human societies evolve, adapt, and emerge, influenced by the geographical, biological, and demographic factors that emerge naturally, within specific moral and ethical rules over long period of time. Regarding Islam, historical facts prove that Prophet Muhammad created a civilization singlehandedly within the span of a decade, inspired and guided by the Qur'an: *"O mankind! Lo! We have created you male and female, and have made you nations and tribes that you may know one another. Lo! The noblest of you, in the sight of Allah, is the best in conduct. Lo! Allah is knower, Aware."*[2]

Islam is generally known as a religion; the Qur'an defines it a *deen* or a way of life. Philosophers and historians, including Ibn Khaldun, Bertrand Russell, Arnold Toynbee, Bernard Lewis, Samuel Huntington, Karen Armstrong, and many more, define it as a civilization. Seen in the light of the history of religions, Islam, revealed to Prophet Muhammad as a *deen,* is a continuation of the messages revealed by God to the earlier Prophets. Its birth as a new ideology of theo-philosophical and socio-political order, explained by the philosophy of history, was neither an imitation nor a revival of the previous civilizations.

Islam was a new and unique development, in which a vast diversity of traditions based on the moral values of the Zoroastrian, Jewish, and Christian faiths and cultured by the ethics of the Babylonian, Egyptian, Greek, Persian and Indian civilizations were homogenized. Islam benefitted from Byzantine statecraft, Hellenistic science and philosophy, Indian arithmetic, and oriental concepts of Persian art and architecture, which were not absorbed "asis" but were filtered and refined into the order of the revealed message of Islam's Divine Truth. Thus, a vast diversity from past and present became fused together into a distinctively and uniquely new civilization. At the same time, intertwined with traditional cultures of local tribes as well as of different races, colors, and ethnic groups, from all those different regions coming under the sway of the Muslims, Islam instituted a great civilization of its own moral, ethical, and spiritual brotherhood amongst its believers, and set a standard of subsistence for the whole humanity. In the Qur'an, God, (Allah *Subhana-wa-Ta'ala*) addressing directly to the people as *yaa-ayyu-allaziina-aamanuu* (O you who believe), as well as *yaa-ayyu-hannaas* (O you mankind) has projected His invocation of a "humanitarian theism" which became the basis of an all-embracing system of life in the form of 'Islamic Civilization.'

Within Islam's unique harmony—of Allah as One Transcendent God, His message revealed in a faultless perfect Arabic language of the Qur'an, His virtuous Messenger Muhammad the Prophet of Islam, and His servants' (believers) charismatic creation of a sacred art of arabesque calligraphy of Qur'anic verses, indicating the presence of Divinity through the symbolism of artistic geometric patterns and rhythmic repetitions pointing to Unity—there exists a cogent appreciation of "Diversity and Unity in Islamic Civilization." It is universally recognized for its social cohesion and spiritual liberty, and by its sacred art of Qur'anic calligraphy and architecture, which has homogenized the traditional heterogeneity into a single socio-religious discipline.

The appeal of Prophet Abraham's Transcendent Monotheism that rose from the fertile valleys of the Tigris and Euphrates rivers, and the calling of Allah echoing from the barren lands of Mecca, gave birth to a moral and spiritual civilization destined to exist for a time beyond the confines of modern man. Its simple message that *"There is no god but Allah, and Muhammad is His Messenger,"* resonating through the sublime rhetoric of the Qur'an—that unique symphony, the very sound that moves the listeners to tears and ecstasy—is the prime miracle persuasive of the fact that it is indeed the word of Allah. This Unity of One God and the inimical Arabic language of the Qur'an hold the key to the mystery of one of the greatest cataclysms in the history of religions which is the heart and soul of the Civilization of Islam.

Today the same call to prayer, in the Arabic of the Qur'an, rings out from the minarets of the Harem Sharif in Mecca as well as from the minarets of millions of mosques throughout the world. The message of Islam has created an everlasting civilizational spirit that includes everything from religion to history, politics to sociology, science to philosophy, and literature to art, from diverse cultures of different races, and ethnic societies of past and present. The reason for its stability and survival during many crises, according to the famous twentieth-century historian Arnold J. Toynbee (1889-1975), is to be found in the spiritual power of Islam's religious message:

> What was the secret of Islam's power to survive the death of
> its founder, the downfall of the primitive Arab empire-builders,
> the decline of the Arab's Iranian supplanters, the overthrow

of the Abbasid Caliphate, and the collapse of the barbarian successor-states that established themselves for their brief day on the Caliphate's ruin? The explanation was to be found in the spiritual experience of the converts to Islam among the non-Arab subjects of the Caliphate in the Umayyad Age. Islam, which they had originally adopted mainly for reasons of social self-interest, struck roots in their hearts, and was taken by them more seriously than the Arabs themselves. ... This spiritual triumph was the more remarkable considering that Islam had borne witness to the spiritual value of the religious message which Muhammad had brought to Mankind.[3]

Prophet Muhammad, the charismatic leader of Islam, left behind God's message, collected into a volume entitled the Qur'an, and died in 632. The gap of leadership shook the united Ummah, exposing signs of differences within the community. After a stormy session, Abu Bakr Siddique, the most respected and close companion of the Prophet was elected his successor as Caliph or *Khalifa* (Arabic for "deputy of God"). In political Islam this means the "Chief Muslim Civil and Religious Ruler," regarded as the successor of Muhammad the Prophet of Islam.

Historical Progression of Islamic Civilization

Upon the announcement of the Prophet's demise, the political edifice erected by him experienced its first tremor. The diversity that thrived under the leadership of the Prophet began to show its separate colors. Some tribes saw themselves released from their treaty obligations, and drove out the tax and zakat collectors in an attempt to return to their old ways. But it is important to note that this falling away was not accompanied by any reanimation of pagan religions or renouncing the name of Allah as One God. Antony Blake in *The History of Islamic Political Thought* reflects:

It is clear, from the Constitution of Medina and the earliest phase of Muhammad's teaching there, his purpose was to construct out of tribal confederacies a new people driven by his own sense of moral mission. Muhammad preached spiritual brotherhood plus an all-embracing law, and universal political control to be achieved, if necessary, by military power. Or at least he acted as if this was what he believed: for the irony was that the Muslims had little in the way of political theory to inform what they were doing. He enabled them to achieve the transition simultaneously from polytheism to monotheism, and from tribalism to nationhood to internationalism.[4]

Since the state of the Prophet was still not a geographically fortified unit but an aggregate of diverse tribal groups and territories, Abu Bakr the first Caliph started administering wisely in the light of the Qur'an and Prophet's precepts, and brought the Arabian Peninsula into geopolitical unity, even using force wherever it was inevitable. Thus, credit for laying a solid foundation of Islamic polity that within a century emerged as a civilization, goes to the first Caliph Abu Bakr.

After Abu Bakr, under the leadership of the second Caliph Umar, Islam spread rapidly, subjugating the Byzantine Empire and overrunning the Persians. During this period the socio-political unity and justice system established by Caliph Umar is an example to be found nowhere else in the history of the world. But the murder of the third Caliph Uthman gave birth to a civil war, creating a wide socio-political schism amongst the Muslims that later on divided the Muslim Ummah into Sunni and Shi'ite factions. In spite of this divergence of political views, the civil war did not destroy the civilizational unity. Rather, in its religious discipline a spiritual inner dimension of human existence evolved from its concept of greater jihad as *jihad-bin-nafs* (cleansing the self-struggle) defined as "Sufism" founded on the universal concept of mysticism. The strand of Sufism ran both in Sunni and Shi'ite factions and even today is a common spiritual bond amongst almost all the religious factions of Islam, except Wahhabism.

In addition to Arabic calligraphy, the art of spiritual music and singing of *hamd* (poetry praising God) and *na'at* (in praise of the Prophet) worked as a balm to the wounded souls of the faithful believers. Though some viewed this addition as a *bid'at* (heresy), the emergence of Sufism worked as an elixir to the distress brought by the civil war and later on to the disaster brought by the savage Mongols. Seyyed Hossein Nasr, in *Islam: Religion, History, and Civilization*, reflects:

In the hands of the Sufis, music became a steed with which the soul could journey from the outward rim of existence to the inner courtyard of the soul, where the Divine Presence resides. Islamic civilization created many musical instruments. ... Furthermore, Islamic philosophers and theoreticians of music [famously al-Farabi] wrote notable works on theory, structure, notation, and the effects of music on the soul as well as the body.[5]

The paradox of the civil war was the birth of many great Sufi Saints and Mystic Poets, who carried the message of Islam to the farthest corners of the world.

By the end of eighth and early ninth century, three main schools of thought—theology (*kalam*), philosophy (*falsafa*), and mysticism (*tasawwuf*)—after much conflict and interactive debates, adapted to an all-embracing harmony. Whereas Arabic literature produced the mystical poets ibn al-Farid and ibn al-Arabi, Persian literature produced in constant succession Sanai, Attar, Rumi, Shabistari, Jami, and Hafiz. Many other poets appeared from Central Asia to India, all over the world of Islam in different regional languages, setting a trend of mysticism far greater than formal theology. It helped rejuvenate Islamic civilization after the appalling catastrophe of the Mongol onslaught, and gave a new perspective to unity in Islam. Nasr, on unity and diversity remarks:

Unity cannot manifest itself without entering into the world of multiplicity, yet this manifestation is the means whereby humanity is led from multiplicity to Unity. Islam's great emphasis on Unity, therefore, could not prevent diversity on the formal level, nor could Islam have integrated a vast segment of humanity with diverse ethnic, linguistic, and cultural backgrounds without making possible diverse interpretations of its teachings. These teachings, nevertheless, lead to the Unity residing at the heart of the Islamic message as long as the interpreters of them remain within the framework of Islamic orthopraxy and orthodoxy considered in their widest and most universal sense. The Islamic religion, therefore, is comprised of diverse schools and interpretations that are deeply rooted and united in the principles of the Islamic revelation.[6]

221

Within a short period, Islam had under its sway the homelands of three out of the four primary civilizations of the Old World—Egypt, Babylon, and Indus—and incorporated them within the folds of its *dar-al-Islam* or the abode of peace. Palestine and Syria were conquered in 640, Mesopotamia in 641, Egypt in 642, Tripolitania in 647, Persia in 650, Khorasan in 661, Tunisia in 693, Algeria and Morocco in 705, and Sind (India) in 712. In the year 661, the capital of the new Empire was moved from Medina to Damascus. Within the first century of Islamic Hijra calendar, Muslims were ruling in Spain. Where for centuries Greek, Latin, Aramaic, and Pahlavi languages had divided the world, the Arabic language of the Qur'an united all the regions from North Africa to Southeast Asia, and from Central Asia and China to Central Africa.

As it is natural amongst conquerors and conquered people, doctrinal arguments, particularly in the matter of a new religion, many new questions arose to be debated. In order to tackle tough debates, Muslim thinkers studied Greek philosophy and logic, exploring them to solve the theoretical problems which arose on how to interpret the Qur'an and Islamic practice in these new environments. Inspired by the Qur'anic injunction, *"Call [the mankind] onto the way of your Lord with wisdom and fair exhortation and reason [argue] with them in the better way"*[7] and guided by the precept of the Prophet of Islam that God has not created anything more beautiful, better, or more perfect than reason, so much so that to *"ponder for an hour, is better than divine service for a year,"*[8] many great Muslim philosophers and religious interpreters appeared during the eighth century. Some of them, believing that philosophy and religion do not contradict each other, explicated many perplexing concepts of Islamic traditions for new converts.

Classical Greek philosophy and science, which had begun to make an impact on Islamic thought, was being translated into the Arabic language. During the period of the Abbasid caliphs' rule, *Bait al Hikmah* (House of Wisdom) was established in Baghdad, the new capital of the empire. Interpretations of Platonic and Aristotelian works triggered an amazing renaissance. Philosophical and scientific literature of the Athenian and Hellenistic schools, as well as Indian arithmetic, Chinese sciences were translated into Arabic. Greek logic helped the theologians in arguing and tackling logically religious and sectarian controversies.

Aristotelian logic (*mantiq* in Arabic) proved very helpful in developing the science of Islamic jurisprudence, which was introduced in their various schools, as well as in recognizing the virtues of induction and deduction. Many books of the ancients were eagerly collected not only in Baghdad but in remote Bokhara where ibn Sina grew to greatness. His *Canon Medicine* was counted as a key text in both the Islamic and the Western medical traditions for many centuries. Medicine, natural sciences, mathematics, and astronomy entered the curricula of the Islamic educational institutions known as *madrasahs*. After the translators came the commentators, such as al-Kindi and al-Rhazes in the east and ibn Bajjah, ibn Tufail, and ibn Rushd in Arab Spain.

Commentaries of Ibn Rushd, or Averroes in Latin, revived Aristotelian philosophy in Europe; his rational and scientific discourses served as a foundation for theoretical openness, political freedom, and religious toleration in Western thought. Ibn al-Hatham, a Muslim mathematician and astronomer, refined the theory of optics, refraction of light, and human sight, which became the basis for the telescope, camera, and even television screen. Another mathematician al-Khwarizmi invented algebra and the elements of the algorithm, which is critical to modern computer's software design as well as for modern science, engineering, and smart electronics. There is a long list of Muslim thinkers appearing from diverse regions, cultures, and religious factions, who made great contributions to social and general sciences.

Islamic Civilization of Today

Today, Islamic civilization stands at a crossroads, torn between the sweeping waves of globalization and cyber-technology. At the same time, it is pulled back and forth by the idea of the clash of civilizations. This has become a source of fear at the world level and a threat facing peoples, nations, governments, and states, pushing them to submit to the will of the sole world superpower for whom Islamic civilizational values are obsolete. Muslims still possess the ingredients and prerequisites for civilizational revival to resume its role in the rejuvenation of a contemporary Islamic civilization.

Muslims, today are better placed than any other nation to play an important part in the current civilizational and cultural spectrum. First, Islamic civilization is not a territorial factor. Instead of a land of Islam or a geo-strategic situation of an Islamic Ummah there is simply a religion, a *deen* or a way of life of immanent universality. Second, there are Muslims of diverse ethnicity, negotiating new identities by consensus as well as conflicting means, usually peacefully, though sometimes violently. Third, sociopolitical Islam throughout the last fourteen centuries has been constantly changing forms. Fourth, in studying and investigating Islamic civilization we find five epoch-making paradigms which Islam has undergone: starting from the paradigm of the original Islamic community, moving on to the paradigm of empires, through the classic paradigm of Islam as a world religions and the paradigm of religious scholars and Sufis, to the Islamic paradigm of modernization.

At the beginning of the modern paradigm, a space is appearing in some Islamic countries to combine the spirit of Islam with the challenges of the twenty-first century. Globalization is reflecting a clear view of this modern paradigm of Islam as we see a majority of Muslims, struggling to create a democratic society and adopt a creative culture of innovative science, are fighting to defeat the terrorist tactics of the orthodox traditionalists. Muslims may have to spend too much time and effort in dealing with terrorism, but radical violence must be placed within the larger framework of modernizing culture and politics by developing a compatible paradigm between the religion of Islam and the innovations of the twenty-first century. Islamic civilization, with its conception of a holistic humanism and its religion's message of love and peace imposes on all Muslim countries an adjustment of their internal situation, setting aside of marginal disagreements, and harnessing of potential within the framework of Islamic solidarity and the spirit of brotherhood.

Today, the same *azan,* or call to prayer, in the Qur'anic Arabic tongue echoes from Mecca to every corner of the world wherever there are Muslims. In spite of a so-called civilizational conflict between the Islamic and Western worlds, conversion to Islam is an ongoing process everywhere in the world. Peoples of many faiths and cultures are embracing Islam and are proudly becoming a part of greater Islamic civilization.

Notes:

1. Armstrong, 2006, p. 385
2. Lewis, 1996, p.17
3. Toynbee, 1957, pp 30-31
4. Blake, 2001, p. 10
5. Nasr, 2002, p. xxi
6. ibid., p.7
7. Qur'an, 18:125
8. Karim, Al-Hadith, vol 1 # 201w, 559

CHAPTER 24

What Went Wrong that the Muslims Abandoned Rationalism

Introduction

What went wrong with Islamic civilization, whose compelling religious idea gave birth to a system of beliefs and morals, to a political and social order that has withstood the test of almost thirteen centuries of history across vast regions, cultures, languages, and peoples from Central Asia to Central Africa and Morocco to Indonesia? Martin Kramer, in his article, "Islam's Sober Millennium," which appeared in the *Jerusalem Post*, propounded that:

> In the year 1000, the Middle East was the crucible of world civilization. One could not lay a claim to true learning if one did not know Arabic, the language of science and philosophy. One could not claim to have seen the world's greatest cities if one had not set eyes upon Baghdad and Cordoba, Cairo and Bukhara. Global trade flourished in the fabulous marketplaces of the Middle East as nowhere else. The scientific scholarship cultivated in its academies was unrivaled. An Islamic empire, established by conquest four centuries earlier, had spawned an Islamic civilization, maintained by the free will of the world's most creative and enterprising spirits.... This supremely urbane civilization cultivated genius. Had there been Nobel prizes in 1000, they would have gone almost exclusively to Moslems.[1]

In the world of Islam, scientific exchange was routine. Religious scholars, physicians, and philosophers debated in the courts, and educational institutions equipped with vast libraries were the pride of every elite group.

On the other hand, according to Martin Kramer, "European knowledge in the sciences paled in comparison, and was sustained through the Middle Ages by crumbs snatched from the Moslem table. From the point of view of a civilized Moslem (or a Jew living under Islam), the lands beyond the Pyrenees were the heart of darkness."[2] The course of history has, in a sense, reversed, and a period similar to Europe's Dark Ages is enveloping much of the Islamic world. One of the various reasons for this downfall is the rise of Arab nationalism, drawing a distinction between Arabs and Turks, not as a reaction to the West but as a critique of Ottoman-Turkish rule. Today, the students and researchers of Muslim philosophical and scientific knowledge ask: Whereas Muslims transmitted knowledge to the Europeans, what went wrong with their civilization's philosophical knowledge and scientific culture that today Muslims lag behind the Western world?

First of all we need to understand what went wrong that the Muslims abandoned rationalism and put an end to ibn Rushd's threefold notion of "truth"—rhetorical (religious); dialectical (reasoning); and philosophical (empirical)? There is no single reason for the decline of Islam's early inventive cultures of scientific and philosophical eminence that for centuries led the world in many areas. It is tragic, both in a historical and a human sense, but many factors contributed to the stagnation of rationalism in Islam. The rationalism of the Mu'tazilites—a school of Islamic theology that flourished in the cities of Basra and Baghdad—who believed that the arbiter of whatever is revealed has to be theoretical reason, was challenged by the Ash'arites, the foremost theological school of Sunni Islam.

The Ash'arites established an orthodox dogmatic guideline based on clerical authority founded by the Arab theologian Abu al-Hasan al-Ash'ari who had laid the foundation of an orthodox Islamic theology. By some, it is also attributed to al-Ghazali (1058-1111), whose arbitral book, *The Incoherence of the Philosophy,* professed that causality was an illusion and rational philosophy futile. Ibn Rushd, on the other hand, in his work *The Incoherence of the Incoherence,* rejoined that God created a logical universe of cause and effect, and argued that he who repudiates causality actually repudiates reason. Al-Ghazali, though, had denounced speculative philosophy, arguing that while philosophical skepticism puts limits on divinity, did not reject scientific investigations.

The biggest blow to Islamic rationalism was the fall of the Arab dynasties at Baghdad in the Middle East and Cordova in Arab Spain. In 1493, the Christians conquered Spain, ending eight centuries of Muslim rule. They massacred Muslims and Jews, and expelled many of them from Spain, but retained their philosophical and scientific works. In Baghdad, the crushing impact on the Muslim heartland by successive waves of invasions, led by the savage Mongols, who threw millions of books in the Euphrates River and burned many libraries in Baghdad to ashes. The Mongols were followed by the Turkic Seljuks, the European Crusaders, the Ayyubid Kurds, the Tamerlane Mughals, and finally the Ottomans, who were all successively promotors of mystical philosophies, and gradually destroyed the centers of rational, philosophical, and scientific knowledge.

Abandoning Rationalism

When the books and libraries of a nation or a society are destroyed, this creates a vacuum of knowledge and cultural emptiness, which results in the new rulers building new societies. One of the most important reasons for the loss of this wealth of knowledge was that the Arab rulers who loved philosophical knowledge did not establish institutions like the House of Wisdom at Baghdad in other parts of their empire. They should have set up universities and colleges all over the world of Islam. After the Abbasids, later caliphs, sultans, and monarchs who could have patronized and supported centers of learning were focused on consolidating their positions and fighting battles. Peoples in all walks of life, fearful of the turmoil of the foreigner's attacks and oppression of the new rulers, looked for solace in religious literacies, specifically in spirituality instead of philosophical argumentation. Muslim lands were now flooded with Sufi saints who were revered for their miracles and teachings of love and peace. Thus, mysticism, known as Sufism, became an inclination and a sigh of relief for the Muslim masses.

Since Sufism provided a new and peaceful ideology to the caliphs and monarchs newly converted to Islam—the Mongols, the Mughal rulers, followed by the Ottoman Turks—instead of patronizing scholars of philosophical learning, began to patronize Sufi saints. The chapter of ibn-Rushd's philosophical thought was closed and that of al-Ghazali's mystical outlook was encouraged. Islamic history of knowledge has been dependent throughout on rulers who preferred to patronize the genre of knowledge which would support them in consolidating their hold on a variety of people, traditions, customs, and cultures. Followers of Sufism would prove peace-loving and submissive subjects, who started seeking the blessings of saints instead of asking for their rights from their rulers. Since reason could challenge the rulers, belief in collective piety, hope, and confidence in God's grace triumphed over the earlier concept of Classical Islam: "submission to God is submission to reason." Thus, a wave of individualistic quests for God engulfed the seekers of love and peace, and masses of Muslims started seeking solace in prayers and in music as *Sama* in the Sufic-inspired services.

With the rise of Central Asian Turkic rulers, the Arabic language, which was the best medium for philosophical cognition, was replaced by the Persian language with the result that most philosophical works started appearing in Persian. Significant philosophical trends after ibn Sina were attempts to reconstruct holistic systems that help refine philosophical propositions and religious questions rather than challenge and refute them. A new trend in philosophy, the "Philosophy of Illumination" of Shihab al-Din Suhrawardy (1153-1191)—second only to ibn Sina—emerged with the rise of Sufism. This system defined a new method, the "Science of Lights," which maintains that human beings obtain the principles of science directly through the "knowledge of presence." Almost half a century after the execution of Suhrawardy, the philosophy of Illumination was viewed as a more complete system. Its aim was to expand the structure of Aristotelian philosophy to include carefully selected religious topics, defending the harmony between philosophy and religion. This gave rise to Mulla Sadra's (1572-1641) theory of the unity or sameness of the knower and the known. His view of theo-philosophy continues to influence Muslim philosophical knowledge even today.

The Socio-political Paradigms

Though the Arabs of the Arabian Peninsula were intelligent people who quickly adopted the new religion of Islam, a discipline intertwined with reason and spirituality had made them warriors first. The way of Islam revealed in social paradigms, cultures, and geo-political circumstances play a very important part in the formation of a literary, socio-political, or even a religious social order. We know that the ethos of pre-Islamic Arabian literary, cultural, and traditional etymology inherited by the people who embraced Islam was devoid of philosophical cognition and rational intellectualism. But the Arabs, living mostly in the Arabian Desert as roaming nomads, had remained engaged in fighting with each other in groups and tribes. If Islam were a dogma, many Arab believers and scholars would never have touched the rationalistic philosophy and free thinking of the pagan Greeks. However, for non-Arabic speaking people the Qur'anic Arabic was as sacred as the messages revealed and collected in the scripture.

After the first four "Rightly Guided Caliphs," when the first Umayyad caliph Mu'awiya established his rule in the seventh century, a period of intellectual activity began. In order to overturn the tradition of electing a caliph, which could have been seen as a type of Socratic democracy or a Roman form of republic, Mu'awiya was tempted by Plato's famous pronouncement, "Until philosophers are kings, or kings and princes of this world have the spirit and power of philosophy" and took Neoplatonism as a rationale to establish a dynasty of hereditary caliphate. For the power-monger Mu'awiya, who was entrusted with the role of scribe by the Prophet to take down the revealed Qur'anic verses during his lifetime, the philosophy of Plato proved a big blessing. However, Mu'awiya did not persecute Jewish, Christian, and Syriac scholars, thinkers and philosophers who had knowledge of Greek philosophy, but gave them protection.

When the Abbasids, who were also Arabs, defeated their ancestral cousins the Umayyads with the help of the Persians, the influence of Persian language and culture started posing a big challenge to the Arabic language. In order to meet this Persian infiltration with a superior intellectual weapon, Caliph al-Ma'mun founded the House of Wisdom known as *Bayt-al-Hikmah* to translate Greek philosophy and sciences into Arabic. Thus, a golden era of Muslim intellectualism began, which also curbed the Persian renaissance of the tenth and eleventh centuries and brought revolutionary changes in Muslim thought and scientific achievements. In short, patronage of the Hellenistic philosophy was not the intrinsic passion of the Arab rulers, but rather a kind of political weapon—used at times to intimidate the theologians or *Fuqaha,* and at other times to subjugate political rebels or curb foreign cultural influences instigated great Muslim thinkers from al-Kindi to ibn Sina, as well as many scientists to involve seriously in the pursuit of scientific exploration and rational thinking.

Unfortunately, first the Crusades and then the Mongol onslaught brought the fall of the Arab Abbasids of Baghdad, and the spectrum of power slipped out of the hands of the Arabs, which also marked the demise of rational and free thinking. The decline of knowledge in the Muslim world dates roughly from the beginning of the twelfth century— at the end of the Crusades—and an irreversible decadence when Baghdad was burned to ashes. When the Mongols sacked Baghdad, the world of Christendom, after having lost the third and final Crusade, proclaimed with great merriment the death of Islam. But the rise of the Ottomans and the Turkic-Mongol race known as the Mughals revived the power of Islam. Since both the Ottomans and the Mughals were patrons of mystical Islam, though they were mostly secular rulers, but banned ibn Rushd's rational and scientific discourses of theoretical openness, intellectual intuitiveness, and political freedom. The Ottomans and Mughals believed that rationalism and the separation of politics and religion would weaken their monarchic and authoritarian rule. They promoted the notion that Islam as a religion was the crucial rationale of Islamic discipline and that the truth of its doctrine lies in spirituality. Since there was neither a sociopolitical inclination nor a cultural requirement for philosophical appreciation, the question of an Islamic renaissance never arose.

The Failure of Enlightenment and *Nahda* in Islam

Today, despite the rising trend of scientific knowledge in the Muslim world, Muslims still construct their polity on the original Islamic rules of community. But an inclination to modernity also exists. Oliver Leaman in *A Brief Introduction to Islamic Philosophy*, argues:

> During the *"Nahda"* or the "Arab Renaissance" movement of the nineteenth century, the challenge to Islamic thought was clear. How can the Muslims develop a view of society which incorporates the principles of modernity, yet at the same time remain Islamic? ... [According to the modernists], "Islamic Renaissance" should

follow the Western Renaissance, and put religion in its place; only in this way can the Islamic world participate in the material and political successes of the West.[3]

Though modern times have seen radical change in the traditional scheme of education, the world of Islam has failed to produce successful "Renaissance men" like Leonardo da Vinci, Pico-della Mirandola, Francis Bacon, and many others. Painting, making sculptures, and many forms of fine artwork have remained forbidden in Islamic discipline, which according to Leonardo is an important medium to express knowledge of the world. Pico, while living in Florence, published a remarkable work *On the Dignity of Man*, portraying man as the spiritual center of the universe, or perhaps man as one focus and God as the other. Such views were offensive for the Muslims who believed in an Omnipotent, Transcendent One God. Bacon's famous boast, "I take all knowledge for my province," means for Muslims to challenge the All-knowing God they believe in and remember daily in their prayers. The solution to all the problems of the Islamic world which exist today rests in understanding and appropriately applying the concept of "reason" in every phase of life. Regarding current problems of the World of Islam, Oliver Leaman is of the opinion:

> What the Islamic world needed was more or less the same sort of passionate involvement with the Enlightenment Project as occurred, in some ways, in Europe and the United States. Critics of the Enlightenment point to the fact that the Enlightenment did not itself provide grounds for believing that reason is the principle of thought to be followed, so that its adherence to reason is itself unreasonable and uncritical. Critics also discuss the terrible things which came into existence as a result of an unthinking adherence to a principle of rationality which is not in itself rich enough to constitute a sufficiently thorough guide to how we should live. Some critics of the Enlightenment and of ibn Rushd's place in it comment on the low status which mysticism has in his thought, suggesting that the glorification of rationality as a form of thought ignores and misrepresents the spiritual aspects of humanity and our links with God.[4]

The Age of Enlightenment is also known as the Age of Reason and rational thinking. In the World of Islam, the period between the ninth and thirteenth centuries was the Age of Enlightenment. It was the heyday of the World of Islam when a series of great philosophers, scholars, thinkers, and scientists appeared who made great impacts on the West. The quest for philosophical knowledge and scientific research of the Arabs dominated the world of ideas even beyond the frontiers of *dar-al-Islam*. Failure to continue the progress of Enlightenment and Rationalism in the World of Islam or a possible revival like the European Renaissance the fall of Arab rule and the end of Arabic as language Franca, a language which could express philosophy by coining new words with innovative-clarity for the Greek words of science and philosophy. Persian language of Central Asian Turkic peoples who had spread as far as the whole sub-continent of India, lacked the innovative-ease of coining new words

During the late nineteenth and early twentieth century, the Islamic Renaissance known as *Nahda*, "the Awakening" in Arabic, which was also referred to as Enlightenment, flourished in Egypt, Lebanon, and Syria, the Arabic-speaking regions of the Ottoman Empire. The *Nahda* was seen as a cultural shock brought about by the invasion of Egypt by Napoleon. The Egyptian scholar Rifa'a al-Tahtawi (1801–1873) is seen as the pioneering figure of the *Nahda*. He was sent to Paris in 1826 by the Turkish Governor Muhammad Ali to study Western sciences and their educational systems. Learning the French language, he translated some important scientific and cultural works into Arabic. This also changed his political views on many matters; in particular, he advocated the parliamentarian system of government and women's education.

Ahmad Faris al-Shidyaq (1806-1887), who was born in Lebanon, went to Great Britain, became a British citizen, and lived there for seven years in pursuit of modern knowledge. From Britain he moved to France and lived there for two years, where he wrote and published some of his most important works. Promoting Arabic language and culture, he is considered to be one of the founding fathers of modern Arabic literature. However, he was more focused on resisting the Ottoman's Turkynizing of the Arab world.

Another scholar, Butus al-Bastami (1819-1893), was also Lebanese and an important figure of the *Nahda* centered in mid-nineteenth century Beirut. Influenced by American missionaries, he became Protestant. In 1863 he founded al-Madrasa al-Wataniya (the National School) on secular principles, employed some leading *Nahda* pioneers of Beirut and produced a generation of *Nahda* thinkers. He compiled and published several textbooks and dictionaries, and thus became known as the Master of the Arabic Renaissance.

Hayreuddin Pasha al-Tunsi (1820-1890), focusing on the writings of European Enlightenment and the Arabic political thought, envisioned in his many writings a seamless blending of Islamic tradition with Western modernization. His theories of modernization made an enormous impact on the Tunisian and Ottoman outlooks. A Syrian physician, publicist, poet, and scholar, Francis Marrash (1835-1874), who had traveled in France and Western Asia, expressed socio-political ideas in *Ghabat-al-Haqq* highlighting his views for the Arabs about two things: Arab patriotism, and modern schooling, free from the religious binding. Saiyid Jamal-al-Din Afghani (1839-1897) advocated Islamic unity and gave a modernist reinterpretation to Islam. Preaching Pan-Islamic solidarity fused with adherence to the faith, he supported an anti-colonial doctrine. Al-Afghani's views influenced many, but his sincere follower Muhammad Abduh (1849-1905) preached that Muslims should return to the "true Islam" of the first four Rightly Guided Caliphs who had been divinely inspired and rationally guided. Rashid Rida ((1885-1935) and Egyptian and one of the students of Abduh continued his legacy and further expanded the view of just Islamic government.

The Birth of Nationalism in Islam

The introduction of the parliamentarian system helped create a political class in the Ottoman-controlled provinces, which rather gave birth to several nationalist movements in Egypt, Lebanon, Syria, and Palestine. The Arabs dreaming to restore Islam to its pristine grandeur and revolted against Ottoman-Turkish rule were deceived. Martin Kramer wrote in his book, *Arab Awakening and Islamic Revival*, "World War I forced a choice upon the adherents of Arabism. After some hesitation, the Ottoman Empire entered the European war on the side of Germany, prompting Britain and France to fan every ember of dissent in the Empire. The Allies held out the prospect of independence for something they called 'the Arab nation,' and they eventually found a partner in a local potentate of Mecca, the Sharif Husayn."[2] Support from the Western powers proved a major political fallacy. The Arabs did not get the real Arab world they had longed for. Graham Fuller, in *Future of Political Islam*, argued:

> The alternative model, imposed by Western colonialism, divided much of the Muslim world into so-called nation-states that were not in reality based on true 'nations' at all as ethnically European states were. The Arab world in particular was 'artificially' divided into units that are perceived by the Arabs as neither traditional, logical, useful, nor successful. On the contrary, this Western principle of reorganization—based on divisive ethnicity rather than moral principles of Muslim unity—is perceived as a key source of contemporary Muslim weakness that only a move toward Islamic unity can overcome—even if the creation of just one single pan-Islamic state is not realistic.[5]

The British and French had replaced the Ottomans, and the Arabs failed to stop the division of Arab land. The Arabs committed a blunder in neglecting the concept of universal Islam, since the sole collective identity Islam offers lies in its faith, in which people of all nations and colors are equal and united as one Ummah under God's banner. By taking the side of the British and French, the Arabs betrayed their fellow Muslims, forgetting that the bond of Islam linked the Arabs and Turks, not the British and French. They were betrayed by their Western allies, now turned masters—a just recompense for those who were believers but placed their trust in nonbelievers of Islam. The Qur'an, giving an account of mighty nations that perished because of their own wrongdoing, says, *"So Allah surly wronged them not, but they did wrong themselves."*[6] Thus, Western civilization succeeded in turning the course of history in its favor by politically dividing the Muslim world into small states.

The doctrine of *dar al-Islam* suffered a big blow from this division, but the ideology of universal Islam remained firmly rooted in the heart of every Muslim. Martin Kramer questioned, "Will it ever be possible again for this region to develop as an independent center of political, economic, and cultural power? Or will it continue, as much of it does now, to nurse old wounds and curse the new world order?"[2] Old wounds of failure and victimization are psychobiological complexes that haunt nations for generations particularly those groups and nations that are oppressed.

Finding themselves hard-pressed under the heels of economic and military power they revolt against the oppressors. Those lacking logistics for warfare express their resentment through terrorism.

The Rise of European Power

In the seventeenth century, when European nations began to colonize the continents of America and Australia, they acquired immense wealth from overseas. This enabled them to undertake colonialism in Africa, Asia, and the Muslim world. European imperialism in the Muslim Middle East, India under Muslim rule, and Southeast Asia, was a final blow to the world of Islam. Colonialism drowned the Muslim world in economic recession and divided it into many nation-states with arbitrary border. Muslim nations were spending money on battles—some on disputes with each other and some fighting for freedom from their European masters—rather than on scientific and educational projects. In the twenty-first century, almost all Muslim nations are part of the developing world, with many problems such as poverty, economic stagnation, educational regression, and above all, political instability.

Throughout the history of Muslim philosophy, Muslim scholars have been arguing and writing mostly for intellectuals and other philosophers. But in the Western world it was understood that there is a need for philosophy to be read, understood, and practiced by intellectuals and non-intellectuals alike. Many complex arguments and multiple contradictions need to be addressed to achieve a simple and clear intellectual vision for the common man and his world. The world is moving rapidly ahead, while Muslims, still basking in their past glories, are struggling to revive their lost golden period of philosophical and scientific eminence.

Today's Islamic World

While the Ottomans, the Safavids, and the Mughals lost their glories, the European nations went from strength to strength, acquiring more and more territories and trade centers, and succeeded in defeating the Muslims on land and sea. Today, Muslims are divided into nations, lacking an understanding of the West's challenges and imperialistic threats. Instead of looking back to their past glory, they need to comprehend that the past cannot be revived. Unfortunately, there still exists in all Muslim societies an "Islamist-Utopia" thinking, which stands as an impediment to scientific and political modernity. It is time to move forward. New IT technology and modern scientific exploration can help them make up quickly the time they have lost.

Since people today are instantly connected by a network of information and knowledge exchange, they are impelled to think and act globally in a world where philosophy is no longer viewed as the "queen of knowledge." The Western world understands that philosophy is now understood through science, phenomenology, and linguistic analysis. Scientific education, research, and the growth of intellectual consortiums, have generated a new scientific form of global interpretation. This should be seen as an act of progressive transformation of philosophy, actualized by the scientific revolution in the West where philosophy has now attained a place in the scientific arenas. The world of Islam today is far behind the West in philosophical and scientific knowledge.

Muslims need to understand that during their Golden Era, the religion of Islam was never an obstacle in their pursuit of philosophical and scientific exploration sponsored by rational thinking, and it should not be an obstacle now. Today, the pace of technology is so fast, its impact so deep, that our lives will be irreversibly transformed. The coming era will neither be utopian nor dystopian; it will drastically transform the concept of human beings relying on conviction to give meaning to their lives. Today, throughout the world IT revolution of "Scientific Enlightenment" is knocking at the door of mankind, an enlightenment where human intelligence will either share or give way to the artificial intelligence of supercomputers.

Today, science is increasing its authority on cultural, religions, and social fields. Science as a technique has presented a different outlook from the one found in theoretical philosophy and the dogmatic approach of religions. Today, instead of looking back to philosophical analysis and rational enquiries, as initiated by al-Kindi, ibn Rushd and many other Muslim philosophers of the ninth century, Muslims need to understand philosophy through science.

Notes:

1. Kramer, 1999.
2. Kramer, 1996, p. 25
3. Leaman, 1999, p. 126.
4. Ibid. p. 177.
5. Fuller. 2003, 3.
6. Pickthall, the Qur'an, 9:70.

CHAPTER 25

Globalization and the World of Islam

Globalization refers to the expansion and intensification of social relations and consciousness across world-time and world-space.—Manfred B. Steger

Introduction

The concept of globalization raises a basic question: is it a process, a condition, a system, a force, or an age? For many nations of the world, and specifically for Muslims, it is important to find out how globalization occurs and which idea is driving it! Is it one cause or a combination of many factors? Is globalization a uniform or an uneven process? Is globalization a continuation of modernity or is it a radical break? How does today's globalization differ from previous social developments? Does globalization create new forms of inequality and hierarchy? Steger argues in his work, *Globalization, A Brief Insight:*

> First, globalization involves the creation of new, and the multiplication of existing, social networks and activities that cut across traditional political, economic, cultural, and geographical boundaries. The second quality of globalization is reflected in the expansion and the stretching of social relations, activities, and interdependencies. Third, globalization involves the intensification and acceleration of social exchanges and activities. As the Spanish sociologist Manuel Castells has pointed out, the creation of a global "network society" required a technological revolution; one that has been powered chiefly by the rapid development of new information and transportation technologies. Fourth, as we emphasized in our discussion of the global imagery, globalization does not occur merely on an objective, material level but also involves the subjective plane of human consciousness. The compression of the world into a single place increasingly makes global the frame of reference for human thought and action.[1]

Steger further argues that globalization involves both the macrostructures of community and the microstructures of personhood. He has defined it in a single sentence: *"Globalization refers to the expansion and intensification of social relations and consciousness across world-time and world-space."* Within this context, universal Islam refers to the unification of Muslims as a global *Ummah*, but perceiving it in a holistic sense in which Islam is more than a religion, it becomes questionable?

Globalization as Universal Culture

Globalization applies to a set of social processes that appear to transform the current social condition of weakening nationality into a strengthened globality. At its core, it is about reframing the forms of human contact. It is a magnetism best captured by the idea of social development or unfolding along discernible patterns. For an ordinary person the forces of globalization include communication, transportation, international commerce, travel and migration, and a growing form of political and economic interdependence fuelled by new technologies like personal computers, the World Wide Web, the internet, cellular phones, digital cameras, high-definition television, satellites, jet planes, and space shuttles—an evolving global reality owned by no one.

But technology provides only a partial explanation for the latest wave of globalization. Muslims, before being divided into nation-states, viewed themselves as a globalizing force. Even today, Islamic culture is universally reflected in its unique commonality from lifestyle, food, clothing, literature, art, architecture, salutation, and greetings to a strong strand of Qur'anic Arabic, binding believers together all around the world. But cultural globalization is not just Islamic, Christian, Jewish, or even what we know as Western culture. It refers to the intensification and expansion of a common cultural flow across the globe that is adaptable by the whole of humanity, irrespective of any specific culture, creed, or ethnicity. Culture is a broad concept, a hard-to-describe human experience making people around the world more alike, particularly in the face of diverse religions and conflicting socio-political ideologies.

Though the internet and the World Wide Web play a pivotal role in facilitating globalization by connecting billions of individuals, civil societies, and governments, the socio-political dimension of globalization refers to the intensification and expansion of social and political interrelation across the globe. It raises important political issues relating to the principle of the state and people's sovereignty, the growing impact of inter-governmental organizations, and future prospects for regional and global governance. Modern democracy, following the fall of the Berlin Wall, is also seen as accelerating the process of globalization and bringing nations into common economic and political ground.

For the Muslim world this new phenomenon is a challenge to its concept of universal Islam and its belief of Divine sovereignty. Therefore, the important question before Muslims today is how universal Islam can mitigate the line between the Islamic political concept and Western secular principles regarding certain key concepts in the process of globalization. These concepts include the compatibility of Islam and modern democracy, responsible forms of government, political accountability, equal citizenship, freedom of choice, and the right of equal say for non-Muslims in matters of political authority.

Globalization as a Contested Concept for Islam

Although the concept of globalization seems to have an interdependent nature, for Islamic civilization it remains a contested concept. One of the reasons for this is because there is no consensus on what social processes constitute its essence, with people's growing consciousness of belonging to a global community. Whereas globalism challenges the ideology of nationalism and the forces of religions, for the Muslims, the first impression is that it is a process of universalizing Western civilization by defeating Islamic civilization's concept of universal Islam. It has, therefore, pitted the universal against the particular and the global against the local, so that many people have trouble recognizing the channels that bind religious traditionalist-fundamentalism to the secular-modernity of today's global age. This phenomenon tempts Muslims to certain forms of globalizing Islam which are clearly fundamentalist, by stressing the need to return to "pure" Islam, that of the *Salaf,* the pious ancestors. Muslims see globalization as a Western way in which their relationship to universal Islam is reshaped, giving an impression of living as a minority in a Westernised global society, fearing that they might lose Islamic universalism.

The early world of Islam represented a form of globalization. Today, not only Islamic countries, but the entire world beyond the Western world, sees modern globalization as a new form of Western or American hegemony in a massive economic, political, and cultural package of questionable benefit. Furthermore, the losers in the globalization process may seek alternative ideologies to resist an American-led globalization, such as some kind of alliance of "anti-hegemonic" states fighting "neoliberalism" (the ideological term for American globalization). Graham E. Fuller argues in *The Future of Political Islam:*

> The Muslim world, representative of the regions of the Third World *par excellence,* and with its strong focus on "social Justice," betrays deep ambivalence toward contemporary globalization that is often perceived as a deliberate Western cultural juggernaut. Islam need not be anti-Western or anti-global by definition, but it functions as a guardian and repository of cultural tradition that emerges from Islamic faith, culture, and tradition.[2]

But while concern about the negative impact of globalization may impact developing and under-developed countries, globalization is believed by Muslims to have a serious bearing on their civilization. For them, it is not a natural process flowing out of modern technological progress; it rather represents a pet project of Western states promoting an institutional infrastructure that the United States, today's only superpower, is monopolizing. Therefore, all Muslim countries, along with many other nations, have reservations about globalization. Additionally, Islam sees the modern West, being in thrall to materialism, as a barrier to the spiritual strand of universal Islam.

The start of the twenty-first century has brought rapid change at an unprecedented rate, creating problems around how to integrate this change into political Islam's concept of universal Islam without any repugnance to the Qur'an and the *Sunnah* of its Prophet. Since religious and political systems are intertwined in Islam, this would mean an Islamic globalization rather than one based on Western humanism and existentialism. Like all social processes, globalization functions on a rational ideology filled with a wide range of norms, claims, beliefs, and narratives about the phenomenon itself, rather than religions. Ideologies of globalism, such as market globalism, justice globalism, and religious globalism, are powerful systems of widely shared ideas and patterns of beliefs that are accepted as truth by liberal democracies, such as neoliberalism (supporting the rights of the individual over those of the state and church) and libertarianism (the advocacy of liberty and free will). They offer people a more or less coherent picture of the world not only as it is, but as it ought to be. The irony is that the West constitutes the most vibrant picture of modernity and creative thinking, corresponding to *ijtihad*, easily available to the Muslims, which can facilitate the Islamic *Ummah* to become part of the globalizing world.

There are, today, three types of globalism. Market globalism seeks to institute globalization with free-market norms and neoliberal meanings. Contesting market globalism from the political "left," justice globalism constructs an alternative vision of globalization based on egalitarian ideals of global solidarity and distributive justice[3]. From the political "right," Islamic fundamentalist *jihadist* globalism struggles against both market and justice globalism. Islamic civilization's concept of universal Islam is in pursuit of mobilizing the global *Ummah,* or the Muslim community of believers, in defence of Islamic values and beliefs that Muslims fear are under attack by the forces of secularism and consumerism. In spite of their considerable differences, however, these three forms of globalism share an important function: they articulate and translate the rising global notions of community, which are increasingly tied into concrete political programs and agendas.

Whereas it is assumed that someone must be in charge and responsible for any movement, the basic truth about globalization is that no one is in charge. "But the global marketplace today is an Electronic Herd of often anonymous stock, bond and currency traders and multinational investors, connected by screens and networks"[4] (Thomas Friedman, an author and *New York Times* correspondent). "The great beauty of globalization is that it is not controlled by any individual, any government, or any institution" (Robert Hormats, vice-chairman of Goldman Sachs International).[5]

Islamic religiously-based organizations have a common perception that Western modes of modernization have failed to put an end to widespread poverty in Muslim regions, and that it has enhanced political instability and strengthened a confused secular tendency in Muslim societies. Steger remarks:

> Thus, jihadist globalism is a response to what is often experienced as a materialistic assault by the liberal or secular world. Drawing on revivalist themes popularized in the eighteenth century by theologian Muhammad Abdal Wahhab, bin Laden and his followers seek to globalize a "pure" and "authentic" form of Islam—by any means necessary. Their enemies are not merely the American-led forces of market globalism, but also those domestic groups who have accepted these alien influences and imposed them on Muslim peoples. ... In principle, the label "jihadist globalism" applies also to the ideology of those violent fundamentalists in the West who seek to turn the whole world into a "Christian empire." [6]

Islamic civilization's necessary Islamization of modernity takes place in a global space emancipated from the confining territoriality of the political framework of religious nationalists fighting modern secular regimes in the twentieth century.

The newly revived concept of an Islamic state under *Khilafat* rule embraces the dualism of a clash of civilizations between its desired *Ummah* and global unbelief or unambiguous globalist ideology. Its *jihadist* attempt to restore a transnational *Ummah* attests to the globalization of the Muslim world just as much as it reflects the Islamization of the world beyond Islam. The ideological claim of Islamic *Khilafat*—to rebuild a unified Muslim global *Ummah* through *jihad* against global unbelief—resonates well with the dynamics of a globalizing world. This concept appeals to the Muslim youth living in the individualized and decultured environment of Westernized Islam. If a purified *Ummah*—imagined to exist in a global space that transcends national and tribal identities—is the final goal of *jihadist* globalism, then *jihad's* offensive and defensive versions alike surely serve as its principal means. That is why Muslims consider *jihad* as their prime obligation, emphasizing that armed struggle against unbelief is the only way toward globalization of Islam.

Cultural and Ethical Dimension of Globalism

The modern age is witnessing a blossoming of Western culture with its new technology, superfast communications and transport systems, and modern social, political, educational, agricultural, scientific, and medical advances. But with these changes have come the strains and tensions of conflicting interests, desires, and values within Islamic countries. Difficulties between the West and the Muslims lie in the "human factor," in their basic attitudes and values, the level of their education and their sense of responsibility to integrate concepts of the scientific worldview into their own pattern of values. Today, Muslims are living in a semi-modernity, in which technological innovations are taken on, but modern political and social values are considered un-Islamic. Muslims need to rediscover a positive Islam, that of their own ibn Rushd, known to the West as Averroes, of critical thought—or in a word, an "enlightened Islam." Islam's globalization cannot be carried out without enlightenment and intellectual freedom, or without a certain degree of political secularism—a complete separation of the political and the religious.

Ethics as the foundation of democracy—and of Islam—should be a global ethics that renders national boundaries insignificant. Peter Singer, in *One World: The Ethics of Globalization*, argues that:

> National sovereignty has no *intrinsic* moral weight. What weight national sovereignty does have comes from the role that an international principle requiring respect for national sovereignty plays, in normal circumstances, in promoting peaceful relationships between states. It is a secondary principle, a rule of thumb that sums up the hard-won experience of many generations in avoiding war. Respect for international law is vital, but the international law regarding the limits of sovereignty is itself evolving in the direction of a stronger global community.[7]

Human societies in the past and nations in modern times have followed the idea of sovereign states not only in terms of relations based on diplomacy and public policy but also of ethics. In the modern concept of globalization, people are moving beyond the era of forging ties between nations, foreseeing something beyond the concept of the nation-state. This shift needs to be reflected in all levels of conception, especially ethics. Peter Singer further argues:

> Sovereignty is no longer simply a matter of the power of the state to control what happens within its borders. The limits of the state's ability and willingness to protect its people are also the limits of

its sovereignty. ... Only the United Nations should attempt to take this responsibility to protect. Otherwise, national interests will again conflict and plunge the world into international conflict. If, however, the world's most powerful nations can accept the authority of the United Nations to be the "protector of last resort" of people whose states are flagrantly failing to protect them, and if those nations will also provide the United Nations with the means to fulfill this responsibility, the world will have taken a crucial step toward becoming a global ethical community.[7]

There is a well understood hypothesis that the free secular state lives by presuppositions which it can no longer guarantee without putting its freedom in question. Therefore, the ideologically neutral state may not decree a meaning in life nor prescribe any supreme value by law; it has to presuppose them if its own mechanisms are to function at all and its laws are to be observed. A democratic state needs a fundamental ethical consensus, supported by all social groups, to which all religions, philosophies, and worldviews contribute. In the Islamic world this consensus is primarily Islam and in countries with Christian characteristics it is Christianity. In such a situation, religion will certainly fall victim to ethically unproductive ideological secularism, which, from a global perspective, represents an exceptional phenomenon in Western and Central Europe and among American elites. However, if they are wise, religious leaders will not strive for a clerical domination of secular spheres. Rather, religion will inspire, motivate, and possibly also improve "security" and "affirmation of the world" from the perspective of faith.

Recently, two forms of global Islam have attracted increasing numbers of Muslims. The first form relates to communities comprised of immigrants, *imams* educated in the West, entrepreneurs, and scholars of Islamic studies living in the West who have created "transnational networks" of solidarity across national and cultural borders. They are helping to develop the idea of a common religious and cultural identity between people living in the West and those living in a variety of Muslim countries. The second form of Islamic globalization concerns those forms of Islam that emphasize the universal ties of communities of believers, or the *Ummah*. A development of electronic religiosity is spreading the message of Islam in contradictory and reformatory forms that are weakening Islamic orthodoxy and its many nationalized versions within Muslim countries. The transnational networks are developing a reconciliationary form of global Islam that is practicable in the modern era. Thus, the growth of rapid communication has made the concept of an invisibly visible Muslim *Ummah* more real than ever before.

Notes:

1. Steger, 2010, p. 10.
2. Fuller, 2003, p. 73.
3. Steger, 2010, p. 10.
4. ibid., p. 14-18.
5. ibid., p. 132.
6. ibid., p. 152-154.
7. Singer, 2002, p. 148-49.

---- CHAPTER 26 ----

The Islamic World's Religious, Political, Cultural, and Modern Aspects

Introduction

Today, observers of world affairs are surprised by the power of the religious, political, and cultural aspects of Islamic civilization which, in spite of sectarian and political differences, still holds Muslims together in a common bond of a shared tradition and a way of life. But if we explain the basic idea and present-day crisis of Islamic civilization within the spectrum of four aspects—religious, political, cultural, and modern—we find its spiritual ideology entwined with rational actualization is as appealing as it was from the seventh to nineteenth centuries. The philosophy of the set of doctrines that came to be known as Islam is interwoven in a complicated spiritual, sociopolitical, cultural, communal, and religious organizational system of a faith. Its function is grounded in the elaboration of practical life amid the maze of spiritual intuition, establishing that the essence of Islam is a combined disposition of intuition and deliberation. Put simply, the religion of Islam is based on a system of belief revealed and enshrined in its scripture, the Qur'an, and its practices supplemented by the traditions of its Prophet Muhammad. Of the Qur'an's 6,235 verses, about 350 or for some five hundred contain discussions of direct legal relevance. However, of these verses at least 140 deal with devotional issues like prayer, religious alms, charity, and fasting. The next most common subjects are marriage and trade, each the focus of an additional seventy verses. Crime and punishment earn just thirty verses, and only five of the infractions mentioned have a punishment prescribed,[1] while the term

Shari'ah appears only once in the Qur'an, "*We have set you on a Shari'ah of command, so follow it.*"[2]

The Religious Aspect of Islam

In Islam, the Qur'an and Sunnah (the precepts and traditions of the Prophet) are the basis of a uniform and codified version of Shari'ah, or "Islamic law." The Shari'ah is a complex ethico-legal tradition, which has emerged as a hot subject of discussion concerning its meanings and application in today's demand for liberal democracy and the separation of religion and state. Though the word Shari'ah is generally defined as Islamic law, and it does indeed contain law, it also embraces elements and aspects that are not, strictly speaking, just law. Shari'ah is a total discourse, one in which all kinds of institutions find simultaneous expression: religion, legal, moral, political, and economic. It offers prescriptions on everything from prayers, diet, and dress to commerce, taxation, and warfare. Rather than law, then, Shari'ah is best understood as God's commanding guidance for an Islamic way of life. Muslim scholars from the early period concluded that the Shari'ah lies at the heart of God's revelation and that it is, in some sense, all-encompassing.

Muhammad was born in c. 570 in a noble family of Banu Hashim of a very influential Quraish tribe in Mecca. In the year 610, at the age of forty, Muhammad received his first revelation as a Messenger of Allah. Confiding only in his wife Khadija, and her literate Christian cousin Waraqa ibn Nawfal, who saw clear signs of prophethood in him, Muhammad kept quiet for two years about the revelation. For him the big question was who would believe and authenticate such an important authority of prophethood to a person who was illiterate and whose life had been ordinary. The history of revealed religions showed him that the legitimacy of a prophet emanates not only from the Divine but—in an important way—from a chain of past prophets descending from Adam, the first Prophet on earth. Finally, in the year 612 he felt encouraged to declare himself a Prophet and Messenger of God by identifying his generational legacy of prophethood descending from Prophet Abraham's son Isma'il. The Torah testifies that Hagar bore a son to Abraham and he named the son Isma'il, about whom God had promised Abraham, "I will make a nation of him, too, for he is your seed."[3] Muhammad was thus assured that his prophethood was authenticated not only through scriptural revelation, but was also genealogically verified by the Biblically acknowledged Abrahamic tradition of the chain of prophets.

Prophet Muhammad appeared as the first Messenger of God amongst the Meccan Arabs and the last and final prophet for the whole of humanity. He started preaching Islam initially not to alter the pre-Islamic tribal rules of *Sunna*, but to warn people against idolatry and to preach the Oneness of God. His opponents argued that he was violating the Meccan tradition and the tribal *Sunna* because even in pre-Islamic ways law and religion were so closely interwoven that an attack on religion would constitute a violation of tribal law. But he taught no new doctrine about one God. His message was in continuum with those of the Jewish prophets descending from Prophet Abraham the Patriarch of three revealed religions.

The Arab elders of Mecca did not understand that revelation was not something that happened only to the prophets in the past, but was an endless continuous progress of human creative consciousness. In the beginning they failed to understand Prophet Muhammad's message of revealed truth, which was symbolic and could not be understood literally. They were shocked by the fresh insight of a way of life revealed to the Prophet verse by verse and *surah* (chapter) by *surah* within a span of twenty-one years. In response to his sermons and call for moral renewal, the Meccans feared that new religion would bring the downfall of the shrine of Ka'ba which was the source of prosperity of the city, and put up fierce resistance to his preaching.

For the first ten years Prophet Muhammad's teachings, embodied in the term "Islam," were to constitute the final and definite religion for the whole of humanity. The *surahs* revealed during the Meccan period addressed social injustice, ethical and moral values, principles of mannerism, and rules to worship Allah the only One Transcendent God of Prophet Abraham instead of hundreds of statues placed inside and outside the Ka'ba. Five pillars of Islam were introduced—profession of faith (*shahada*), five daily prayers (*salat*), fasting during the month of Ramadan (*sawm*), alms tax (*zakat*), and pilgrimage to Mecca (*hajj*). These pillars were referred to in technical language as the basic articles of the religious practice and worship—a believer's individual obligations. These obligations are not to be enforced by the state; they must be observed by the individual believers regardless of the sanction of any authority.

The first adherents of the Prophet were limited to his family members and close friends, later joined by the oppressed, poor, and desperate people. Though the influential and wealthy Meccans did not foresee any political threat from the Prophet Muhammad's new religion during his twelve years of preaching, they strongly antagonized him and his followers. For the safety of the new believers the Prophet dispatched a group of his followers to Abyssinia, while he himself started spreading the message of Islam to the people of Taif as well as to the pilgrims visiting from different tribes, most importantly from Yathrib, today's Medina. He succeeded in converting some people of Yathrib to Islam, which proved a turning point in the establishment of the faith. The people of Yathrib needed an arbitrator to settle disputes that had broken out in the city between different tribes and groups. Apart from the newly converted Muslims, all other non-Muslim groups believed in the honesty and wisdom of Prophet Muhammad. The growing number of Muslims, posing a danger to their shrine of Ka'ba and a clear blow to their businesses, alerted the Meccans. They decided to finish Prophet Muhammad, who seeing forewarning signs of danger to his life, left his native city Mecca in the summer of 622 to settle in Yathrib.

Political Aspect of Islam

Prophet Muhammad's migration to Yathrib, referred to as the *Hijra*, or emigration, was later declared the beginning of the Islamic calendar, marking a new stage of development for the Islamic community. It changed the Prophet and his followers from a persecuted minority into a fear-free peacefully settled community. Most importantly, settling in Yathrib—renamed Medina or the "city of the Prophet"—helped the Prophet change from a mere preacher to an administrator, a politician, a statesman, a soldier, and a field marshal. He grew from his role as a spiritual guide to a political and military leader ready to lay the foundation of a state that would grow into an empire.

The first step he took to end the internal chaos and lawlessness in Medina was to frame the so-called Charter of Medina—also known as the Constitution of Medina, the first written constitution in the history of world. This helped him to govern politically by uniting the polytheists, non-Muslims, Jewish communities, and Muslims of local tribes as *Ansar* or helpers and the *Muhajirun* or immigrants into one community named "Muslim Ummah" which accepted citizens of the city-state of Medina, to be administered without any discrimination under a secular rule. The details of the Charter are still disputed among scholars on the basis that the constitution's authority was both spiritual and secular. It includes the phrase, "Whenever you differ about a matter, it must be referred to God and Muhammad" and also invokes God's name in many places; however, its rules and legal terms were secular, based on the traditional tribal laws of the Arabian Peninsula.

The Constitution of Medina addressed the rights and duties of every group within the community regarding the rule of law, as well as the issue of war. It recognized the Jewish community of Medina as separate tribes, and agreed on reciprocal obligations with them. Among its edicts, it obliged all the believers of any faith, including polytheist tribes, to fight unitedly as citizens of Medina if it came under threat of an attack. The large and powerful Jewish community living in Medina—probably from the time of Roman occupation of Palestine—was organized into several tribes, out of which three large tribes played an important role in signing the Charter of Medina. In spite of the agreed-upon terms of the Charter, they sparked conflicts that ended with the expulsion of some of the Jews from the State of Medina. Some Jews converted to Islam, some were killed, and a Jewish tribe was massacred, which according to some historians the Prophet had not ordered but had in fact condoned.

Though the Qur'an reveals more detail on religious and moral duties than political matters, Islam is described as a peace-loving *deen* but not a pacifist faith. The Prophet repeatedly stressed that Islam should be defended from the attacks of unbelievers, which may in some cases mean taking preemptive action. The Qur'an instructs, *"Fighting has been enjoined upon you while it is hateful to you."* This means, although the believers in Islam abhor violence, it can be a necessary evil for the protection and advancement of Islam.

A year and half after having settled in Medina, Muslims started making preemptive raids on caravans carrying merchandise to Mecca, to fracture the economy of the Meccans as well as to acquire goods for sustenance. These raids also served as training missions and provided confidence in their ability to face any attack on their city. In the Qur'anic revelations of the Medina period, the word *jihad* appears in many forms, but where *jihad* is a form of struggle with an external enemy posing a challenge it is interpreted as "*jihad* for war." In certain verses the concept of *jihad* is synonymous with war and fighting, testifying to the Prophet that war is a stratagem, which in the nineteenth century was phrased by Clausewitz: "war is a continuation of politics by other means." While the Qur'an prescribes all forms of *jihad* as a religious duty and fighting as hateful but necessary, it also states strict rules governing the conduct of a "just war."

Prophet Muhammad's ultimate goal was to restore Ka'ba to its original status of the house of Allah as established by Prophet Abraham and his son Isma'il. As a first step, it was revealed to the Prophet that one must face Mecca for the direction of prayer toward Ka'ba as *qibla*, rescinding the earlier direction of facing toward Jerusalem. Thus, conferring the location of *qibla* ordained a clear vision of distinct sanctity and idealization of Ka'ba. This also set a course of distinguished identity of Islam. In 630 Mecca was conquered by Prophet Muhammad and his followers without shedding a single drop of blood. The Prophet destroyed the idols in and around Ka'ba with his own hands, re-establishing the monotheistic legacy of Prophet Abraham. Soon the larger part of the Arabian Peninsula came under the sway of Islam.

When Prophet Muhammad died after a short illness on June 8, 632, at the age of sixty-three, nearly all of Arabia was under his control. His successors, the four "Rightly Guided Caliphs" carried on a wave of conquest, and within three decades the first expansion of the Islamic state arose as *dar-al-Islam*: a structure with an ability to transform itself from a religious community into a commonwealth of culture which soon developed into a civilization. The Arabs, who were originally a religious community and primarily non-political, became a determining factor in laying the foundation of political Islam during the second phase of Islamic world's expansion under the Umayyad and Abbasid dynasties.

The Muslims of the Arabian Peninsula, imposing their own qualities upon the ancient cultures of Egyptian, Babylonian, and Indus civilizations, and at the same time learning from the Greco-Roman, Persian, Chinese and Indian arts and sciences, appropriated a dynamic culture of their own and developed their *dar-al-Islam* into the Islamic civilization. It was not only the physical domination of these ancient civilizations but the power of knowledge and teaching acquired from regions beyond Arabia that helped the Muslims to develop a culture uniquely religious and universal.

The Cultural Aspect of Islam

Culture, according to *The Blackwell Dictionary of Sociology*, is the complex whole that consists of all the ways people think and act in the fields of knowledge, belief, art, morals, law, custom, and other capabilities and habits acquired by them as members of a society. Culture has both material and non-material aspects. Material aspects of culture include everything that is made, fashioned, or transformed as part of collective social life. Nonmaterial aspects include symbols from language, art, and ideas that shape and inform people's lives in relation to one another and the social systems in which they participate—most importantly, the ideas relating to attitudes, beliefs, values, and norms. Historians define culture as a higher achievement by the people of a group or a period of history—specifically in art, literature, philosophy, religion, and science.

The Bedouins of the Arabian Peninsula had no such cultural assets. In the genre of literature they had only poetry and the articulate Arabic language, to which religion was later added. The Qur'an was their only book of prose. They acquired all the important assets of culture from the people they conquered. They adopted and adapted what did not conflict with their religion, the injunctions of the Qur'an, and the Sunnah of their Prophet. They would teach their new faith to the conquered peoples and at the same time would learn from them the best part of their knowledge. Thus, Muslim conquerors were at the same time culturally conquered by the peoples of the diverse regions who had become their subjects, whether they had converted to Islam or were believers of some other faith.

Islamic culture is Islamic in the sense that it developed under the aegis of the Muslim rulers. The first success of the Arabs in their quest for a culture was adoption of a religion or an ideological way of life. After embracing Islam and declaring themselves Muslims instead of Arabs, their second success was the establishment of a state through the ideology of multiple forms of *jihad*, "jihad for war" being the lowest form. But the most important factor in facilitating the development of Islamic culture was the perfection of the Arabic language, the language in which the Qur'an was revealed. The perfect grammar and faultless language of the Qur'an soon became a cultural asset of the Muslims. It helped pave the way for the translation of almost every available philosophical, scientific, and literary text from any language into Arabic.

Within a short period, the spiritual believers of Islam succeeded in refining their culture and many great grammarians, philosophers, physicians, mathematicians, astronomers, and alchemists arose among them. However, as *lingua franca*, Arabic did not necessarily supersede the vernacular languages in home use as well as in the regions conquered by the Muslims. The Arabic language achieved importance when the Egyptians, Syrians, Berbers, and most importantly the Persians started using the language of the Qur'an in expressing their thoughts and feelings. Art, literature, and sciences of various regions, as well as customs, traditions, and subcultures of people that interacted with Islam, were cultivated to assimilate into an Islamic culture.

An important contribution of the Syrians and Persians to Muslim culture was art and architecture. The Persians tended to express their aesthetic feelings through their hands in the form of painting, sculpture, and architecture, whereas the Arabs expressed their feelings only through written poetry or their tongue. Since Islam strictly forbade representation of animate objects through sculpture or painting, newly converted Persian Muslims, using Arabic letters and verses from the Qur'an, raised calligraphy to the rank of a unique art. Art for art's sake or art for the sake of morality was spiritually cultivated and introduced as "art for the sake of religion." Qur'anic verses adorned mosques, mausoleums, and many important institutions. The Syrian Muslims under the Umayyad Caliphs, by modifying the Christian cathedral style, created a new and uniquely Islamic form of architecture for their mosques. The Syrians, who were familiar with the Hellenistic tradition—a fusion of Greco-Roman culture—helped their new masters understand science, philosophy, and many branches of knowledge which were unknown to the early Muslims from Arabia.

Islamic culture during its first six centuries rose to a sublime level and elevated Baghdad in Iraq and Cordova in Arab Spain to centers of its civilization. What historians define as culture was the way and lifestyle of the Muslims. The magnetism of spiritual Islam attracted and absorbed diverse cultures, customs, traditions, and knowledge of diverse arts and sciences. Its material and non-material culture was capable of setting Islamic civilization to an enlightened way to modernity. But at the dawn of the nineteenth century, the glory of Islamic civilization faded and its culture found itself stuck in rigid religious beliefs rather than the spiritually enlightening rationalism of the faith of Islam. The lifeline of the Islamic civilization is today in a state of confusion. Muslims are looking back to the lost glory of their religious, political, and cultural achievements, without realizing that the past can neither be revived nor modernized; it is the present which has to be modernized.

Modern Aspects of Islam—From Past to Present

As we know, the religion of Islam was initially spread by illiterate Arab Bedouin warriors who lived at a low level of material and non-material culture. During the pre-Islamic period, their cultural activity was limited and parochial, producing only poetry in the literary sphere and nothing worth mentioning in the fields of fine art, architecture, music, and science. Even when most of the Arabian Peninsula was under Muslim rule, there was no art, science or philosophy. Literate Jews and Christians lived in Mecca and Yathrib, but no Arabic translation of the Bible existed. The psalms and the gospels were accessible in Arabic in the eighth century at the earliest, and a definitive translation of the whole Bible was not available in Arabic even in the tenth century. At the advent of Islam, the Qur'an became the first book in the Arabic language and its Prophet's tradition was Islam's first cultural identity. Muslims, in the eyes of cultured Persians and Byzantines, were known as barbarian Bedouins. They desperately needed to gain new knowledge and adopt modernity in the context of their contemporary period.

When Islam, revealed in the Qur'an as a *deen* or a way of life, interacted with the Hellenistic Greco-Roman and Persian cultures, it receptively responded to the modernizing influences of the sophisticated lifestyles and knowledge of the world beyond the Arabian Peninsula. Islamic culture was hungry for knowledge. Its spiritual aspect was a kind of recipient culture offering hospitality to other cultures which Muslims felt to be useful. Modernization in Islamic culture started soon after Muslims moved out of the deserts of Arabia. It was due to their quest for modernity that within couple of centuries the towering and finely developed structure of an Islamic culture and civilization arose on the foundation of a pagan Bedouin desert society. It was their concept of *deen* which proved more inflammatory than their religion's prayers. Within a few centuries, Islamic civilization was ready to transmit modernity to the West. From the tenth to the sixteenth century, a new awakening in Europe laid the foundation of modern Western civilization.

At the beginning of nineteenth century, Islamic civilization was plunged into a state of blackout. European colonization of the world of Islam was on its height. Islamic regions were subjugated by the Europeans and divided into small nation-states. Throughout the twentieth century the pace of modernity kept accelerating—not in the Islamic civilization, but in Western civilization. After the two world wars, the Europeans, unable to maintain control of their colonized regions, started liberating their colonies, including the Muslim regions. Though the sunset of the twentieth century brought an end to European colonization of Muslim lands, the light of modernization has yet to shine on Islamic regions as in the West.

Today, Islamic civilization needs a secular based forward movement to modernity more than just an Islamic renaissance. In the present age of science and technological progress, Muslims are reaping the benefits of modernity but have lost the vigor of modernizing their civilization through their own *jihad* for modernity. Instead of boasting about their glorious past, the only thing for the Muslims of today should be to learn from their past as the early Arabs, while remaining passionate believers in Islam, embraced the modernity of the contemporary period by benefitting from Classical Greek philosophy and science, and Roman political and legal systems. In doing so, neither was their culture destroyed nor their religious belief fractured. As in the past, today there is an open door for Muslims to modernize through the cybernetic technologies available to them which are incessantly releasing a chain of new ideas in every field of knowledge. But there is a big difference between the interest in embracing modernity by the Muslims of today and the appetite for modernity of the Muslims of a thousand year earlier.

Notes:

1. Hefner, 2011, p.12.
2. Qur'an, 45:18
3. Torah, Genesis.

CHAPTER 27

Western Muslims and Impact of Conflicts in the Muslim World

(A Study within the Geopolitical Spectrum)

What if Islam had never existed? To some, it's a comforting thought: No clash of civilizations, no holy wars, no terrorists. Would Christianity have taken over the world? Would Middle East be a peaceful beacon of democracy? Would 9/11 have happened? In fact, remove Islam from the path of history and world ends up exactly where it is today.[*]

Introduction

Most immigrants who came to Europe during the twentieth century were Muslims from the European post-colonial nations of North Africa, the Middle East, and South Asia, who were invited as workers. With worsening economic conditions in Muslim countries, a new wave of immigrants suffering from poverty and unemployment started pouring into Europe, Canada, and the United States to seek better life. Though a majority of them were Muslims, peoples of other faiths from the southern and eastern Mediterranean and the Indian subcontinent started migrating to Western countries as well. After World War II, highly educated professionals, mostly Muslims, started immigrating to European countries, but the war in Vietnam invited many well qualified and highly learned persons to the United States. They were followed by their relatives, both skilled and unskilled workers. Many asylum seekers found a chance to enter the United States and make a better living. Today millions of Muslim refugees from the war-torn Middle East and North Africa are pouring into Europe, and some heading toward the United States. Their militant tendencies and growing numbers, overwhelming police in the small European continent, has created a fear of cultural collision. For the Muslims, the big question is who has created chaos in their countries by bombing their cities and homes, forcing them to flee to regions where they can find shelter and peace.

Migrants and Their New Generation

As compared to Europeans, the image of the United States and Canada as immigrant nations delineates Americans as much more self-assured, confident, and less nervous about the cultural and religious importance of Islam. Prior to the September 11 attacks, a majority of Americans seem to find it normal and natural that immigrants, most of them highly educated, come to their great country by choice. For them, identifying with America cannot be a problem either for the host society or for the newcomer immigrants. Therefore, immigrants, after being naturalized as American citizens, lived in peace. But after the attacks of September 11, 2001, Islam is now viewed more as a militant ideology than a peaceful faith. At the same time, in spite of anti-Islamic sentiments, Islam is the fastest growing religion by conversion in Europe and America. Islamic culture, anchored on spirituality and powered by its centuries-old traditions, tempts Western people to change rather than the other way around.

Today, throughout the Western world, white supremacists are criticizing Islam, threatening to send Muslims back to the countries from which they came. American Muslims, therefore, are naturally concerned about the chaos in the Muslim world which is impacting their status in the West. They are not looking toward Muslims of the world of Islam to sympathize with them, but rather to seek help from them if they are forced to leave the West.

The Intense Form of Islamic Revival

Until the last decades of the twentieth century, many Western thinkers believed that Muslims were becoming secularized because many Islamic countries were ruled by apparent Marxist-type regimes, such as Libya, Egypt, Yemen, Syria, Iraq, Indonesia, and Pakistan under Benazir Bhutto.

These Western thinkers held that since secularization was the wave of the future and the inevitable result of modernization, the clock could not be turned back. Peter Berger, the Boston University sociologist, told the *New York Times* in 1968 that by "the 21st century, religious believers are likely to be found only in small sects, huddled together to resist a worldwide secular culture." He later recanted, saying, "I think what I and most other sociologists of religion wrote in the 1960s about secularization was a mistake. ... Most of the world today is certainly not secular. It's very religious."[1] Today, as Rodney Stark, a professor of Social Sciences at Baylor University, argues in his latest book, *The Triumph of Faith*:

> The world is more religious than it has ever been. ... Meanwhile, although not growing as rapidly as Christianity, Islam enjoys far higher levels of member commitment than it has ever before, and the same is true for Hinduism. In fact, of all the great world religions, only Buddhism may not be growing. ... Indeed in combination with globalization, the worldwide intensification of religiousness [particularly of Muslims, including those living in the West] is causing what Samuel Huntington called Clash of Civilization.[2]

In the 1960s there erupted a massive revival of an intense and strict form of pristine Islam from Saudi Arabia—also defined as Islamic fanaticism—founded on the theological outlook of Abdel Wahhab. The great strength of fanaticism is that it demands the individual be prepared to lay down his life for his faith. With the start of Soviet-Afghan war, Wahhabism spread throughout the world of Islam. It was taught in *madrasahs* set up in many Muslim and Western countries, financed by the oil money of Saudi Arabia. This revival hit mostly Egypt and the Gulf States, as well as India, Pakistan, Bangladesh, and Indonesia. Its impact also succeeded in rolling back Ataturk-era secular measures when Turkey lifted the ban against *hijabs* for universities and offices in 2011. Moreover, the call to prayer now is done in Arabic instead of Turkish. Facilitated by safe and fast air travel, a huge increase in the number of pilgrims visiting Mecca from 100,000 a year in the 1960s to three million in 2015 reflects a wave of Muslim revival. Muslims coming back from Mecca after *Hajj* and *Umra* would bring for themselves and for their families and friends Arabian dresses like *hijabs, abayas,* and other souvenirs considered sacred. Above all, they would start using Arabic words: *inshallah* instead of sure, *jazakallah* for thanks, *maashallah* for great or well done, and *Allah-hafiz* for take care. This movement to Arabize the Muslims living in the West is seen as a challenge to Western culture and traditions.

Islam has ever been understood as a mighty and hyper-identity faith by Westerners, who have noticed its followers shaping every aspect of their life in the way of Islam and reducing allegiances to obligations beyond their faith. Christopher Caldwell, in his work, *Reflections on the Revolution in Europe: Immigration, Islam and the West,* referring to what Ernest Renan wrote in 1883, argues, "Certain habits inculcated by the Muslim faith are so strong that all differences of race and nationality disappear before the fact of conversion to Islam. The Berber, the Sudanese, the Circassian, the Malay, the Egyptian, the Nubian, once they have become Muslim, are no longer Berbers, Sudanese, Egyptians, etc.— they are Muslims." [3] This view is not just held by Islam's detractors but by its adherents, especially when they are trying to present Islam as a source of brotherhood that can serve as an antidote to Western racism or nationalism. When Malcolm X converted to orthodox Islam, he undertook the pilgrimage to Mecca in 1964. In his autobiography he included a letter sent from Mecca to his loyal assistants in Harlem, written from his heart, relating his experience of color- and race-blind Muslim solidarity that came to him as a revelation:

> For the past week, I have been utterly speechless and spellbound by the graciousness I see displayed all around me by people of all colors. ... America needs to understand Islam, because this is the one religion that erases from its society the race problem. There were tens of thousands of pilgrims, from all over the world. They were of all colors, from blue-eyed blonds to black-skinned Africans. But we were all participating in the same ritual, displaying a spirit of unity and brotherhood that my experiences in America had led me to believe never could exist between the white and the non-white. America needs to understand Islam, because this is the one religion that erases from its society the race problem. [4]

Unfortunately, while there are still positive engagements with Islam in the West, the overall trend in Europe and the United States today is becoming much more negative.

Muslims, mainly in the Islamic countries inflamed by the bogey of Machiavellian Western political philosophy and culture, espoused anti-Western sentiments—inherited from anti-colonialism—which became another aspect of Muslim revival. When the Soviet Union invaded Afghanistan in 1979, millions of Afghan refugees poured over the border into Pakistan. Refugee camps and *madrasahs* were ostensibly set up to educate them as well as to provide a recruiting ground for a new brand of soldiers impregnated with pristine Arab traditions. Known as *mujahedeen* or warriors, they were trained to fight the proxy war for the United States with the infidel invader the Soviet Union. A turn to the radical concept of *jihad* from the past for a solution to current conditions revived the strict form of Islam. A Chechen terrorist calling himself *mujahid* said during the siege of the theater in Moscow: "We will win in the end, because we are willing to die—and you are not." With the help of the United States' warfare logistics, and the *jihadi* spirit of the young warrior *mujahedeen* recruited from the Muslim lands, the Soviets were defeated, leading to the demise of Communism.

The end of the Cold War rejuvenated radical Islam, and Muslim *jihadists* found themselves leaders of Islamic civilization. Emboldened by their success against a global superpower, the *mujahedeen*, believing in the charismatic power of their faith, heralded a move to fulfill their dream of a "Universal Islam." They revolted against the Western-appointed corrupt and tyrannical leaders in Muslim countries and turned against Western culture and its modern customs. Terrorism in Muslim countries erupted as a new form of revolt against the appointed and protected rulers—brutal kings and dictators with the titles of presidents and prime ministers, supported by the West in former Islamic colonies. They started destroying any institutions in their own Muslim lands where Western education was imparted. They triggered a wave of terror within Muslim countries, forcing them to turn against the Western world. The 9/11 attacks on the United States exposed this intense and fanatic form of Islamic revival, and warnings of its dangerous consequences alerted Americans and Europeans. On the other hand, the Arabized Muslims envisioned it as a great step toward their dream of "Universal Islam."

Islam under Siege

After 9/11, Muslim *mujahedeen,* who had been the pride of the Western world, became its enemies. They understood that Islamic fanaticism is a formidable weapon in the struggle for cultural survival. Throughout Islamic history, it has served as a powerful mechanism to thwart all attempts by rival cultures to conquer, dominate, or even influence Islam. At the same time, it has given Islam the capacity to expand, not merely through conquest of territories but through the conquest of hearts and minds.

Fundamentalist Muslims are well aware that throughout history, wherever Islam has spread, there occurred a total revolutionary transformation in the culture of the conquered or converted—a transformation so thorough that it becomes difficult even to imagine a time when those lands were not Muslim. The fundamentalist would destroy ancient pre-Islamic relics, archaeological sites, and monuments to claim the regions as purely their own by erasing all signs of pre-Islamic cultures. Therefore, by interpreting Qur'anic injunctions in their own way and using suicidal tactics, declaring themselves *mujahedeen,* they exposed themselves as terrorists in the eyes of the Western world and fixed a label of disgrace for the Muslim world. The modern West understood the power of their intense and fanatical form of Islam as a potent weapon in the struggle for their religious and cultural survival and supremacy, as good a weapon in the war with the Soviets in Afghanistan as it was in the distant past. Their terrorist attacks provided an ample justification for the Westerners to bring Islam under siege in the West, suspecting both radical and traditional Muslims.

Though there is no Muslim world, many Muslim states and countries with diverse sects existing within those religious and cultural commonalities now defined as Islamic Civilization—a Westernized definition of *Dar-al-Salam*—came under assault in Europe and the United States. Policies of Western nations, particularly the United States, in order to fracture the unity of Islamic Civilization, have paradoxically helped forge a committed and Islam-minded community of Muslims. Micah Zenko, resident of the Council of Foreign Relations recently tallied up how many bombs the United States has dropped on other countries and the results are very depressing. Zenko determined that since January 2015, the United States has dropped around 23,144 bombs on Iraq, Syria, Afghanistan, Pakistan, Yemen, and Somalia, all Muslim-majority countries. Whether or not one thinks such bombing is justified, it's a blunt illustration of how much damage in life and property the West has inflicted on Muslim populations. Killing millions of Muslims and displacing millions more from their homelands became a suspicious act of the United States and its European allies. At the same time, many scholars of international affairs and humanitarian activists in the West have accused the United States of playing a double game. The role of Western powers in the Muslim world has caused great concern for Western Muslims and even their second and third generations are feeling great consternation regarding their future in the West.

Reactive Conflict Spillovers

After the 9/11 attacks, discussion around Islam has been shrill, which is a matter of great concern for the historians and thinkers of socio-political philosophy: Why are Muslims who were born, raised, and living in the West impacted by the conflicts abroad in the Muslim world? Why is there a reactive spillover of violence or strong sympathy with the Muslim regions where the Western military is involved? Whatever Western Muslims are displaying as the impact of conflicts in their home countries or in the Muslim world is in fact a product of "reflective conflict spillover." According to Professor Juris Pupcenoks, it happens when violence in domestic migrant-background communities occurs in response to conflicts abroad. Arguing on reflective conflict spillover in his book, *Western Muslims and Conflicts Abroad* he remarks:

> Reactive conflict spillover is an episode of protracted violence within a diasporic [dispersion of people from their original homeland] community in response to conflicts abroad. Frequently, spillovers occur following trigger events, which can be either violent (e.g. the beginning of the Second Intifada in Palestinian territories in 2000) or non-violent (e.g. the publication of Prophet Muhammad caricatures in 2005). In instances of planned terrorist acts and other cases of premeditated hostilities,

violent acts can occur without an immediate proceeding specific trigger event. However, more frequently, spillovers happen spontaneously following a vivid triggering event, such as news reports of horrifying crimes committed by a perceived adversary. Thus, spillovers can involve radicalization and acts by national liberation or ideological movements—as long as such behavior involves violent actions and is committed in response to an event taking place in another country.[5]

Reactive conflict spillovers happen when violence in domestic migrant-background communities occurs in response to conflicts abroad. Some believe that Muslims in the West are different, not only religiously but also socially and culturally. They appear less likely to fit into the cultural and socio-political ethos of the Western countries where they have been citizens for many decades. They are more likely to follow or give preference to their religious teachings and Islamic cultural heritage than the ways of the states of their newly naturalized citizenship.

The tragic events of 9/11 also opened a chapter of grave concern for Europeans and Americans over whether Muslims living in the West are loyal citizens or a fifth column. Fifth column, as it is well known, is any group of people who undermine a larger group—such as a nation or a besieged city—from within, usually in favor of an enemy group or nation. The activities of a fifth column can be overt or clandestine. Forces gathered in secret can mobilize openly to assist an external attack. The dramatic force of 9/11 was focused on Muslims, as they became seen as enemies inside the tent, as fifth columnists lying in wait for the signal to strike. Violence in the form of terrorism did come to Europe and the United States, but the conspirators were traced to Muslims linked with Saudi Arabian ideology of an intense form of fundamental Islam.

It is an irony that Saudi Arabia is still seen as a best friend of the United States and Europe when eighteen out of nineteen terrorists involved in the 9/11 attack were from Saudi Arabia. An important question facing both Western Muslims and Muslims worldwide is that whereas attacks were launched by the United States and its allies against Afghanistan, Iraq, and Syria, why was not even a finger pointed toward the Saudis or a warning issued? On the other hand, Muslims in the West have never appreciated the support provided by Saudi Arabia to the terrorist groups.

Islamophobia

The standard definition of Islamophobia is "prejudice against, hatred toward, or irrational fear of Muslims." Islamophobia is enshrined in many hate speeches in the United States as well as in Europe. Just as some people are anti-Semitic or hate evangelical Christians or African Americans, today in the West some are Islamophobic. Famous evangelist Franklin Graham told NBC news following the 9/11 attacks: We're not attacking Islam but Islam has attacked us. The God of Islam is not the same God. He's not the son of God of the Christian or Judeo-Christian faith. It's a different God, and I believe it is a very evil and wicked religion." Pastor R. Parsley of the huge World Harvest Church of Columbus, Ohio, a spiritual adviser to John McCain, said: "The fact is that America was founded, in part, with the intention of seeing this false religion [Islam] destroyed, and I believe 9/11 was a generational call to arms that we can no longer ignore." Many Christians have expressed hate against Islam, while former president Donald Trump, while still a presidential candidate was a blunt critic of Islam, behaving as an enemy of Muslims living in the West.

President Barack Obama was impelled to take aim at nativism in his final State of the Union address on Tuesday, January 12, 2016, offering a not-so-veiled jab at politicians, specifically GOP presidential candidates, who called for keeping Muslims from entering the country and have denigrated other minorities. President Obama said: "[The U.S. needs] to reject any politics that targets people because of race or religion, [not as] a matter of political correctness, [but to maintain the country's values.] It's a matter of understanding what makes us strong....The world respects us not just for our arsenal; it respects us for our diversity and our openness and the way we respect every faith....When politicians insult Muslims, when a mosque is vandalized, or a kid bullied, that doesn't make us safer. That's not telling it like it is. It's just wrong. It diminishes us in the eyes of the world. It makes it harder to achieve our goals."

Noam Chomsky, the noted activist and MIT professor emeritus, remarked in an interview on January 22, 2016 with *The Huffington Post*, "The Republican Party has become so extreme in its rhetoric and policies that it poses a serious danger to human survival. ... Today, the Republican Party has drifted off the rails." Chomsky said the GOP and its presidential candidates are "literally a serious danger to decent human survival." GOP presidential candidates are aggravating the situation in their debates by making commitments that Muslims should be banned from immigrating to the United States; and that those already living, even as citizens, should be sent back to the countries from where they came. Such rhetoric is creating unrest amongst the Muslims, and what we see in Western Muslims and the impact of conflicts in the Muslim world will consequentially be a dangerous situation as visualized by Professor Chomsky.

Efforts to deny any link between violent acts of terrorism and Islam are widespread, in the news media as well as government circles. It is an acknowledged fact that terrorism in the West is usually perpetrated by a handful of misguided individuals, mostly with connections to radical networks abroad, as has been proved in the case of the woman terrorist Tashfeen who had connections in Saudi Arabia. Many experts in foreign affairs do not believe that Islam is on a collision course with the West or that it is inherently inimical to the modern age. It is, rather, the negative attitude of the West toward Islam which has created Islamophobia, scaring the Western Muslims.

Is Something Going Wrong with the Muslims?

We are aware that billions of Muslims are not motivated by their faith even to hate, let alone to kill, those who do not fully share their religious outlook. Many Muslim religious scholars teach that Islam is a religion of peace. But we cannot ignore that many terrorists today are Muslims who justify their atrocities on religious grounds. Rodney Stark in *The Triumph of Faith* argues:

> Responses to Muslim terrorism have long generated confessions that terrorism exists because Americans, and Westerners in general, have offended Muslims in many ways, including by supporting Israel, that they really have only themselves to blame. In the immediate wake of the 9/11 attack, former president Bill Clinton cited the Crusades as one of "our crimes against Islam." More recently, while speaking at the National Prayer Breakfast in Washington, and in the aftermath of televised beheadings by ISIS terrorists, President Obama also stressed Christian guilt for the Crusades.[6]

But it also seems important to point out that most Muslim terrorism is against *other Muslims*. It seems unlikely that even the most ardent apologists for Islam would suppose that either Western or American misdeeds are the reason why Sunni Muslims kill and are killed by Shi'ite Muslims. It is time to raise an important question: Is something going wrong with the Muslims that every terrorist act points toward them? One of many reasons is that the rise of a far more intense and militant Islam—justified and promoted as the need of the hour during America's proxy war with the Soviets—seems primarily to have been a source of modern terrorism.

Traditional Islam, isolated during the European colonial rule until the end of the nineteenth century, was relatively lax and accommodative to worldliness. When modernity broke down and isolation and oil money enriched the Arabs, the result was not the proliferation of a new rational "enlightenment" focused on secular political ideology, but the rise of national and international Islamic religious leadership. These new religious leaders and scholars of Islamic *Shari'ah*, such as Maulana Maudoodi, generated a kind of militant commitment to a variety of intense forms of Islam, partly in a reaction against secularism and partly in response to Muslim economic/industrial backwardness. It appeared in the form of intensification rather than a regression into a peaceful and pious past. We can say that modernity in the world of Islam resulted in an increase of religiousness instead of a modernity of rational and scientific enlightenment.

What Is in Store for the Muslims?

The prospects for a harmonious relationship between Islam and the West seem uncertain. A period of cordial relation between the fanatically intense and militant Muslims and the allied American and British Westerners lasted for a very short period of a decade or so. Soon after the fall of the Soviet Union, voices were being raised by thinkers and politicians in the West that this was the time to take care of "Islamic Civilization." I remember reading an article in the *Los Angeles Times* in 1990 stating that after the demise of Marxism the only ideology that could pose a threat to American supremacy is Islam. Works and interviews with Bernard Lewis appeared, followed by Samuel Huntington's famous book,

The Clash of Civilizations and the Making of World Order, followed by many debates and discussions.

Before a well-planned clash of civilization could be ignited, the "Desert Storm" campaign against Saddam Hussein was administered as a testing ground. For me it is neither pride nor a matter of glorification—as since my childhood I have hated war from the core of my heart—that the concept of *"Jihad* for war" is so powerful in Islam that within a short period it shattered two great empires soon after the advent of Islam, and went a long way toward bringing the Soviet empire to its knees. It took ten years for the U.S. think tank to find a new way to tackle the *jihadi* ideology by turning the *mujahedeen* into terrorists, engaging them to destroy their own believers of liberal and traditional Islam. The West has created an atmosphere of uncertain chaos in the Muslim world by adopting a careful and safe role for themselves and the deadly start of a horrible World War for the Muslims, right from the footage of September 11, 2001.

Notes:

*   Graham Fuller, former Vice Chairman of National Intelligence Council at CIA, in his article "A World Without Islam," Foreign Policy Magazine, Jan/Feb 2008.

1.   Stark, 2015, p. 5 and 9
2.   Ibid., p. 1 and 9.
3.   Caldwell, 2009, p.129.
4.   Malcolm X, letter from his autobiography.
5.   Pupcenoks, 2016, p. 2.
6.   Stark, 2015, p. 104.

CHAPTER 28

The Western World, Racial Intolerance And Islamophobia

Introduction

Throughout human history—more emphatically during the past five hundred years—we have been taught by intellectuals, politicians, statesmen, businessmen, and economic leaders that human racial biology reveals certain races are biologically rather than morally and culturally better or inferior than others. These teachings have led to major injustices to Jews, Muslims, and non-Christians during the Spanish Inquisition; to Native Americans and others during colonial times; to Black Africans during slavery and Reconstruction; to Jews and other Europeans during the reign of the Nazis in Germany; and to groups from Latin America and the Middle East, and many others, during modern political times.

The Spanish Inquisition—which had its greatest impact on the formation of the newfound Western world known as America—has not been researched and discussed by the thinkers of social sciences. The Spanish Inquisition did not focus on religion alone, but expanded to include ethnicity or race, introducing the notion of "impurity of blood." It was about classes of people rather than just categories of belief. It was run by those in political power who ruled and defined religion, ideology, and race or ethnicity. Columbus's voyage to America was made at the peak of the Inquisition. Thus, the conquistadores justified their maltreatment of Native Americans by declaring them subhuman and incapable of having and understanding rational or abstract ideas and of running their own world. They were deemed morally incapable of becoming Christian. Thus, the inhuman conquest of America continued. Racial theories remained crucial in justifying the maltreatment of the local peoples.[1]

The European settlers committed all sorts of atrocities to wipe out the aborigines of the newfound continent. Years later, enslaved Africans were brought in as cattle to replace the rapidly dying indigenous Americans as a work force for exploiting the New World. The first African slave ship to reach America was called *The Good Ship Jesus* captained by Sir John Hawkins, a cousin of Sir Frances Drake, who was granted permission from Queen Elizabeth I for his first voyage in 1562. Hawkins, who had a reputation for being a religious man who required his crew to "serve God daily" and to love one another, was allowed to carry Africans to the Americas with their own free consent. Religious services were held on board the ship twice a day.

Thus, *The Good Ship Jesus* became involved in the Atlantic slave trade under Sir John Hawkins, who organized four voyages to West Africa and the West Indies between 1562 and 1568. Off the coast of Africa, near Sierra Leone, Hawkins captured three to five hundred slaves, mostly by plundering Portuguese ships, but also through violence and subterfuge, promising Africans free land and riches in the new world. He sold most of the slaves in what is now known as the Dominican Republic. He returned home with a profit and ships laden with ivory, hides, and sugar. And thus began the slave trade!

The Race Phenomenon

The Spanish Inquisition's theories to explain human differences, pre-Adamite and degenerate, were later adopted mainly by the English, Anglo-Americans, and the French in the seventeenth and eighteenth centuries. These views provided the basis of racist thought in regard to people of color and are still with us in twenty-first century, both in the general public and in Western sciences. Today, perhaps, because of the European settlers in America, the same biological myth of human race is being revived to make "America great again." However, one of the important lessons that may be derived from the meaning of race phenomenon in relation to human experience is associated with the archetypal energy of "wisdom" and its connection to the archetypal energies of "compassion, love, oneness, truth."

Wisdom, as we know, is the ability to be conscious of what is happening around us, to see the higher truth, and express ourself with compassion.

Feeling love rather than judgment changes negative energy into harmless energy. The wise heart embraces others with a feeling of compassion for whatever stage human beings are at in their march of spiritual and rational evolution. It approaches with a feeling of "love and oneness" rather than cultural judgment.[2] Within this perspective, to bind mankind together as one humanity, words of wisdom by the Persian sage Sheikh Sa'adi Sherazi were chosen to grace the Hall of Nations at the United Nations building in New York:

Of one Essence is the human race,
Thusly has creation put the Base;
One Limb impacted is sufficient,
For all Others to feel the Mace.[3]

بنی‌آدم اعضای یک پیکرند
که در آفرینش ز یک گوهرند
چو عضوی به درد آورَد روزگار
دگر عضوها را نمانَد قرار

Secretary-General Ban Ki-moon said in Tehran: "[...] At the entrance of the United Nations there is a magnificent carpet – I think the largest carpet the United Nations has – that adorns the wall of the United Nations, a gift from the people of Iran. Alongside it are the wonderful words of the great Persian poet, Sa'adi:

All human beings are members of one frame,
Since all, at first, from the same essence came.
When time afflicts a limb with pain
The other limbs at rest cannot remain.
If thou feel not for other's misery
A human being is no name for thee.

These verses [of Sa'adi Sherazi] were inspired by a Hadith, or saying, of the Prophet Mohammed in which he says: 'The example of the believers (Muslims) in their affection, mercy, and compassion for each other is that of a body. When any limb aches, the whole body reacts with sleeplessness and fever.'"[4]

On December 10, 1948, what was affirmed by the United Nations General Assembly was just not a Declaration of Human Rights, but the Universal Declaration of Human Rights— irrespective of race, color, or culture—based on natural moral and legal rights of the whole of mankind. In 1950, UNESCO issued a statement asserting that all humans belong to the same species and the phenomenon of "race" is not a biological reality but a myth.[5] If this is true, then why is the rhetoric of racism spoken throughout the world and especially the United States today? So far, facts prove that the appeal of "universal human rights" and the intrinsic rectitude of "*of one essence is the human race*" failed when President Trump during his election campaign declared that he would ban the entry of Muslims into the U.S., and also build a wall to keep the Mexicans and the Latinos—as if to keep the barbarians away—from crossing the border; that he was in favor of water-boarding and even worse torture. Such behavior of the President and the ruling party of the U.S. poses a big question: Is the U.S. exempt from the declaration of Universal Human Rights and the statement of UNESCO?

Racial Discrimination in America

When President Trump, with all his racist remarks, raised his slogan to make "America great again" it was no surprise to realize he meant that America was "great" when its foundation was laid on racism, first by Columbus and then by the early European settlers. Underlying the grand experiment that is called America or the United States has been an ongoing struggle regarding the meaning of race and culture. Historically, a common human heritage has never been accepted to design American identity within the framework that all human beings belong to the same species and that "race" is not a biological reality but a myth. The United States of America, in the name of progress was initially an attempt to evolve as a unique future-oriented, fast-paced "one culture" based on immigrants from every corner of the world. But those who were in control, unfortunately, overlooked how capitalist forces were based on a value-exchange of energy. The British philosopher and Nobel Prize in winner Bertrand Russell Bertrand in the *Russell's America*: Volume II 1945–1970,

Part II, *The Entire American People Are On Trial, Ramparts magazine* (March 1970), p. 474 has remarked:

> Violence is not new to America. White men of European stock seized the lands of indigenous Indians with a ferocity which endured until our own times. The institution of slavery shaped the character of the nation and leaves its mark everywhere. Countless "local" wars were mounted throughout the twentieth century to protect commercial interests abroad. Finally, the United States emerged at Hiroshima as the arbiter of world affairs and self-appointed policeman of the globe.[6]

The concept of race was dissected and divided, to become a tool for manipulating people and controlling the exchange of energy, and a whole group of people, African slaves in particular, were devalued as human beings. In the United States, a future-oriented culture, people became too busy looking forward, often failing to appreciate the beauty of the present by distorting the past to justify a present sense of the self. In this context, the idea of race and culture as a celebratory concept was never allowed to fully emerge.

Today, it is an irony of all mankind that people are excessively suckered by what is called "the reality of technique," or "the theory of human behavior." Instead of following great intellectuals who possess qualities of human excellence and heroes of instantiative ideals, people are being educated to believe and follow the bionic types controlled by wires and IT gadgets.[7] Ignoring human wisdom and dependence on information technology and artificial intelligence is leading, particularly in the U.S., to convictions without the ideals *"of one essence is the human race."*

> *Man is a bowl so finely made that Reason*
> *Cannot but praises him with kisses. . .*
> *Yet Time the potter, who has made this bowl*
> *So well, then smashes it to bits again.* — Omar Khayyam

Notes:

1. Robert Wald Sussman: *The Myth of Race,*
2. Carroy Ferguson: *Evolving the Human Race: A Spiritual and Soul Centered Perspective.*

3. Wikipedia: *Saadi Shirazi.*
4. Saying of Prophet Muhammad: *Sahih Bukhari.*
5. A Magazine of Ideas: *Philosophy Now, Talking about Human Rights, issue # 118.*
6. Bertrand Russell's America: Volume II 1945–1970, Part II, The Entire American People Are On Trial, Ramparts magazine (March 1970), p. 474
7. William J. Bennett: *The Book of Man.*

CHAPTER 29

Islam and Modernity:
Muslims in Search of
Modern Ummah

A synthesis of modernist and traditionalist interpretations of Islam
can make it compatible with changing modes of time.

Reviving Muslim *Ummah*

Muslims, in their quest for the revival of an *Ummah* of the Prophet of Islam's time, need to evolve a modernized *Ummah*. In spite of many complications, Muslims are realizing that modernization requires a spiritual reorientation. Over the past several decades, Islamic paradigms of Pan-Arabism, Pan-Islamism, socialism, fundamentalism, and in some states secularism, have proved unhelpful in rejuvenating a Muslim *Ummah*—a universal community of Muslims—to be appropriate within the Islamic paradigm of modernization. Though today Muslim nation-states are in shackles, there is a silent majority within as well as outside Islamic regions, struggling to revive, recultivate, and harmonize *Shari'ah* and universal morality, *haquq al abad* and human rights, Islamic economy and the Western financial system, state and religion, and most importantly Islam and the modern world. But the problem is how to integrate modern values into the society of traditional Islam. If change is not smoothly homogenized it can disrupt socio-political systems and pose a challenge to moral values. Abdolkarim Soroush, an Iranian philosopher, currently a visiting scholar at the University of Maryland, has expressed this challenge in sharp antitheses:

> A modern person is critical and demanding (not placid and inert),
> in search of change (not merely of understanding), in favour of
> revolution (not just reform), active (not passive), at home with

scepticism and anxiety (not certitude), interested in clarity and causality (not bewilderment and enchantment), prone to pride and joy (no sorrow of separation), mindful of life (not death), in pursuit of rights (not only duties), sponsor of creative (not imitative) art, oriented to the external (not just the internal) world, a lover (not a despiser) of life, an intervener in (not merely user of) the world, a user of reason in the service of criticism (not just for understanding). Modern humanity is, in few words, oblivious to its limits and proud of its creative possibilities.[1]

Thus, change in a society is brought about by many factors. But traditional Islamic society is faced with the outside world and more severely with decisions to modernize from within. Though the seeds of change were sowed in the Muslim world by the European colonization of Muslim regions, their influence was received as a greater challenge from the outside world to the centuries-old traditions of the Islamic way of life and the practices of its religious tenets.

Modernization began in the West with industrialization and commercialization. It was introduced and inducted into the artefacts of contemporary life in the European colonies, including electricity, railways, and new forms of communications, industries, and household consumer goods. But modernity in its political, social, and cultural processes needs an integration with, or in certain cases a replacement of existing religious ways of life with new ideas of political, cultural, and educational systems. It begins when a society, or in the case of Islam an *Ummah,* assumes an inclination of enquiry into how people are free to make their choices in political, economic, religious, moral, and personal affairs. In an attempt to introduce modernity to the Muslim *Ummah*—the term *Ummah* serving here as a substitute for communities—the freedom to doubt the efficacy of available religious traditions and institutionalize the implication of rationality, debate, and discussion, would lead to conclusions over which rational men and women may agree or disagree.

The Road to Modernization

The first road leading to modernism is the will and capacity of Muslims to control and change their existing social phenomena with the power of human reason. Instead of leading a fight against the movement to modernity and seeing it as a corruption of their Islamic cultural values, Muslims need to understand that their present stagnation is not an interval between their glorious past and the re-establishment of that glorious past. Past glories can neither be revived nor are they applicable to the modern age. As the universe is changing and evolving every moment, the needs and ways of humanity demand a new system for every age. Therefore, modernity has to be carved out of the foundations laid by the past. Fazlur Rahman, who was professor of Islamic thought at the University of Chicago, argues in *Islam & Modernity: Transformation of an Intellectual Tradition*:

> There are basically two aspects of reformist orientation. One approach is to accept modern secular education as it has developed generally speaking in the West and to attempt to "Islamize" it— that is, to inform it with certain key concepts of Islam. This approach has two distinct goals, although they are not always distinguished from one another: first to mold the *character* of students with Islamic values for individual and collective life, and second, to enable the adepts of modern education to imbue their respective fields of learning at higher levels, using an Islamic perspective to transform, where necessary, both the content and the orientation of these fields. The two goals are closely connected in the sense that molding character with Islamic values is naturally undertaken at the primary level of education when students are young and impressionable. However, if nothing is done to imbue fields of higher learning with an Islamic orientation, or if attempts to do so are unsuccessful, when young boys and girls reach the higher stages of education their outlook is bound to be secularized, or they are likely to shed whatever Islamic orientation they have had—which has been happening on a large scale.[2]

Returning to the Qur'an as a touchstone of true Islam, as introduced by Muhammad ibn Abdal Wahhab, resonated to some degree in freeing Islam from unnecessary superstitions and accretions, but it also blocked the road to modernity. Abdel Wahhab's religious appropriation, instead of bringing *Shari'ah* into alignment with modern realities and the traditions of scientific knowledge, pushed Muslims back to the age when Islam had first appeared as a new faith.

The doctrine of Wahhabism is "scripture alone" and the rejection of interpretations of *Shari'ah* law which had evolved through the centuries, and the canonical clarification of theology gave birth to Saudi-inspired Salafism and Wahhabism. Abu Jaffar al Mansur (754-775), a great Muslim ruler who was in power for over twenty-five years as a Caliph in the beginning of the Abbasid regime, and who had dissociated from radical *Shari'ah*, once requested Imam Malik (711-795) to write a comprehensive book outlining verdicts on matters of daily life. He wanted that book to be the standard by which all matters were resolved in the way of Islam. Imam Malik argued: "The Prophet's companions settled in different provinces with each of them having his share of knowledge about Islam. If you were now to enforce a single opinion on them all, this will inevitably lead to a great deal of chaos and trouble." These words of wisdom by Imam Malik apply today in greater measure. We have a wealth of Islamic knowledge, research, and scholarship, which has interpreted the *Shari'ah* law in a manner that is compatible with the social and political ethos of contemporary society. Hans Kung, in *Islam, Past, Present & Future*, is of the view that:

> Many Muslims recognize that Arab-Islamic [Wahhabism] culture, insistently fixated on its heyday long past, suppressed all tendencies toward reform and enlightenment which could have led to a paradigm change and thus remained in permanent crisis. It is not by a chance happening of history that in contrast to European countries, Islamic countries did not manage to develop from trade capitalism to an industrial society. The well-known consequence was a complete isolation from scientific and technological progress and thus a scientific, technical, military and cultural subordination to the West, which some individual Muslim groups still compensate for by fighting against the "unbelieving West." A dependence on European colonial powers, which lasted into the twentieth century, made this fatal situation worse.[3]

The search for the development of a modern *Ummah* by the Muslims needs to be actualized through the "human factor": Muslim people, their attitudes and humanistic values, their sense of responsibility, and their quest to modernize their education. Concepts of a scientific worldview and a way of shaping their own lives must be integrated within the paradigm of Islamic values. In some Islamic countries, a pattern of semi-modernity based on technological innovations with the help of petro-dollars, or in some cases foreign aid, is adopted from Western countries, but their socio-political ways and intellectual freedom are not wanted.

The first step toward modernization of the Muslim *Ummah* is "Reformation" based on a synthesis of modernist and traditionalist interpretations of the way of Islam to make it compatible with the changing modes of time. Reformation will help Islamic culture to proceed to the next stage, which is "Enlightenment." This leads to intellectual freedom, human dignity, and human rights, and guarantees against the attacks of religious fundamentalism and exploitation by the state. Because of a lack of intellectual freedom, many Muslim scholars of science and liberal arts had to immigrate to Western countries. The results of this emigration include the fact that on account of their intellectual freedom and equal rights for women, the next generation will not be following an orthodox and excessively literal interpretation of Islam.

Hans Kung in his work, *Islam Past, Present & Future* quotes the Muslim scholar Malek Chebel, who said, "One must recall the hope of millions of Muslims who reject radical Islam and who attach importance to rediscovering a positive Islam, that of Averroes, of critical thought or of the nineteenth-century 'Renaissance' (*nahdah*), in a word an Islam of the Enlightenment, an enlightened Islam." [4] The subject of enlightenment may have been troubled by the question of faith, but it is not anti-religious. It is important to note that the modernization of the Muslim *Ummah*, as in the past, can only be carried out through enlightenment and political secularization—not to be confused with general secularism—based on privatization of faith and the separation of religion from the political system, which has to include modern science, technology, and liberal democracy.

Islam and Modernity

The Muslim *Ummah's* first five to seven centuries of progress took place on account of its gaining scientific and philosophical knowledge from foreign civilizations. Today, modern Muslims can learn the process of modernization from the West in the same way the West learned how to get out of their dark age from the Muslims. If Muslims fear that the Western secular system can turn into a rational atheism or agnostic secularism, they first have to understand the difference between it and the "Way of Islam" or *deen,* which in its essence is holistic and whose sum is greater than the religious tenants. It is difficult for the Muslims, as it was difficult for the religious Western nations, to adopt a modern civilization by compromising belief in the traditions of Judaism and Christianity. Those who follow Islam as a religion must understand that religions in the twenty-first century are no longer followed in the same way as they were in the pre-reformation ages. For Islamic faith to be understood as one part-system among diverse others is to be set today within the broader social system of Muslim nations as a guarantee of its "civilizational unity" alone.

A Muslim today is individually modernized, but holistically with all his ideas and functions he is integrated into a unitary religious and moral system. Unfortunately, he fears he will be ideologically colonized by the godless Western modernity. Therefore, Muslim *Ummah's* march to modernization and secularization is a complex process, but it is not impracticable. For Islamic countries, modernity is not a harmful Western penetration into the faith of Islam. Modernity has embraced the whole world and cannot be reversed, even by the Islamic countries where it is there in one way or another. It is not just a phase, but an epistemic shift which Muslim intellectuals have to recognize; and they must understand that the way of Islam assists rather than impedes the modernization process. Today there is neither one Muslim world nor one Muslim *Ummah* because of Muslims judging themselves through the lens of Islam as a religion. Muslims all over the world must understand that only modernization rather than the fundamental principles of Islamic religion, can establish a new Muslim *Ummah.* It is time to accept that the way of Islam is congruent with modernity.

In order to revitalize Islam, Muslims have to revive their relationship between Islam and science. They need to open up the mundane subject of the compatibility of Islam with modern science in the light of Albert Einstein's famous saying: "Science without religion is lame, religion without science is blind." It is time to discard the view that modern science, including space exploration, is anti-religion. For some two centuries, the world of Islam has confronted the assault of alien civilizations and worldviews which have challenged the very tenets of Islam itself. This assault has also destroyed much of the civilization created by Islam over the centuries. From the family to the state, from economics to mosque architecture, from poetry to medicine, all are affected by the alien worldview of the modern world, as its ethos was first incubated and nurtured in the West and then spread to other continents, and has also been imposed upon the Islamic world and its peoples.[5]

Muslims, with the message of a transcendent truth, undiluted by human error or historical accident, slumbering as passive victims, are now facing the active aggression of the modern Western world's rational, materialistic, skeptical, agnostic, and atheistic challenges. As a solution, the sociologist Shmuel Eisenstadt has coined the term "multiple modernities," arguing that the cultural program of transformation and basic institutional constellations that emerged in Europe are not the only path to modernity. Other cultures and regions will travel diverse pathways and have varied experiences in their modernization process.[6] This means one model does not fit all the nations and cultures of the world. When it comes to reconciling the deep tensions and contradictions between religion, democracy, and modernization, it is not necessary for them to follow the Western model. Muslims, therefore, can either set their own pathway or adopt a process which is befitting the way of Islam and suitable to its religion in order to modernize the Muslim *Ummah*.

Bernard Lewis argues in *From Babel to Dragomans*, "Islamic history [which] provides its own models of revolution [as well as change]; its own prescriptions on the theory and practice of dissent, disobedience, resistance, and revolt." He further adds, "It is now a truism that in Islam there is no distinction between church and state, unlike Christendom [where] the existence of two authorities goes back to the founder of Christianity, who enjoined his followers to render to Caesar that which is Caesar's and to God that which is God's. There are two powers: God and Caesar." [7] But for the Prophet of Islam both powers are conjoined; he was a Messenger of God and a head of a state who dispensed justice, raised taxes, promulgated laws, and made both war and peace. This is a sacred paradigm of Islamic history which chronicles the way of the Prophet, enshrined in scripture, tradition, and social order. Thus, the main hurdle in the way of modernization of the Muslim *Ummah* is the belief of "Islamic exceptionalism," describing an essentialized conception of Muslim politics and history. However, a post-Islamist transformation is silently taking place, focused on a new Muslim identity which is challenging and facing the challenges of the fundamentalists.

Muslim scholars have long argued that Islamic societies are uniquely resistant to secularism and liberal democracy due to an inner antimodern, religious cultural dynamic that has few parallels with other religious traditions or civilizations. Modern technological innovations which have arguably brought about drastic social changes in diverse societies more far-reaching than those caused by the industrial revolution for the Muslims living in the West, a reformist trend is beginning to emerge which is also being transmitted to the motherlands from where they emigrated. The trend of reformation in thought is particularly visible in the United States, which has a large presence of Muslim elites from various Islamic countries and cultures. For them it is easier to express their ideas and methodologies in the West than in their home countries, where free expression of thought is difficult and in some cases impossible.

Notes:

1. Soroush, 2000, p. 54-69:56.
2. Rahman, 1984, p. 130-31
3. Kung, 2007, p. 645-46.
4. Chebel, Quoted by Kung, 2007, p. 647.
5. Nasr, 1994, p. vii.
6. Eisenstaedt, p. 1-29.
7. Lewis, 2004, p. 300 and 303.

CHAPTER 30

Rumi the Philosopher

*". . . A mystic who is capable of philosophizing and penetrating
into the meaning of physical and spiritual phenomena."*
(Nicholson: *Rumi Poet and Mystic*)

The Physical and Spiritual Phenomena

After many years of pondering, I believe that the mystical poet-saint-literary genius Jalaluddin Rumi, in the field of Islamic literature and philosophy, stands high above other sages (*hukama*), philosophers, and religious scholars of the past or present. The magnitude and insight of his thought, and his instinctive and experiential approaches supported by his formal education, have proved Rumi fully capable of inquiring, penetrating, and philosophizing deeply into the meanings of both physical and spiritual phenomena. His profound understanding and addressing of the complexities of a coherent philosophy is at least comparable with that of any contemporary philosopher of his period. Though a passionately practicing Muslim, he was by temperament still a non-conformist, making his life an example of the creative unity that reconciles opposites.

Although he does not stand in the order of a particular school of philosophers, he was fully aware of the commentaries and interpretations of Muslim thinkers about Classical Greek philosophy. Rumi's *Mathnawi* is sufficient testimony that he comprehends the wisdom of the rational philosophy of classical Greek thinkers, while remaining ever conscious that logic is a poor substitute for life. When Rumi argues, he is no less a dialectician than Socrates or Plato. He places the guiding role of spiritual wisdom over and above that of worldly wisdom. In one simple verse in the *Mathnawi*, he appreciates and praises the stellar figures of Greek philosophy, in rhyming poetry within an overarching holistic frame of Love:

Hail! O Love that brings us good gain—
you that are the physician of all our ills,

The remedy of our pride and vainglory—
O Love, you are our Plato and our Galen.[1]

Rumi may sometimes seem to deviate from the wisdom of the Greeks, as he places high value on a philosophy of faith and the study of the wisdom of the faithful rather than relying on logic. This does not mean that he is against rational philosophy; rather, he is concerned about its insufficiency to resolve the ontological problems of existence, to be sufficiently helpful in the course of a true human development toward "perfection" or "wholeness." He argues specifically that the fruits of reason alone are neither stable nor complete enough to grasp ultimate truths. Speaking of the intellect's suggestibility, Rumi remarks in the *Mathnawi* about its instability:

This vacillation is a prison and a motive
that will not let the soul go in any direction.

This motive draws in one direction, and that in another,
each motive saying, "I am the right way."[2]

These verses project the core of Rumi's cognitive philosophy, maintaining that the resulting uncertainty causes an unavoidable skepticism when one impulse draws toward the materialistic life while the other is drawing toward spiritual life. For him, true knowledge is "double winged," a faith that incorporates reason, while reason and opinion (without a spiritual company) are single-winged. He proposes that knowledge is complete and eternal only when wedded with spiritual truth; otherwise, its approach is both materialistic and partial, and thus remains in physical confinement.

Knowledge has two wings, Opinion one wing:
Opinion is defective and curtailed in flight.

The one-winged bird soon falls headlong;
then again it flies up some two paces or a little more.

> *The bird Opinion, falling and rising,*
> *goes on with one wing in hope of reaching the nest.*

> *When he has been delivered from Opinion, Knowledge shows its face*
> *to him:*
> *That one-winged bird becomes two-winged and spreads his wings.*[3]

By knowledge, however, Rumi does not mean only religious knowledge, but also scientific knowledge that in the long run may lead to knowledge of the Creator or God. Rumi's view on knowledge is particularly significant, given the schism in our time between some scientists and religious people who adhere to "one wing"; i.e., schism tends to occur when both types first intellectualize and then harden their positions.

A uniqueness in Rumi's thought is his view of the unification of reason with spiritual experience which is closer to the human soul. According to Rumi, man the animal is actualized holistically as a "complete human" when the proper integration of all his energies—physical, emotional, and intellectual—are in harmony and unified with spiritual energies within the space of one body. The actualized complete being, as one whole, is not only greater than the sum of disparate (and dysfunctional) parts, but even greater than the sum of functioning but still not integrated parts (physical, emotional and intellectual, and spiritual). The solely intellectual person, no matter how smart or educated, cannot fully understand the actions of one endowed with spirit until he himself is spiritualized. For Rumi, the spirit is exalted above intellectual apprehension. He reflects upon this difficulty,

> *The spirit of prophecy also has actions conformable to reason,*
> *the Intellect does not apprehend them,*

> *For the spirit is exalted above intellectual apprehension.*
> *Sometimes the intellectual regards actions of the spiritual as madness,*

> *While sometimes he is bewildered,*
> *since it all depends on his becoming the other one.*[4]

Realizing that the nature of form is secondary to spirit, Rumi, though a believing and practicing Muslim, nevertheless remains temperamentally a non-conformist. Divinity for him is not a dogma, but a reality to be comprehended and experienced as more real than the objects of mere sense experience. The holistically driven integration of these four components: 1) embracing reason and faith (intellect and spirit) together with the emotional and physical support from whirling and music, 2) prayers and meditation, 3) not throwing away dismissively the old obedience and role in society, and 4) the emphasis upon the experiential, begin to distinguish Rumi's philosophy as one that embraces the development of a complete human.

The translation of Rumi's poems and sermons into English and other Western languages that assisted in their proliferation over the past century has tempted many readers to browse web sites, library shelves, and bookstores to explore "Rumi the Teacher," or "Rumi the Poet," or "Rumi the Preacher," or "Rumi the Pious Mystic," or "Rumi the Humanist." But Rumi himself was not known as an analytical intellect dissecting reality into fragments and presenting them piecemeal. Rather he was known and loved by Muslims and non-Muslims alike as a remarkably open-minded saint who loved without discrimination. Rumi himself believed that the "man of heart" is holistic: ". . . when you have seen him you have seen the whole universe."

Although Rumi's approach to reality is highly intuitive, it is still clearly presented through the lens of Islam and is not a depiction of mysticism alone. While portraying cultural traditions of Muslims in all their manifold aspects, it also reflects the wisdom of Hellenistic epistemology, the richness of Babylonian, Indian, and Egyptian cultures, the dualism of good and evil of Zoroastrianism, the deliberations of Judaism, and the formal ceremonial manners of Christianity. In the Foreword to Khalifa Abdul Hakim's *The Metaphysics of Rumi*, Bashir Ahmad Dar, a Pakistani scholar and writer, claims that Rumi's approach reflects the ideal of philosophical and cultural unity of humanity:

> The scholastic philosophy of Philo, the illuminative mysticism of Plotinus and his followers, the Hellenistic interpretation of Christianity, the mystic experiences of a host of Christian and Gnostic hermits are found beautifully woven into the texture of a system of thought which is from beginning to end purely Islamic.[5]

In the same foreword Dar, arguing upon the trends of voluntarism and spiritual pluralism that emerged in the post-Kantian period of European philosophies, including Nietzsche, Schopenhauer, Bergson, Lloyd Morgan, William James, and James Ward, reflects that they are a developed form of some of the characteristic features of Rumi's thought. Dar further says:

> Rumi's advocacy of activism and voluntarism; his effort to uphold the individuality and separate identity of the finite self, and yet in deep and intimate relationship with the Ultimate Ego, that together forms a spiritual kingdom of free self-determined individuals; his emphasis on intuition and 'love' as opposed to barren intellectualism; his theory of emergent evolution and creative development—are all different lines of thought that converge in the supreme *weltanschauung* of Rumi and, like pearls, are strung together in a single rosary.[5]

Before Rumi, Islamic interpretation and development of Greek philosophy had started with al-Kindi (c. 801-873) and reached its highest point of perfection in the philosophy of Averroes (1126-1198). Mystic thought and life had also experienced a long and sustained tradition from the first known ascetic in Islam, Abu Hashim (d. 767 CE) of Syria to whom the word "Sufi" was applied, to Sanai (c.1044-1150) and Farid-ud-din Attar (c.1120-1193) of Persia, and to Mohi-ud-Din ibn Arabi (1165-1240) of Arab Spain, a contemporary of Rumi (1207-1273). Thus Rumi, appearing at a relative high point in the development and perfection of philosophical thought and religious experience in Islam, inherited an exceptional intellectual and spiritual wealth.

With the theoretical influences of Greek philosophical interpretation, Jewish and Christian religious life, and Islamic jurisprudence on the one hand and the influences of Persian and Indian traditions on the other (Rumi was born, raised, and educated in his very early youth in Afghanistan, a region bordering both India and Iran), it becomes easy to understand the extent, variety, and richness of thought and experience that met in Rumi. He was not merely a great mystical poet, but as has been said, a philosopher of unique *weltanschauung*. Khalifa A. Hakim, presenting a sketch in his work, *The Metaphysics of Rumi*, put forward this argument in support of Rumi's philosophical greatness:

> His *Mathnawi* is a crystal of many facets in which we see reflected the broken lights of Semitic monotheism, Greek intellectualism

with Pythagorean elements and Eleatic theories of Being and Becoming, Plato's theory of Ideas and Aristotle's theory of Causation and Development, the "One" of Plotinus and the ecstasy that unites with the "One,"... [We see] problems of ibn Sina and al-Farabi, Ghazali's theory of prophetic consciousness and ibn Arabi's Monism. With all this wealth of thought, the *Mathnavi* of Rumi is neither a system of [mere] philosophy, nor of theology nor of mysticism nor it is pure eclecticism. ... The study of Rumi is interesting not because he is the greatest mystic poet of Islam but because of the fact that in him we find a man who has left no problem of philosophical and religious life untouched.[6]

At the core of the complexity of Rumi's outlook is the problematic dualistic nature of man's personality—divine and human. This complexity sub-divides into several fundamental philosophical questions about the nature of the soul, free will, immortality, and the relation between man and the divine. Rumi deeply realized that in spite of these and other profound questions, spirituality is universal, and whatever one's faith, the soul of every person is from the same Source. By expanding one's vision with a willingness to open oneself to the inner potential (and with firm determination and patience), anyone may unlock the door to the attainment of spiritual bliss. In his *Divan-i-Shams*, Rumi comments on this transformation from an incomplete, partial self to a whole self:

> *Make a journey out of self into Self, O master*
> *For such a journey earth becomes a quarry of gold*
>
> *From sourness and bitterness advance to sweetness,*
> *Even as from briny soil a thousand sorts of fruit spring up.[7]*

Here Rumi argues that a person should submit his self to higher Self, as the real worth of a person submitting to God is judged by the virtue of his inner sincerity. This reflects that, logically, once a person is sincerely in perfect submission to God, any other appellation becomes insignificant. Rumi had been guided by the Qur'anic injunction: "Those who believe [in Islam] and those who are Jewish, Christian, or Sabian, whoever believes in God and the Last Day and who does what's morally right, their reward will be with their Lord, and they'll have no cause to fear or regret."[8] Rumi, perceiving far beyond the small crusty circle of dogma, emphasized that the core of the issue, the sound of one's heart, is the Divine Language that needs no tongue to speak out and no ear to hear. On this theme he said:

> *That voice which is the origin of every cry and sound:*
> *that indeed is the only voice, and the rest are echoes.*

> *Turk and Kurd and Persian-speaking man and Arab*
> *have understood that voice without help of ear or lip.*

> *Ay, but what of Turk, Tajik or an Ethiopian?*
> *Even wood and stones have understood that voice.*[9]

Rumi believed that the basis of all existence is "spiritual," a complex term in his worldview that bears elaboration. According to modern philosophical outlook, the term "'spirit" or "soul" in its traditional sense refers to everything that is characterized in the inner life of a human being. When human beings think, reason, and form beliefs, it denotes that they have minds; when they have desires based on emotions and sensations, it reveals that they have will. However, when they are cognizant of their mental conditions and decisions with an exceptional spontaneity, clarity, and certainty, it determines that they are self-conscious or self-aware. This last, according to Rumi, is a special self-consciousness that can establish for the human being a distinctive non-dualistic realization of the unity of the mind, passion, will, and self, which is identified as "spirit" or "soul." And the rationale of the human being's existence is correspondent with what he or she feels in himself/herself as spirit or ego. The famous philosopher of the eighteenth century, Emmanuel Kant (1724-1804) defined this concept of Rumi's (though not taking it directly from him) as a "transcendental unity of perception or self-consciousness." Rumi believes that it is this human spirit or soul whose windows can open to embrace all directions in unlimited dimension and their contents. Therefore, he refers to his magnum opus, the *Mathnawi*, as a "Shop of Unity," where all the diversities of life are welcomed, admitted, and harmonized, where the contradictions vanish or lose their contrary sting, and are left behind by creative unity.

Rumi argues that rationalism has not only permeated philosophic tradition but also influences the practice of scholastic theology and religious jurisprudence, "irradiating" human beings with a wrongful pride that drives them away from spiritual truth, humility, and even kindness. The intellectual pursuit of the rationalist, however fine and important it may be, is incomparable to the spiritual quest that includes it. The intellect and senses see only cause and effect, whereas the spirit apprehends limitless wonder upon wonder. One may possess intellectual capability and yet be totally devoid of spiritual perception. But when one finally realizes spirit and truth, the principles of logic become unnecessary. Indeed, the reasoning that may have helped in the beginning now becomes an attachment, a habit and a barrier to human development. Rumi expresses this poetically:

> *The intellectual quest, though it be fine as pearls and corals,*
> *is other than the spiritual quest.*
>
> *The spiritual quest is on another plane:*
> *the spiritual wine has another consistency.*
>
> *Know that the quest of the intellect and the senses*
> *is concerned with effects or secondary causes.*
>
> *The spiritual quest is either wonder or the father of wonder;*
> *it's either wonderful or beyond wonder.*[10]

Rumi has warned that without humility, obedience, respect, and love of human beings, both logic and religious fervor may prove a treacherous guide:

> *Partial and discursive reason is a denier of Love,*
> *though it may reflect to know many realities.*
>
> *It [partial reason] is our friend in word and deed,*
> *But when you come to ecstatic feeling, it is not.*[11]

According to Rumi the ground of existence is spiritual; even substance is spiritual. There is no lifeless matter: "earth and water, fire and air are alive in the view of God, though they appear to be dead to us." His conception of soul is the same as the spirit or ego, which is striving to evolve. Infinite numbers of souls or egos emanating out of the Cosmic

Ego or God comprise the entirety of existence, which is constantly in the process of creation. Presenting his interpretation of an evolutionary reincarnation he writes about himself, "I—meaning my soul or ego— existed when there were neither names nor the things that are named." Here, a Western thinker comparable to Rumi is the German philosopher Gottfried Wilhelm von Leibniz (1646-1716) who, centuries after Rumi, speculated that all existence is constituted of infinite numbers of egos at various levels of consciousness. Rumi's conception of God as a universal cosmic Monad is the same as that reflected in the metaphysics of Leibniz. Rumi seeks his God not through self-denial but through a process of self-transcendence where the indestructible ego is purified again and again to ultimately become fit for its union with God. Affirming the integrity of ego, Rumi projects the core of his Islamic belief.

Rumi, like Plotinus (204-270), was an emanationist in the great traditions of al-Farabi (870-950) and ibn-Sina (980-1037). Like Aristotle (384-322 BCE), he held that love of God is the motivating force of the universe. Islam, as heir to earlier biblical traditions and incorporator of Hellenistic thought, attempted a synthesis of reason, love, and law. But for Rumi, love is far greater than reason and law: "Gamble everything for love, if you're a true human being." Rumi's conception of God is a reality to be experienced and apprehended beyond a mere object of sense experience. Man's relation to his God is not an assertion of an article of faith, but a realization in the depth of one's own being where man is tuned with the divine and the finite is embraced by the infinite. His God is the first ground as well as the final goal of all existence.

Rumi's philosophy of holistic humanism is grounded in love. He believes that the force that creates heavenly bodies like stars and planets also creates life. As atoms begin incorporating into molecules, so in their evolutionary urge they emerge as living cells, which in an initial stage appear in vegetation and later in animality. According to G. W. Friedrich Hegel (1770-1809), creation starts through a synthesis of the opposites. Rumi, many centuries before Hegel, propounded that the opposites, which are already akin, are attracted by love. Love, as Rumi believes, originates in God and moves toward God the creator of everything. As love advances from one phase to another in the process of creation, it proliferates by generating new forms of existence at each phase.

According to Rumi, the universe is a realm of love in which law and reason are secondary phenomena. Love is the creative stimulus and reason enters to look at it retrospectively, introducing law to establish unity in the diversities of manifested life. Rumi, intuiting the gravitational pull of atoms and masses of matter, resorts to love as the primary urge that creates attractions and affinities. His remarkable poetical rendition of this thought in the *Mathnawi* is philosophically paraphrased and explained by Khalifa Abdul Hakim in *A History of Muslim Philosophy,* edited and compiled by Mian Muhammad Sharif:

> All atoms in the cosmos are attracted to one another like lovers; everyone is drawn toward its mate by the magnetic pull of love. Heavenly bodies draw the earth toward them in a welcoming embrace. It is on account of this cosmic pull of love that earth remains suspended in space like a lamp, the forces from all directions pulling it by equilibrated attraction not allowing it fly away or drop down in space, as if the stellar dome of heaven were a magnetic dome inside which a piece of iron is suspended without visible cords.[12]

Here one finds in Rumi an intuitive anticipation of Isaac Newton's (1643-1727) definition of the movement of celestial bodies by physical gravitation, propounding that the same force that creates heavenly bodies also creates life by Love. Instead of explaining the gravitation of Love by mechanical dynamics, Rumi views it as a basic impulse initiating attractions and affinities.

Rumi's projection of metaphysical possibilities has been as strong as his attraction to the mystical ones. In the spheres of scientific propositions and philosophical conceptions he appears as a prophetic intellectual. One finds in Rumi traces of Kant's nebular hypothesis explaining the origin of celestial bodies out of incandescent vapor as well as the subjectivity of time, space, and causality. Rumi recognized that "The same force that creates heavenly bodies out of a nebulae resulting in stars and planets and systems, proceeds further and generates life because love by its essence is creative."[13] Long before Hegel's ever-progressing dynamism of Nature and Mind, and his assertion that creation proceeds through a synthesis of the opposites, Rumi had already viewed that, ". . . these apparent opposites were already akin by the affinity of love. Love originates in God and also moves back toward God who is essentially a creator: therefore, love as it advances from phase to phase in the upward movement of creation brings into being new forms of existence at every step."[12]

Rumi, in an illuminating description of his philosophy of evolution in the *Mathnawi*, has beautifully portrayed the systematic process of man emerging from lifeless matter to his present status of a holistic human being. Rumi's exposition remarkably reflects an anticipation of Darwin's (1809-1892) biological view of the evolution of species by the blind urges of the struggle for existence and life's adaptation to its environment. In the same description Rumi has also summed up Bergson's (1859-1941) conception of *elan vital* and his view of creative evolution. Delineating diverse modes and stages of the nature of man, as presented by Hakim, Rumi says:

> For several epochs I was flying about in space like atoms of dust without a will, after which I entered the inorganic realm of matter. Crossing over to the vegetable kingdom I lost all memory of my struggle on the material plane. From there I stepped into the animal kingdom, forgetting all my life as a plant, feeling only an instinctive and unconscious urge toward the growth of plants and flowers, particularly during the springtime as suckling babies feel toward the mother that gave them birth. Rising in the scale of animality I became a man pulled up by the creative urge of the Creator whom one knows. I continued advancing from realm to realm developing my reason and strengthening the organism. There was ground for ever getting above the previous types of reason.[13]

Rumi does not stop here, but also transcends Friedrich Nietzsche's (1844-1900) view that present humanity must be superseded in a further advance toward new dimensions of being. Hakim further speculates on Rumi's view of man's evolutionary ascent:

> Even my present rationality is not a culmination of mental evolution. This too has to be transcended, because it is contaminated with self-seeking, egoistic biological urges. A thousand other types of reason and consciousness shall emerge during the further course of my ascent; a wonder of wonders! [13]

Whereas Rene Descartes (1596-1650) could not be certain that his body was real and summed up his insight in his famous "*cogito, ergo sum* (I think therefore I am)*"*, Rumi had already envisioned this in his own unique way:

> *O brother, you are that same thought of yours;*
> *as for the rest of you, you are only bone and fiber.*
>
> *If your thought is a rose, you are a rose-garden;*
> *And if it is a thorn, you are fuel for the bath-stove.* [14]

Even epistemologically, Rumi left his footprint. A man of conventional religious beliefs before he met the mystical figure of Shams of Tabriz, with Shams's guidance Rumi awakened to the realization that there is a unitive state beyond orthodox religion. His teaching system in its essence is based upon unitive realization and is composed of mental drill, thought, meditation and prayer, work and play, and above all, action and inaction. The body-mind movements of the Whirling Dervishes, accompanied by the music of the reed pipe, is Rumi's special method to help bring the seeker into affinity with the mystical current, to transcend in order to be transformed. Rumi says, "Prayer has a form, a sound and a physical reality. Everything which has a word has a physical equivalent. And every thought has an action."

> *Hence philosophers have said that we received these harmonies*
> *from the rotating of the celestial sphere.*
>
> *And the melody people play on tambours and sing*
> *is the sound of the revolutions of the sphere;*
>
> *The true believers say that the influence of Paradise*
> *made every unpleasant sound to be beautiful.*
>
> *We all have been parts of Adam,*
> *we have heard those melodies in Paradise.*
>
> *Although the water and earth of our bodies has covered us with doubt*
> *yet something of those melodies comes back to our memories.* [15]

Rumi, an adept in the science of mystical tradition, wrote poetry that reflected and encouraged this process and taught his followers to open their hearts to the dynamism of human existence through mystical experiences. In today's parlance, it is tempting to think of Rumi as one who "innerly" danced to his own spiritual drum, in both the fields of philosophy and religion, and yet remained devoted to God and the forms of Muslim worship. All in all, it is difficult to truly label his supreme *weltanschauung* or to classify the genre of his oeuvre. While philosophizing about Rumi's intellectual and spiritual experience, one always feels one has fallen short and has not done full justice to Rumi's philosophical and spiritual brilliance.

Notes:

1. *Mathnawi* Book I, 24.
2. Ibid., Book III, 488-90
3. Ibid., Book III, 1510-13.
4. Ibid., Book II, 3260-61.
5. Dar, *The Metaphysics of Rumi* by Hakim, 2006, a-b.
6. Ibid., 2006, ii.
7. Nicholson, *Divan* 1898, p. 111.
8. The Qur'an, 2:62
9. *Mathnawi* Book I, 2107-09.
10. Ibid., Book I, 1501-1506.
11. Ibid., Book I, 1982 and 1985.
12. Sharif, *A History of Muslim Philosophy*, vol. 2, page 833.
13. Ibid., vol. 2, page 833 and also *Mathnawi* Book IV, 3637-48.
14. *Mathnawi* Book II, 277-78.
15. Ibid., Book IV, 733-37.

ABOUT THE AUTHOR

Mirza Iqbal Ashraf is a retired professor of English Language and Literature. He was born at Chiniot, a town situated on the bank of river Chenab. He began his education with home schooling by his father Mirza Sharqui, his first teacher and his mentor, who acquainted him with the works of Confucius, Socrates, Plato, Aristotle, and the Muslim philosophers from al-Kindi to Avicenna and Averroes. His father helped Ashraf understand Rumi's Persian poetry and philosophy by reading Masnavi's coherent commentary in six volumes by Ashraf's grandfather Maulana Mirza Muhammad Nazir Arshi (Shaheed). Tutored by his father, Ashraf achieved his bachelor's degree with honors in Persian literature and Islamic philosophy. He was fifteen years old when his father retired as an English teacher, and at a very young age he got a job teaching in the same school where his father had taught. When he was twenty-one years old, he was accepted at Punjab University Lahore where he earned his Master's degree in English Language and Literature. It was his first experience as a student in an institution.

While in his home country of Pakistan, Ashraf remained involved with his family's tradition of *"learning to teach and teaching to learn,"* He taught both graduate and post-graduate students and lectured on English language, literature, and philosophical issues in his native Pakistan. Before taking up the teaching profession, he worked as a sub-editor with the English daily newspaper, *Civil and Military Gazette,* in Lahore. Ashraf wrote many articles on philosophical, sociological, religious, and cultural topics for *The Pakistan Times* and *Civil and Military Gazette,* English daily newspapers of Pakistan, until his passion to seek knowledge brought him to the USA in 1990. He set his heart on being an independent reader and writer, and authored his first landmark work, *Introduction to World Philosophies: A Chronological Progression* (iUniverse), which was published in 2007, followed by the *Islamic Philosophy of War and Peace,* (iUniverse, 2008), *Rumi's Holistic Humanism: The Timeless Appeal of the Great Mystic Poet,* (Codhill Press, 2012), *Diversity and Unity in Islamic Civilization,* (iUniverse, 2017), and *Human Existence and Identity in the Modern Age: A Socio-Philosophical Reflection,* (Peter-Lang, Berlin, Germany, 2019).

Since immigrating to the United States of America, Ashraf works as an independent research scholar of world philosophies, as well as sociopolitical, cross-cultural, inter-faith, and Islamic philosophy and religious subjects. He is a popular speaker and lecturer at many institutions and organizations in and around Poughkeepsie, New York, including the following institutions and organizations (not a complete list):

1. Marist College, Hyde Park, New York.
2. Vassar College, Poughkeepsie, New York.
3. Bards College, Red Hook, New York.
4. State University of New York, Albany, New York.
5. Center for Lifetime Study, Marist College, New York.
6. World Affairs Council of Mid-Hudson Valley, New York.
7. Thinkers Forum, Haverstraw, New York.
8. Mid-Hudson Islamic Association, Wappinger Fall, New York.

Ashraf holds a Master's degree in English Language and Literature, and Bachelor's degree of Honours in Persian language, literature, and Islamic Philosophy. He lives in Poughkeepsie, New York (USA).

Mirza Iqbal Ashraf
mirzashraf@hotmail.com

BOOKS CITED AND RECOMMENDED

A Magazine of Ideas: *Philosophy Now, Talking about Human Rights, issue # 118.*

1. Adamson, Peter and Taylor, Richard C.: *The Cambridge Companion to Arabic Philosophy*, 2005.

2. Ahmad, Israr: *The Qur'an and the World Peace*, Markezi Anjuman Khuddam-ul Qur'an, Lahore, Pakistan, 1980.

3. Allen, Berry: *Knowledge and Civilization*, Work view Press, USA, 2004.

4. Allen, Reginald E.: *Greek Philosophy: Thales to Aristotle*, 1966.

5. Armstrong, Karen: *A Short History of Islam*, Modern Library, New York, 2002.

6. Armstrong, Karen: *Muhammad: A Prophet of Our Time*, Harper-Collins, NY, 2006.

7. Armstrong, Karen: *The Great Transformation*, 2006.

8. Armstrong, Karen: *A History of God*, Alfred A. Knopf, New York, 1994.

9. Asad, Muhammad: *Islam at the Crossroads*, Islamic Book Service, New Delhi, India, 2006.

10. Asad, Muhammad: *The Principles of State and Government in Islam*, Berkley: University of California Press, 1961.

11. Asad, Muhammad: *The Message of the Qur'an*, Bristol, UK Book Foundation, 2003.

12. Ashraf, Mirza Iqbal: *Introduction to World Philosophies: A Chronological Progression*, iUniverse, 2007.

13. Ashraf, Mirza Iqbal/Yaldur, Hulya (eds.): *Human Existence and Identity in Modern Age: A Socio-philosophical Reflection*, Peter Lang GmbH, Berlin, Germany, 2019.

14. Attenborough, David: https://cnnespanol.cnn.com/2018/12/03/david-attenborough-el-colapso-de-nuestras-civilizaciones-esta-en-el-horizonte/

15. Barker, Dan: *Free Will Explained*, Sterling, New York, 2018.

16. Barrat, James: *Our Final Invention*, Thomas Dunne Books, New York, 2013.

17. Bashir, Zakaria: *War and Peace in the Life of the Prophet Muhammad*, The Islamic Foundation, Markfield Leicestershire, UK, 2006.

18. Bennet, William J.: *The Book of Man*, Nelson Books, Nashville, Tennessee, 2013.

19. Berlin, Isaiah: *The Age of Enlightenment*, A Meridian Book, New York, 1984.

20. Black, Antony: *The History of Islamic Political Thought, From the Prophet to Present*, Routledge, New York, 2001.

21. Blackmore, Susan: *Consciousness*, Sterling, New York, 2005.

22. Bronstein. Jay Daniel, and Schulweis, Harold M.: *Approaches to the Philosophy of Religion,* Books For Libraries Press, Freeport, New York, 1954.

23. Butchvarov, Panayot: *The Concept of Knowledge,* Northwestern University Press, Evanston, 1970.

24. Carroll, Sean: *The Big Picture,* Dutton, New York, 2016.

25. Chittick, William: *The Heart of Islamic Philosophy,*

26. Chou, Mark: *Democracy and Tragedy,* Philosophy Now, Issue # 94, Jan-Feb 2013.

27. Chossudovsky, Michel: *Toward A World War III Scenario,* Global Research Publishers, 2012.

28. Chossudovsky, Michel: *The Globalization of War,* Global Research Publishers 2015.

29. Christensen, Thomas: *The River of Ink--Literature, History, Art,* Counterpoint, Berkley, CA 2014.

30. Clarke, Richard A. and Knake, Robert K.: *Cyber War,* HarperCollins Publishers, New York, 2010.

31. Curnow, Trevor: *Wisdom: A History,* Reaktion Books Ltd., London, UK 2015.

32. Darwin, Charles: *The Descent of Man,* Prometheus Books, New York, 1998.

33. DK Editors: *The History Book,* DK Penguin Random House, New York, 2016.

34. DK Editors: *The Literature Book,* DK Penguin Random House, New York, 2016.

35. DK Editors: *The Politics Book,* DK Penguin Random House, New York, 2013.

36. Dennett, Daniel C.: *Consciousness Explained,* Little Brown Company, NY, 1994.

37. Dewey, John: *Human Nature and Conduct,* Barnes & Noble, New York, 2008.

38. Doren, Charles Van: *A History of Knowledge,* Ballantine Books, New York, 1991.

39. Dunn, Philip trans. *Sun Tzu's The Art of Peace*: Jeremy P. Tracer/Putnam-Penguin, New York, 2003.

40. Edelman, Gerald M., and Tonoi, Giulio: *A Universe of Consciousness.*

41. Eagleman, David: *The Brain,* Pantheon Books, New York, 2015.

42. Einstein, Albert: The Philosophy of Albert Einstein, Fall River Press, NY, 2013.

43. Eams, Elizabeth Ramsden: *Bertrand Russell's Theory of Knowledge,* George Braziller, New York, 1967.

44. Farah, Caesar E.: Islam: Beliefs and Observances, Barron's Educational Series, Hauppauge, New York, 1968.

45. Ferrone, Vincenzo: *The Enlightenment: History of an Idea,* Princeton University Press, NJ, 2015.

46. Ferrucci, Piero (Editor): Aldous Huxley, *The Human Situation,* Harper & Row Publishers, New York, 1977.

47. Ferry, Luc: *A Brief History of Thought*

48. Feser, Edward: *Philosophy of Mind,* Oneworld Publications, England, 2010

49. Foer, Franklin: *World Without Mind,* Penguin Press, New York, 2017.

50. Franklin, Daniel: *Megatech-Technology in 2050,* Profile Books Lt., London, 2017.

51. Fuller, Graham: *The Future of Political Islam,* Palgrave McMillan, NY 2003

52. Goldblatt, Mark: *On Soul,* in the Magazine *Philosophy Now* issue # 82.

53. Grayling, A. C.: *The Age of Genius,* Bloomsbury Publishing, London, 2016.

54. Gregor, Thomas ed.: *A Natural History of Peace*: Vanderbilt University Press, Nashville, USA, 1996.

55. Goodman, Lenn E.: *Islamic Humanism,* Oxford University Press, NY, 2003.

56. Gottlieb, Anthony: *The Dream of Enlightenment,* Liveright Publishing, NY, 2016.

57. Grunebaum, Von G. E.: *Classical Islam: A History 600-1258,* 1960.

58. Hakim, Khalifa A.: *Islamic Ideology,* Institute of Islamic Culture, Lahore, 1951.

59. Hall, Stephen S: *Wisdom: From Philosophy to Neuroscience,* Vintage Books, New York, 2011

60. Harari, Yuval Noah: *Homo Deus: A Brief History of Tomorrow*: Harper Collins, New York, 2017.

61. Harari, Yuval Noah: *Sapiens; A Brief History of Humankind,* Harper Collins, New York 2015.

62. Hashemi, Nader: *Islam, Secularism, and Liberal Democracy,* Oxford University Press, New York, 2009.

63. Hedges, Chris: *War is a Force that Gives us Meaning,* Public Affairs, N Y, 2014.

64. Heimans, Jeremy and Timms, Henry: *New Power,* Doubleday, New York, 2018.

65. Hobbes, Thomas: *Leviathan,* Barnes & Noble Books, New York, 2004.

66. Hoover, Herbert and Gibson, Hugh. *The Problems of Lasting Peace*: Doubleday, Doran, USA, 1943.

67. Huxley, Aldous: *The Human Situation,* Harper & Row Publishers, New York, 1977.

68. Huxley, Aldous: *The Perennial Philosophy,* HarperCollins, New York, 1945.

69. Isaacson, Walter: *Einstein, His Life and Universe,* Simon & Schuster, NY 2007.

70. Issawi, Charles: *An Arab Philosophy of History.* Darwin Press, Princeton, New Jersey, 1987.

71. Jaspers, Karl: *The Origin and Goal of History,* Routledge, NY 2021.

72. Joy, Bill: *The Future Does Not Need Us,* Fourth Estate New York, 2004.

73. Jouvenel, Bertrand de: *On Power*; Its Nature and the History of its Growth, Beacon Press, Boston, 1962.

74. Kaku, Michio: *The Future of the Mind,* Anchor Books, New York, 2014.

75. Kant, Emanuel: *On History.* Pearson, London, 1963.

76. Kant, Emanuel: *Basic Writings of Kant,* The Modern Library, New York, 2001.

77. Kaplan, Robert: *The Return of Marco Polo's World,* Random House NY, 2018.

78. Keegan, John: *A History of Warfare,* Vintage Books, New York, 1994.

79. Keegan, John: *War and Our World,* Vintage Books, New York, 2001.

80. Kenny, Anthony: *A New History of Western Philosophy,* Clarendon Press, Oxford, UK, 2010.

81. Kellogg, Ronald T: *The Making of the Mind: The Neuroscience of Human Nature,* Prometheus Books, NY, 2013.

82. Khadduri, Majid: *War and Peace in the Law of Islam,* Johns Hopkins Press, Baltimore, 1955.

83. Khadduri, Majid, (trans): *The Islamic Law of Nations: Shaybani's Siyar,* Johns Hopkins Press, Baltimore, USA, 1966.

84. Knoles, George H., and Snyder, Rixford K.: *Readings in Western Civilization,* J. B. Lippincott Company, New York, 1960.

85. Kramer, Martin. *"Arab Nationalism: Mistaken Identity."* Daedalus, Summer, 1993. www.geocities.com/martinkramerorg/ArabNationalism.htm

86. Kramer, Martin. *Arab Awakening & Islamic Revival.* New Brunswick (USA): Transaction Publishers, 1996.

87. Kramer, Martin. *"Islam's Sober Millennium."* Jerusalem Post, 30 December, 1999. www.geocities.com/martinkramerorg/Millenium.htm.

88. Kung, Hans, trans. John Bowden. *Islam, Past, Present and Future.* Oxford, UK: Oneworld Oxford, 2007.

89. Kurtz, Paul: *Embracing the Power of Humanism,* Rowman & Littlefield Publishers Inc., New York, 2000.

90. Kurzweil, Ray: *The Singularity is Near,* Viking Penguin, New York, 2005.

91. Laszlo, Ervin-Houston, Jean and Dossey, Larry: *What is Consciousness,* Select Books, Inc., New York, 2016.

92. Law, Stephen: *Philosophy, Visual Reference Guide,* Metro Books, New York, 2007.

93. Leaman, Oliver: *Islamic Philosophy,*

94. Leaman, Oliver: *A Brief Introduction to Islamic Philosophy;* 1999.

95. Levine, Peter: *The Future of Democracy,* Tufts University Press, Medford, MA, 2007.

96. Lewis, Bernard: *The Middle East and West,* Weidenfeld & Nicolson, UK, 1964.

97. Lings, Martin: *Shakespeare's Window into the Soul,* Inner Tradition, Rochester VR, USA, 2006.

98. Lings, Martin: *Shakespeare's Window into the Soul,* Inner Tradition, Rochester VR, USA, 2006.

99. Machiavelli, Niccolo: *The Prince and Other writings,* Barnes & Noble Classics, New York, 2003.

100. Mahdi, Muhsin S.: *Al-Farabi and the Foundation of Islamic Political Philosophy, University of Chicago Press, Chicago, 2001.*

101. May/June 2014 issue: *Scientific American Mind.*

102. Morgan, Michael Hamilton: *Lost History, The Enduring Legacy of Muslim, Scientists, Thinkers and Artists,* 2007.

103. Maitzen, Stephen, *A Philosopher Panelist of Ask Philosophy.*

104. Martin, Richard C. (editor): *Encyclopedia of Islam and the Muslim World*

105. May/June 2014 issue: *Scientific American Mind.*

106. Michael Shermer: *The Moral Arc,* Henry Holt & Co., New York, 2015.

107. Miller, Kenneth R.: *The Human Instinct,* Simon & Schuster, New York, 2018.

108. Naim, Moises: *The End of Power,* Basic Books, New York, 2013.

109. Nasr, Seyyed Hossein: *The Heart of Islam, Enduring Values for Humanity,* HarperCollins, New York, 2004.

110. National Geographic: *Your Brain 100 Things You Never Knew, (Special Edition)* Washington D. C., 2011.

111. National Geographic: *Brain the Complete Mind.*

112. Nietzsche, Friedrich: *Thus Spoke Zarathustra,* Barnes & Noble Classics, NY, 2005.

113. New York Times (October 30, 2001): *How Islam Won, and Lost, the Lead in Science*: By Dennis Overbye.

114. Nye, Jr., Joseph S.: *Soft Power,* Public Affairs, New York, 2004.

115. Philosophy Now: *A Magazine of Ideas,* Issue 82, Jan/Feb 2011.

116. Pinker, Steven: *The Stuff of Thought,* Penguin Books, New York, 2007.

117. Pinker, Arthur Steven: *How the Brain Works,* W. W. Norton & Company, NY, 2009.

118. Rand, Ayn: *Philosophy Who Needs It,* Signet Book by New American Library, 1984.

119. Rauch, Jonathan: *The Constitution of Knowledge,* Brooking Institute Press, Washington, D.C., 2021.

120. Reese, Byron: *The Fourth Age,* Atria Books, New York, 2018.

121. Revonsuo, Antti and Kamppinen, Matti: *Consciousness in Philosophy & Cognitive Neuroscience.*

122. Rosenthal, Franz (Translator): *The Muqaddimah,* Princeton University Press, New Jersey, 2005.

123. Rousseau, Jean-Jacques: *The Social Contract,* Translated by G.D.H. Cole, Barnes & Noble, New York, 2005, Original 1762.

124. Russell, Bertrand: *The Principles of Mathematics,* Cambridge University Press, Cambridge UK, 1903.

125. Russell, Bertrand: *Human Knowledge: Its Scope and Limits,* Simon and Schuster, New York, 1948

126. Russell, Bertrand: *The Problems of Philosophy,* Henry Holt and Company, New York, 1912.

127. Russell, Bertrand: *Sceptical Essays* 1928, Unwin Books, London, 1962.

128. Russell, Bertrand: *Power*: Unwin Books, London, 1967.

129. Russell, Bertrand: *History of Western Philosophy*, Unwin University Book, London, 1946 and 1961.

130. Saiyidain, K. G.: *Iqbal's Educational Philosophy*, Sh. Muhammad Ashraf, Lahore (Pakistan) 1938.

131. Sanger, David E.: The Perfect Weapon, Broadway Books, New York, 2018.

132. Scruton, Roger: *On Human Nature*, Princeton University Press, New Jersey, 2017

133. Selby-Bigge, L. A.: *British Moralists,* The Bobbs-Merrill Company, Inc., NY, 1964.

134. Sharif, M.M.: *History of Muslim Philosophy*, Lahore. Pakistan, 1961.

135. Scheler, Max; translator Hans Meyerhoff: *Man's Place in Nature*, The Noonday Press. A Division of Farrar, Straus and Cudahy, New York.

136. Shermer, Michael: *The Moral Arc*, Henry Holt and Company, New York, 2016.

137. Skeptic Magazine: *Extraordinary Claims, Revolutionary Ideas & the Promotion of Science.* Vol.22, No.2, 2017

138. Smart, Ninian: *World Philosophies*, Routledge, New York, 2001.

139. Smuts, General Jan Christian, *Holism and Evolution,* The MacMillan Company, New York, 1926.

140. Spielvogel, Jackson J.: *Western Civilization*, Thomson, Wadsworth, Canada, 2006.

141. Stevenson, Leslie and Haberman, David L.: *Ten Theories of Human Nature*, Oxford University Press, New York, 2004.

142. Sweeney, Michael S.: *Brain the Complete Mind*, National Geographic, Washington D. C., 2014.

143. Tarnas, Richard: *The Passion of the Western Mind,* 1993.

144. Temes, Peter S.: *The Just War*, Ivan R. Dee, Chicago, 2003.

145. Toynbee, Arnold: *A Study of History,*

146. Tzu, Sun: *The Art of War*, Barnes and Noble Classics, New York, 2013.

147. VandenBos, Gary R., editor: *Dictionary of Psychology*, American Psychology Association, Washington, USA, 1931.

148. Walzer, Michael: *Just and Unjust Wars*, Basic Books, New York, 2015

149. Walsh, Toby: *Machines the Think*, Prometheus Books, New York, 2018.

150. Wilson, Edward O.: *The Meaning of Human Existence*, W. W. Norton & Company, New York, 2014.

151. Wilson, Edward: *Origins of Creativity*, Liveright Publishing Corp., New York, 2018.

152. Yaldir, Hulya/Onkal, Guncel (eds.): *New Horizons in Philosophy and Sociology*, Peter Lang GmbH, Frankfurt, Germany, 2017.

153. Yaldir, Hulya/Ashraf, Mirza Iqbal (eds.): *Human Existence and Identity in Modern Age: A Socio-philosophical Reflection*, Peter Lang GmbH, Berlin, Germany, 2019.

154. Zakaria, Fareed: *The Future of Freedom*, Norton & Co., New York, 2003.